Rosemary Conley's
Low Fat
Cookbook

Rosemary Conley's
Low Fat
Cookbook

Century Publishing

Published by Century in 1998

1 3 5 7 9 10 8 6 4 2

Copyright © Rosemary Conley Enterprises, 1998

Rosemary Conley has asserted her right under the Copyright, Designs and Patents Act, 1988 to be identified as the author of this work

First published in the United Kingdom in 1998 by Century
Random House UK Limited
20 Vauxhall Bridge Road, London SW1V 2SA

Random House Australia (Pty) Limited
20 Alfred Street, Milsons Point, Sydney,
New South Wales 2061, Australia

Random House New Zealand Limited
18 Poland Road, Glenfield
Auckland 10, New Zealand

Random House South Africa (Pty) Limited
Endulini, 5a Jubilee Road, Parktown 2193, South Africa

Random House UK Limited Reg. No. 954009

A CIP catalogue record for this book is available
from the British Library

Papers used by Random House UK Limited are natural, recyclable products made from wood grown in sustainable forests. The manufacturing processes conform to the environmental regulations of the country of origin

ISBN 0 7126 7964 2

Photography by Peter Barry
Food styling by Dean Simpole-Clarke
Designed by Roger Walker

Printed and bound in Great Britain by
Butler & Tanner Ltd, Frome and London

Also by Rosemary Conley

Rosemary Conley's Hip and Thigh Diet
Rosemary Conley's Complete Hip and Thigh Diet
Rosemary Conley's Inch Loss Plan
Rosemary Conley's Hip and Thigh Diet Cookbook (with Patricia Bourne)
Rosemary Conley's Metabolism Booster Diet
Rosemary Conley's Whole Body Programme
Rosemary Conley's New Hip and Thigh Diet Cookbook (with Patricia Bourne)
Shape Up for Summer
Rosemary Conley's Beach Body Plan
Rosemary Conley's Flat Stomach Plan
Be Slim! Be Fit!
Rosemary Conley's Complete Flat Stomach Plan
Rosemary Conley's New Body Plan
Rosemary Conley's New Inch Loss Plan

Contents

Foreword

Over the last ten years Rosemary Conley has introduced millions of people trying to control their weight to the benefits of low-fat eating. Today there is strong scientific evidence that in general we all eat too much fat for good health. Reducing the fat in our diet can reduce the risk of our becoming overweight and decrease the chances of our suffering a heart attack or developing other serious diseases.

These recipes encapsulate the current government recommendations for a healthy diet based on independent scientific advice. This book offers an eating plan which is low in fat, high in carbohydrate to reduce hunger and provide important fibre, and with plenty of fruit and vegetables to ensure a good intake of vitamins and minerals.

I hope that this book will introduce many more people to the idea that low-fat cookery is not just about losing weight but an enjoyable way of eating for everyone which can make a real contribution to a healthier life.

Susan A Jebb SRD, PhD
MRC Dunn Clinical Nutrition Centre, Cambridge, 1998

Acknowledgements

This book has been a most enjoyable challenge and I hope that everyone who uses it — and their family and dinner guests — enjoys the recipes. A book like this is a team effort and I want to publicly thank all those who helped me.

Dean Simpole-Clarke is a chef and home economist with whom I have had the pleasure of working in my Granada Sky television daytime show, Rosemary Conley's Cookbook. When I asked Dean if he would help me with this book, he not only agreed but also brought with him his enthusiasm, skill, talent and attention to detail. Without Dean, this book would not be the magnificent volume that it has turned out to be. Many of the recipes are Dean's own creations. Thank you so much, Dean.

Thanks also to my assistant, Melody Patterson, who made this book her life work for the last ten months; to my PA, Louise Cowell, for her valuable contribution; to Becky Morris for doing the nutrition calculations; and to Dr Susan Jebb who has given her support to this book. Another major player, as always, is my editor, Jan Bowmer, who has worked so hard to make the book work logically and easily for the reader.

Thanks, too, to photographer Peter Barry, to art director Dennis Barker for designing the cover, to Roger Walker for designing the inside pages, and to Simon King and Andy McKillop at Arrow Books for their support and encouragement throughout.

Thanks must also go to members of Rosemary Conley Diet & Fitness Clubs and to the Meat and Livestock Commission for supplying some of the recipes.

Last, but by no means least, thank you to my husband, Mike, for his positive encouragement and support throughout the writing and preparation of this book.

Useful Information

Weight conversions

All weights are given in imperial and metric. All conversions are approximate. Use only one set of measures and do not mix the two. The table below shows the conversions used.

Ounce (oz)	Pound (lb)	Gram (g)
1		25
2		50
3		75
4	$^1/_4$	100
6		175
8	$^1/_2$	225
16	1	450
	$1^1/_2$	675
	2	900

Liquid measures

1 tablespoon = 3 teaspoons =	$^1/_2$fl oz	= 15ml	
2 tablespoons = 1fl oz	= 30ml		
4 tablespoons = $^1/_4$ cup	= 2fl oz	= 50ml	
5 tablespoons = $^1/_3$ cup	= $2^1/_2$fl oz	= 75ml	
8 tablespoons = $^1/_2$ cup	= 4fl oz	= 120ml	
10 tablespoons = $^2/_3$ cup	= 5fl oz ($^1/_4$ pint)	= 150ml	
12 tablespoons = $^3/_4$ cup	= 6fl oz	= 175ml	
16 tablespoons = 1 cup	= 8fl oz	= 250ml ($^1/_2$ US pint)	

Note: A UK pint contains 20fl oz

American cup measures can be convenient to use, especially when making large quantities. However, although the volume remains the same, the weight may vary, as illustrated opposite.

Imperial	American
Flour	*Flour*
plain and self-raising	all purpose
1oz	$1/4$ cup
4oz	1 cup
Cornflour	*Cornstarch*
1oz	$1/4$ cup
generous 2oz	$1/2$ cup
$4^1/_2$ oz	1 cup
Sugar (granulated/caster)	*Sugar (granulated)*
4oz	$1/2$ cup
$7^1/_2$ oz	1 cup
Sugar (icing)	*Sugar (confectioner's)*
1oz	$1/4$ cup
$4^1/_2$ oz	1 cup
Sugar (soft brown)	*Sugar (light and dark brown)*
4oz	$1/2$ cup firmly packed
8oz	1 cup firmly packed

Useful measures

1 egg	56ml	2fl oz
1 egg white	28ml	1fl oz
2 rounded tablespoons breadcrumbs	30g	1oz
2 level teaspoons gelatine	8g	$1/4$oz

1oz (25g) granular aspic sets 1 pint (600ml).
$1/2$oz (15g) powdered gelatine or 4 leaves sets 1 pint (600ml).
All spoon measures are level unless otherwise stated.

Wine quantities

Average serving	ml	fl oz
1 glass wine	90ml	3fl oz
1 glass port or sherry	60ml	2fl oz
1 glass liqueur	30ml	1fl oz

Oven temperature conversions

Celsius (Centigrade)	Fahrenheit	Gas Mark	Definition
130	250	$^{1}/_{2}$	very cool
140	275	1	cool
150	300	2	warm
170	325	3	moderate
180	350	4	moderate
190	375	5	moderately hot
200	400	6	hot
220	425	7	hot
230	450	8	very hot
240	475	9	very hot

Abbreviations

oz	ounce
lb	pound
kg	kilogram
fl oz	fluid ounce
ml	millilitre
C	Celsius (Centigrade)
F	Fahrenheit
kcal	kilocalorie (calorie)

Equipment and terms

British	American
baking tin	baking pan
base	bottom
cocktail stick	toothpick
dough or mixture	batter
frying pan	skillet
greaseproof paper	waxed paper
grill/grilled	broil/broiled
knock back dough	punch back dough
liquidiser	blender
muslin	cheesecloth
pudding basin	ovenproof bowl
stoned	pitted
top and tail (gooseberries)	clean (gooseberries)
whip/whisk	beat/whip

Ingredients

British	American
aubergine	egg plant
bacon rashers	bacon slices
bicarbonate of soda	baking soda
black cherries	bing cherries
boiling chicken	stewing chicken
broad beans	fava or lima beans
capsicum pepper	sweet pepper
cauliflower florets	cauliflowerets
celery stick	celery stalk
stock cube	bouillon cube
chicory	belgium endive
chilli	chile pepper

British	American
cooking apple	baking apple
coriander	cilantro
cornflour	cornstarch
courgette	zucchini
crystallised ginger	candied ginger
curly endive	chicory
demerara sugar	light brown sugar
essence	extracts
fresh beetroot	raw beets
gelatine	gelatin
head celery	bunch celery
icing	frosting
icing sugar	confectioner's sugar
plain flour	all purpose flour
root ginger	ginger root
self-raising flour	all purpose flour sifted with baking powder
soft brown sugar	light brown sugar
spring onion	scallion
stem ginger	preserved ginger
sultanas	seedless white raisins
wholemeal	wholewheat

Introduction

'I adore food – in fact I like it much too much. I really want to be slim, but I don't want to "diet" because as soon as I'm told I can't have certain foods, I want them even more! I don't want to feel hungry, I want the food that I eat to look good and taste superb, and I want to be able to eat large portions.' If this could be you speaking, then this book is for you.

Since 1986 when I first discovered the enormous benefits of eating low fat (I had to follow a low-fat diet in order to avoid surgery for gallstones), a great deal of research has been done. We now know why the body becomes so much leaner when following a diet low in fat and how it gets even leaner if we undertake regular aerobic exercise. (Don't panic – aerobic exercise is any activity that makes you puff a bit, from walking to running.)

The problem is that I am basically greedy where food is concerned. In the late 60s, just after I'd got married, I undertook a cordon bleu cookery course which was published in weekly parts. I read them from cover to cover, cooked lots of the wonderful recipes and served them up to my husband. He ate a normal portion – and I ate the rest!

Soon I had gained over 30lb (13.6kg) and was overweight for the first time in my life. I had discovered how delicious food could be, and I just couldn't get enough of it. As the weight crept on, panic set in. I hated being overweight. Was I pregnant? friends asked. 'Rose has put on some weight, hasn't she?' was a regular comment. I binged and starved with great regularity. I felt out of control. I hated myself.

Then I started reading every diet book I could find. I became fascinated by the subject and calorie-counted my way down to a respectable weight of 8st 7lb (54kg) for my 5ft 2in height and then started my own slimming club. I still struggled with my weight, but I never returned to the 10st 3lb (65kg) I weighed at my heaviest. Then, 15 years on, I discovered low-fat eating.

When I fell ill one day and was rushed to hospital, the surgeon told me I should have my gall bladder removed and that I'd only be out of action for three months. I asked what alternative there was, as I really couldn't be out of action for so long. Rather sniffily, he said the only alternative was to eat an extremely low-fat diet. 'Fine', I said. 'I'll do it'. The hospital dietician gave me a list of foods to avoid and I was soon to rearrange my eating pattern. No more butter or cream – of which I used to eat loads. No more crisps or chips. No more cheese or skin off the chicken. The future looked bleak indeed. Then a miracle happened. As I continued with a will of iron to stick to my new diet there appeared an amazing change in my shape.

All my adult life I had endured a huge posterior and voluptuous thighs. My mother and my grandmother had been the same. I always had to buy skirts and trousers in a size 12, while I was a size ten above the waist. But now things were changing dramatically. Inches fell away from my hips and thighs. I could now slip easily into a size ten trousers or skirts. It was quite remarkable.

The ladies who attended my slimming classes noticed the transformation in my shape and pleaded with me to share my secret, so I designed a diet sheet for them, offering low-fat meals. What happened to their shapes exactly replicated what had happened to mine. Inches were falling off those places previously ignored by other diets. To test the effectiveness of the diet even further I ran an eight-week trial, with hundreds of volunteers recruited through local radio. The results were a resounding thumbs up for low-fat eating. The comments from my volunteer trial team were a real tonic. One lady wrote telling me how her husband had commented that she now had the figure she had when she married him 30 years ago. Another had put her husband on the diet. 'He's regained his boyish figure again', she said. One lady was so thrilled with what the diet had done for her, she wrote: 'I can't stop looking in the mirror'. This lady was 79 years old!

With the trial complete and the results conclusive, I set about writing my Hip and Thigh Diet. This was to become the diet sensation of the decade, selling in excess of two million copies and appearing in the UK bestseller charts for ten years. Low-fat eating became fashionable and the food manufacturers responded to the dramatic increase in the demand for low-fat foods.

Low-fat eating wasn't new. We'd been told long before that we should eat less fat for our health. Sadly, we either couldn't believe that we would suffer from heart disease ('that always happens to someone else'), or we just enjoyed high-fat foods too much to say no. But this was different. Here was proof that if you ate low fat you could lose lots of fat from your body and you could look loads better. The nation bought into the philosophy and found it definitely worked.

It's now almost 11 years since my Hip and Thigh Diet was first published. Subsequently there have been further books, videos, TV programmes, and the launch of my Diet & Fitness Clubs and my Diet & Fitness Magazine. Millions of people are now eating a low-fat diet as a way of life. They know it makes sense.

I have already had two Hip and Thigh Cookbooks published offering delicious low-fat recipes, but this low-fat cookbook is different. I wanted to write a book that would teach people *how* to cook low fat and to offer a low-fat option to those family favourites that form part of our staple diet, as well as more ambitious recipes.

If you've lost weight, or are still in the process of doing so, your best chance of achieving long-term success is by satisfying your taste buds, your appetite, and your family's appetite. This can only be achieved by eating foods you enjoy, foods that will work for you by making and keeping you healthy rather than work against you by making you fat.

I want you to enjoy using this book. You don't need to be an expert cook. The recipes will work for everyone, irrespective of your level of competence as a cook. In each recipe, the fat and calorie content per serving is given as an indication only – I do not want you to start counting fat grams, only to be mindful of your daily calorie intake. Because almost all the ingredients used in the recipes contain 4 per cent or less fat, the fat content will look after itself. The only exceptions to this rule are foods such as oily fish or lean cuts of meat, which contain valuable nutrients, or items such as mustard or curry powder that are used in such small quantities that the fat content is immaterial. Calories do count – if you eat too many, you will gain weight, and if you eat fewer than your body expends, you will lose weight. It really is as simple as that.

The secrets of successful slimming

Even on a low-fat diet, calories play a vital role in determining whether or not we lose weight.

If you look at the nutrition panel printed on the packaging of foods, the 'energy' value is given in kJ (kilojoules) and kcal (kilocalories). The kcal (kilocalories) figure will tell you the number of calories per 100g. A kilogram calorie is a unit of energy derived from food. For ease of reference I shall simply refer to kilocalories as 'calories'.

Are all calories equal?

It used to be thought that, providing you stuck to a reduced-calorie intake, you would lose weight, and it didn't matter what made up those calories – it could be chocolate and

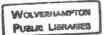

chips as long as you didn't exceed your calorie allowance. It's certainly true that if we eat fewer calories than our body burns up as energy each day, we will lose weight. BUT – and it's a big but – this old way of thinking didn't take into account the fact that weight loss on the scales is not representative of fat loss from the body. We can lose weight by a reduction in bodily fluids, muscle tissue and fat, but fat has the greatest volume. Test it for yourself. Go to your butcher and buy 1 lb (450g) of lean meat such as steak or chicken breast without the skin. Then buy a 1 lb chunk of beef fat (not lard, as that is too condensed). When you get home, weigh out 1 lb of water on your kitchen scales. Line up the water, lean muscle meat and the lump of fat and see the difference.

On a weight-loss plan, there are three main reasons why we want to lose fat. Firstly, we don't need so much of it. Secondly, it uses fewer calories than muscle to sustain it and, thirdly, it's ugly and unhealthy.

To sustain an efficiently working body machine, we need water, and lean muscle tissue is something to be treasured, as it demands lots of calories to sustain it. In fact, it burns three times as many calories as fat per unit weight. Muscle is hungry tissue that keeps our metabolic rate buoyant and uses energy even when we're not exercising. During exercise, the energy expenditure of muscle increases dramatically, but there is very little change in the energy expenditure of fat. Muscle burns 13 calories per kilogram of weight per day. Fat, on the other hand, burns just 4.5 calories per kilogram. Interestingly, a kilogram of fat contains 9,000 calories, whereas a kilogram of muscle has about 1,000 calories.

Fat is very easily stored by the body for emergencies. In its evolutionary process, the body was designed to store fat to keep energy supplies ready for times of famine. Sounds far-fetched? Well, here's further proof.

In 1996 I made a series of films for ITV's highly popular This Morning programme. I went along with the film crew to the Dunn Nutrition Centre in Cambridge, where Dr Andrew Prentice, who at that time was Head of the Energy Metabolism Research Group, showed us an experiment.

A volunteer was given a high-carbohydrate meal – a plate of pasta. After eating it, a plastic hood with a breathing tube connected to a computer (called a metabolic hood) was placed over the volunteer's head. As he continued to breathe quite normally the computerised machine registered an increase in energy expenditure, signifying metabolic activity by the volunteer's body in digesting the calories supplied by the carbohydrate in the pasta.

A similar test was run on another volunteer. This time the volunteer was given a bar of chocolate that was high in fat but which contained the same number of calories as the plate of pasta. Again, the metabolic hood was placed over the volunteer's head to check the energy expenditure created by the eating of the chocolate. There was, however, almost no recognition by the computer that the volunteer had eaten anything! In other words, the body had digested and absorbed the high-fat chocolate without burning any extra calories.

It was by accident that I discovered that low-fat eating leads to a leaner body. I didn't know how or why it happened. Fortunately, scientists are now able to illustrate how the body uses carbohydrate calories and burns them off rather than storing them, while the body is extremely efficient at storing fat for emergencies.

Most people who decide to shed a few pounds want to do it fast! There is an understandable temptation to eat fewer and fewer calories in the belief that the less you eat, the more weight you will lose. There are three main problems with this theory. Firstly, eating too little stretches your willpower to its limits, leaves you feeling very hungry and deprived and always, yes always, ends in disaster when the inevitable eating binge takes over. Feelings of failure, desperation and disappointment follow, and your good intentions are replaced with a feeling of resignation that you're meant to be overweight!

The second problem is that the body doesn't like being starved and automatically changes down a gear towards self-preservation. Believing it may be starved, your body becomes as efficient as possible and tries not to waste a single calorie. In fact, on the most severe diets, your metabolic rate can actually decrease by up to 20 per cent.

There is yet another problem. Since there isn't enough energy in your food, the body takes the

energy it needs from its reserves. We hope that this will be from our fat stores, but during rapid weight loss the energy also comes from our muscles. Yes, we lose weight on the scales – possibly lots of it, but it's weight from the wrong places. And the worst news of all is the fact that the less muscle we have, the lower our metabolic rate. Crash dieting – that's eating less than 800 calories a day or less – is bad news on all sides. It doesn't re-educate our eating habits. It is counter-productive and doesn't work in the long term.

So how many calories should we take in? The average woman burns around 1,400 calories a day, just by being alive. She'd burn up that many if she stayed in bed all day. As soon as she gets out of bed and goes about her daily work, she burns even more. The more active she is, the more calories she burns.

Another interesting fact is that the heavier you are, the more calories your body needs to carry out your daily activities. On pages 21–26 you will find tables giving approximate calculations of your basic daily calorie requirements, depending on your weight and age. Use these to calculate your daily calorie allowance. They cater for men too.

Losing weight is simply a matter of physics. Your body needs a certain number of calories to keep you alive and give you the energy to live your daily life. If you eat more calories than your body uses, you will gain weight. If you eat an equal number of calories to those you use, your body weight remains constant. If you eat fewer calories than your body uses, you lose weight. If your weight is remaining constant when you think you should be losing it, then I'm afraid you are eating more calories than you think and are not being active enough!

You can lose body fat *more* effectively by eating sufficient low-fat calories to make your body believe it's not dieting and you can burn more calories by doing more activity.

The most efficient way to lose body fat is to eat a low-fat diet of around 1,400 calories a day for women and 1,750 for men and combine this with 30 minutes of physical activity, at a level that makes you slightly breathless, three to five times a week.

All my diets are based on two key criteria. They offer 1,400 calories a day (men may increase the quantities by 25 per cent), and each ingredient usually contains a maximum of 4 per cent fat, although vegetarians are allowed a tiny amount of additional fat.

As a rough guide, this is how I make up one of my diets.

Daily allowance

	kcal
¾ pint (450ml) skimmed or semi-skimmed milk:	200–275
1 unit alcohol (average)	100
Breakfast	250
Lunch	350
Dinner:	
main course	400
dessert	100
TOTAL (approx.)	1400

The calories can be moved around, and the alcoholic drink is optional. If on one day you eat 1,300 calories and on another day 1,500, it doesn't matter. To lose 2lb (1kg) a week you need to consume 7,000 fewer calories than your body spends. This is how it works. See it as a balance sheet.

ENERGY OUTGOINGS PER DAY	Debit (kcal)	ENERGY INCOME PER DAY	Credit (kcal)
Energy used in being alive	1400	Food consumed	1400
Energy used in going about your everyday tasks	800		
Exercise 3 to 5 times a week, plus additional physical activity – average per day	200		
		TOTAL INCOME	1400
		POTENTIAL FAT LOSS	1000
TOTAL OUTGOINGS	2400		2400

An energy deficit of 1,000 kcal per day = 7,000 kcal a week = 2lb (1kg) weight loss which will mostly be body fat.

So can you do it by diet alone? By following a diet of 1,400 calories a day, you would go into debt by only 5,600 calories a week. To reach your target of 2lb (1kg) fat loss per week, you would need to spend another 1,400 calories during the course of the week. This is where exercise comes in. The average woman burns around 100 calories to briskly walk a mile (at a 3mph pace). Interestingly, she would burn the same number of calories if she jogged or ran the same distance – the only difference is that, at a more energetic pace, she would burn the calories in less time. The good news for the moderate exerciser is that they can continue for longer, so it pays to take it at a gentle pace. Whatever exercise you do, you will lose weight faster and lose fat more efficiently. You'll look and feel so good that you will be greatly encouraged to continue. Get into the habit of doing some exercise on a regular basis, but don't feel you have to train for a marathon. Exercise is recommended on only three or five days a week, as the body needs two rest days to restock its energy stores, rather like charging a battery!

Now, here's some more good news. If you are very overweight you will actually burn more calories than your slim friend for the same amount of activity, because it requires more energy to move a bigger body. This means you won't have to work as hard to achieve the same results as your friend, so don't exhaust yourself.

Just walk at a moderate level that is comfortable for you. Remember, any activity is better than none, and the one you enjoy doing is the very best one for you because you are more likely to keep on doing it.

Metabolism

Our metabolic rate is the rate at which we burn our food, rather like the number of miles per gallon a car can do. Like a car, the bigger the body, the more fuel it uses. Our bodies use a lot of energy just to tick over – to keep the heart beating, tissue renewing, hair growing, and so on. The approximate number of calories used by the body for this process is between 1,200 and 2,000 a day for women and between 1,500 and 2,500 for men.

This basic energy requirement is described as our basal metabolic rate (BMR). On pages 21–26 there are tables illustrating what your BMR is likely to be, based on your age, weight and also how many calories you are likely to burn up each day in your daily activities. From these you can calculate your personal calorie allowance for weight maintenance. If you want to lose weight, you must eat less than your maintenance requirement, but make sure your daily calorie allowance does not fall below your BMR, so that you give your body sufficient fuel. Failure to do this may result in your muscles being utilised to make up the starvation rations, which, in turn, will lower your metabolic rate. Obviously, you want to avoid this at all costs.

Daily energy (kilocalorie) requirements of women aged 18–29 years

Body Weight (Stones)	Basal Metabolic Rate	Total energy requirement(kcal per day)		
		Sedentary	Active	Very Active
7	1146	1720	1950	2180
7.5	1193	1790	2030	2270
8	1240	1860	2110	2360
8.5	1288	1930	2190	2450
9	1335	2000	2270	2540
9.5	1382	2070	2350	2630
10	1428	2140	2430	2710
10.5	1476	2210	2510	2800
11	1523	2880	2590	2890
11.5	1570	2360	2670	2980
12	1618	2430	2750	3070
12.5	1664	2500	2830	3160
13	1711	2570	2830	3250
13.5	1758	2640	2990	3340
14	1806	2710	3070	3430
14.5	1853	2780	3150	3520
15	1900	2850	3230	3610
15.5	1945	2918	3306	3696
16	1992	2988	3386	3785
16.5	2040	3060	3468	3876
17	2087	3130	3548	3965
17.5	2133	3200	3628	4053
18	2180	3270	3706	4142
18.5	2228	3342	3788	4233
19	2274	3411	3866	4321
19.5	2320	3480	3944	4408
20	2370	3555	4029	4503

Body Weight (Stones)	Basal Metabolic Rate	Total energy requirement (kcal per day)		
		Sedentary	Active	Very Active
7	1215	1820	2070	2310
7.5	1242	1860	2110	2360
8	1268	1900	2160	2410
8.5	1295	1940	2200	2460
9	1323	1980	2250	2510
9.5	1348	2020	2290	2560
10	1374	2060	2340	2610
10.5	1400	2100	2380	2660
11	1427	2140	2430	2710
11.5	1454	2180	2470	2760
12	1480	2220	2520	2810
12.5	1505	2260	2560	2860
13	1532	2300	2600	2910
13.5	1559	2340	2650	2960
14	1586	2380	2700	3010
14.5	1612	2420	2740	3060
15	1639	2460	2790	3110
15.5	1645	2468	2796	3126
16	1671	2506	2841	3175
16.5	1700	2550	2890	3230
17	1723	2584	2929	3274
17.5	1750	2625	2975	3325
18	1774	2661	3016	3371
18.5	1800	2700	3060	3420
19	1825	2738	3102	3468
19.5	1852	2778	3148	3519
20	1880	2820	3196	3572

Daily energy (kilocalorie) requirements of women aged 30–59 years

Daily energy (kilocalorie) requirements of women aged 60 years and over

Body Weight (Stones)	Basal Metabolic Rate	Total energy requirement (kcal per day)		
		Sedentary	Active	Very Active
7	998	1500	1700	1900
7.5	1028	1542	1750	1950
8	1057	1590	1800	2010
8.5	1087	1630	1850	2070
9	1116	1670	1900	2120
9.5	1146	1720	1950	2180
10	1174	1760	2000	2230
10.5	1204	1810	2050	2290
11	1233	1850	2100	2340
11.5	1263	1890	2150	2400
12	1292	1940	2200	2450
12.5	1320	1980	2240	2510
13	1350	2030	2300	2570
13.5	1380	2070	2350	2620
14	1409	2110	2400	2680
14.5	1439	2160	2450	2730
15	1469	2200	2500	2790
15.5	1552	2328	2638	2949
16	1581	2372	2688	3004
16.5	1610	2415	2737	3059
17	1639	2458	2786	3114
17.5	1667	2500	2834	3167
18	1697	2546	2885	3224
18.5	1726	2589	2934	3279
19	1754	2631	2982	3333
19.5	1783	2674	3031	3388
20	1810	2715	3077	3439

Body Weight (Stones)	Basal Metabolic Rate	Total energy requirement (kcal per day)		
		Sedentary	Active	Very Active
8	1456	2180	2480	2770
8.5	1509	2260	2570	2870
9	1557	2340	2650	2960
9.5	1606	2410	2730	3050
10	1652	2480	2810	3140
10.5	1701	2550	2890	3230
11	1749	2620	2970	3320
11.5	1797	2700	3060	3410
12	1846	2770	3140	3510
12.5	1892	2840	3220	3600
13	1940	2910	3300	3690
13.5	1990	2980	3380	3780
14	2037	3060	3460	3870
14.5	2086	3130	3550	3960
15	2134	3200	3630	4050
15.5	2180	3270	3710	4140
16	2220	3330	3770	4220
16.5	2278	3420	3870	4330
17	2330	3490	3950	4420
17.5	2365	3548	4020	4494
18	2410	3615	4097	4579
18.5	2460	3690	4182	4674
19	2510	3765	4267	4769
19.5	2555	3832	4344	4854
20	2605	3908	4428	4950

Daily energy (kilocalorie) requirements of men aged 18–29 years

Daily energy (kilocalorie) requirements of men aged 30–59 years

Body Weight (Stones)	Basal Metabolic Rate	Total energy requirement (kcal per day)		
		Sedentary	Active	Very Active
8	1458	2190	2480	2770
8.5	1495	2240	2540	2840
9	1532	2300	2600	2910
9.5	1569	2350	2670	2980
10	1604	2410	2730	3050
10.5	1641	2460	2790	3120
11	1678	2520	2850	3190
11.5	1715	2570	2920	3260
12	1752	2630	2980	3330
12.5	1787	2680	3040	3400
13	1824	2740	3100	3470
13.5	1861	2790	3160	3540
14	1898	2850	3230	3640
14.5	1934	2900	3290	3680
15	1970	2960	3350	3750
15.5	2007	3010	3410	3810
16	2037	3060	3460	3870
16.5	2080	3120	3540	3950
17	2117	3180	3600	4020
17.5	2150	3225	3655	4085
18	2184	3276	3713	4150
18.5	2220	3330	3774	4218
19	2260	3390	3842	4294
19.5	2295	3442	3902	4360
20	2330	3495	3961	4427

Body Weight (Stones)	Basal Metabolic Rate	Total energy requirement (kcal per day)		
		Sedentary	Active	Very Active
8	1182	1773	2009	2246
8.5	1220	1830	2074	2318
9	1256	1884	2135	2386
9.5	1294	1941	2200	2459
10	1331	1996	2263	2529
10.5	1368	2052	2326	2599
11	1406	2109	2390	2671
11.5	1443	2164	2453	2742
12	1480	2220	2516	2812
12.5	1517	2276	2579	2882
13	1555	2332	2644	2954
13.5	1591	2386	2705	3023
14	1629	2444	2769	3095
14.5	1666	2499	2832	3165
15	1704	2556	2897	3238
15.5	1740	2610	2958	3306
16	1777	2666	3021	3376
16.5	1815	2722	3086	3448
17	1852	2778	3148	3519
17.5	1888	2832	3210	3587
18	1926	2889	3274	3659
18.5	1964	2946	3339	3732
19	2000	3000	3400	3800
19.5	2038	3057	3465	3872
20	2075	3112	3528	3942

Daily energy (kilocalorie) requirements of men aged 60 years and over

Excuses, excuses . . .

Overweight people blame many things for their size. Here are the top ten excuses I've heard in my 25 years in the business.

1 I've a slow metabolism
2 I can't exercise
3 It's because I'm on HRT
4 It's my glands
5 I don't have time to diet
6 I hardly eat anything
7 It's my job – irregular hours
8 It's not fat, it's muscle
9 It's in my genes
10 I can't lose it since I had the children

At the Dunn Nutrition Centre in Cambridge, many and varied studies and clinical tests have been undertaken on metabolism and weight loss. Firstly, it's extraordinarily rare for anyone to have a slow metabolism. Secondly, in tests where overweight and slim people were asked to keep daily diet diaries, the results were very interesting. Slim people accurately recorded what they ate, while the overweight volunteers, on average, underestimated how much they ate by a third!

While many overweight people may think they have a slow metabolic rate, in actual fact the reverse is true. Think of it like this. If you had to carry around the equivalent of several heavy suitcases, 24 hours a day, 365 days a year, you would obviously burn more calories than usual. The more weight you carry, the harder the body has to work. But as we shed our excess weight our muscles don't have to work as hard to enable us to move around. After a while, a suitcase can be eliminated, the body adjusts, muscles slowly get smaller and our basal metabolic rate falls. To keep our metabolic rate up, we need to work on building more muscle. Remember, unlike fat, muscle is an energy-hungry tissue.

It is really important for you to use all your muscles if you are to maintain their size and strength. To do this, you need to do additional exercise that puts pressure on the muscles to become stronger. This type of exercise can be done in a class, in a gymnasium or, indeed, at home to a fitness video.

The good news is that you can lose weight without starving. You can maintain your metabolic rate so that you can still eat plenty of food when you're slim and look fit and feel healthy into the bargain.

In my opinion the problem of excess weight arises not from a slow metabolism, HRT or lack of exercise. It comes from our attitude to food. If we really love food – any food – then the chances are we'll have a weight problem, because it takes willpower to stop eating when we're enjoying ourselves. Some people just keep on eating; some people can't stop spending money, even when they can't afford to; others can't stop drinking when they've had more than enough. Addiction? Possibly, but we have to eat food because if we don't, we'll die, so we have to learn to control our urges.

I often tell people that it is much harder to control their weight – or appetite – than it is to stop smoking. For smoking, the advice is straightforward – stop. But, in the case of eating, it's much more difficult. We not only have to break old habits but develop new ones too.

I hope that the recipes in this book will enable you to get your attitude to food back on line. I hope you'll stop seeing food as an enemy, a danger area, and make it your friend. I want you to learn to relax about food but stay in control.

Eating low-fat foods has changed my life. I never thought I would ever be able to control my eating to maintain my lower weight. It's now 12 years since I was out of control. What's changed? I now eat large healthy, low-fat meals, three times a day, and I've become more active.

Creating a healthy diet

We only need to walk into our doctor's surgery to see an abundance of leaflets and posters recommending that we eat a healthy diet. But so often we associate things that are healthy with foods that are boring. Well, it needn't be that way.

We need to eat a variety of foods to obtain the nutrients we need for good health. I find it easier to think of nutrients as falling into two categories – tangible and intangible. Tangible nutrients are carbohydrates (bread, potatoes, rice, pasta, cereal), proteins (meat, fish, poultry, eggs, cheese, milk) and fats (oil, butter,

margarine, cream, lard). Minerals and vitamins fall into the intangible category because they are found *within* carbohydrates, proteins and fats. The key to good nutrition is getting the balance right. Eating too much of one thing can be as bad as eating too little of another. Another item for consideration is alcohol. In essence, a little is good, and too much is bad for you.

Here are some basic nutritional guidelines.

Carbohydrates
Primary use: To give us energy
Calories per gram: 4
Fattening power (i.e. storage potential as body fat): Poor. Carbohydrates will only be stored as fat if eaten in great excess
Food types: Bread, potatoes, cereal, pasta, rice, fruit, vegetables
How much should we eat? Carbohydrates should form the bulk of each meal, and most of the calories we consume each day should come from this food group

Proteins
Primary use: To help the body grow, renew, and repair
Calories per gram: 4
Fattening power: Poor. Excess protein cannot be stored, but instead will be used to provide energy, therefore delaying the burning of fat
How much should we eat? Protein should be eaten in moderation, forming about a seventh of our daily calorie intake. Too much can be harmful

because it has to be metabolised by our kidneys. Part of the protein is excreted from the body; the remainder is used to provide energy

Fats

Primary use: A concentrated form of energy, efficiently stored for later use in case of. Also supplies some valuable nutrients for health

Calories per gram: 9

Fattening power: Excellent. This is the prime purpose of fat

How much should we eat? Allow 20–40g per day on a weight-reducing diet. Eat no more than 70g per day when seeking to maintain weight and for good health

Alcohol

Alcohol is a mixture of good and bad. It is a relaxant and has been acknowledged by the medical profession as having a real benefit in relieving stress. Alcohol also helps to reduce the risk of heart disease. It is, nevertheless, a mild form of poison and the body works hard to get rid of it. On my diets, I allow a single unit of alcohol each day for women and two for men, plus three bonus drinks that can be taken at any time during the week, but not all at once! Remember, too, that, alcohol can be addictive, and we need to be mindful of the dangers. As with all things, moderation is the key.

There has been much debate and many trials to determine the benefits and disadvantages of consuming alcohol, ranging from whether it helps your heart to whether it makes you fat. It was even suggested at one point that the calories from alcohol didn't count because the body processed calories from alcohol in a different way from other calories. But alcohol calories *do* count.

In its neat form, alcohol yields 7 calories per gram, but of course we never consume alcohol in its pure state. It is always diluted by water, even in the strongest spirits. The calories in your favourite tipple may not always be directly related to the alcohol content, since many drinks contain sugar, carbohydrate and sometimes even fat.

Alcohol is easily absorbed by the stomach, but the only way the body can rid itself of alcohol is by burning it in the liver and other tissues. Since alcohol is essentially a toxin and the body has no useful purpose for storing it, the body prioritises the elimination of it at the cost of processing other foods you have eaten. Consequently, other foods may be converted to fat more readily than usual, thereby increasing your fat stores.

In the many trials I have carried out for my diets I have always found that slimmers who do drink a little alcohol while following the diet do at least as well as those who don't and, in some cases, lose more weight. But rather than suggesting that alcohol has any miracle effect, I believe it's down to the fact that if you are allowed a drink you feel less restricted, can still socialise and feel as if you are leading a 'normal' life.

The key is to have a little each day, rather than drinking a lot on the occasional drinking binge. Perhaps the greatest danger from drinking alcohol when you are dieting is that it is extremely effective at diluting your willpower. Because it is a relaxant, it's so easy to think, 'oh, what the heck, I'll diet tomorrow,' and then really overindulge on the food front!

Minerals

There are many minerals, all of which play an important role in helping us achieve good health. In most cases, a varied and healthy diet will ensure we are not missing out. However, there are two important minerals – calcium and iron – that require special mention. Since dairy products are the richest source of calcium, and red meat is the richest source of iron, on a low-fat diet it is particularly important to make sure you are taking in sufficient amounts. If you consume $3/4$ pint (450ml) of skimmed or semi-skimmed milk plus a small pot of yogurt (5oz/150g) each day and eat red meat four times a week, you will probably meet your needs.

We need calcium to help maintain our bones and teeth and we need iron to make haemoglobin which carries oxygen around the body in the red blood cells. Too little iron, and we become anaemic. Too little calcium, and we get osteoporosis. The tables on pages 31 and 32 will help you check if you are getting enough of each nutrient. If you're not, you need to amend your diet accordingly.

Please note, these tables are intended as a rough guide only, since the iron and calcium content of foods may differ slightly for different cuts of meat and different brands of cereals, especially if they have been fortified.

Vitamins

Vitamins fall into two categories: fat soluble and water soluble. Vitamins A, D, E and K are fat soluble and do not need to be consumed daily, since the body is able to store them. However, the B complex vitamins and vitamin C are water soluble. Since these cannot be stored by the body, they need to be consumed daily. Each vitamin has its own special function and all are essential for good health.

Even though my diets are designed to be healthy and balanced, I do recommend you take a multivitamin tablet daily, just to make doubly sure you have all the vitamins you need. This will ensure that you always get all the micronutrients your body needs. The time-released type of vitamin tablet is best and they are widely available from healthfood stores and chemists. Always follow the recommended dose.

These days much attention has been focused on the antioxidant vitamins (vitamins A, C, and E). These vitamins help to zap the free radicals that occur naturally in the body. For thousands of years, the balance between antioxidants and free radicals in the body has been just fine, naturally. But now, with increased pollution, radiation from microwaves, TVs and computers and even

Iron content of foods

Food	Serving size	MG	
Liver	100g cooked weight	8	
Kidney	100g cooked weight	7	
Venison	100g cooked weight	8	
Lean beef	100g cooked weight	3	
Lean lamb	100g cooked weight	2	
Pork	100g cooked weight	1	
Ham	100g cooked weight	1	
Duck	100g cooked weight	3	
Chicken/turkey	100g cooked weight	1	
Egg	1	1	
Chickpeas	100g cooked weight	3	
Lentils	100g cooked weight	2.5	
Baked beans	1 small can	2	
Potatoes	100g	0.5	
Spinach	50g cooked weight	2	
Watercress	50g	1	
Cabbage	50g cooked weight	0.5	
Broccoli	50g cooked weight	0.5	
Dried fruit	50g	1	
White bread	1 slice	0.5	
Wholemeal bread	1 slice	0.8	
Branflakes	25g	7	(fortified)
Weetabix	25g	4	(fortified)

The reference nutrient intake (RNI) for the female population is 14.8mg per day.

Calcium content of foods

Food	Weight	MG
Milk	600ml	680
Cheddar cheese	25g	225
Cottage cheese	1 small pot	60
Yogurt	1 small pot	360
Egg	1	25
Sardines	50g cooked weight	250
Pilchards (canned)	50g	150
Prawns	50g cooked weight	75
Tofu	100g	500
Ice cream	50g	70
White bread	1 slice	30 (fortified)
Wholemeal bread	1 slice	7
Weetabix	25g	10
Shredded wheat	25g	12
Spinach	50g cooked weight	300
Watercress	50g	110
Dried fruit	50g	30

The reference nutrient intake (RNI) for the female population is 700mg per day (800mg per day for 15- to 18-year-olds).

electric light bulbs, as well as increased exposure to stress, the body is producing more free radicals. These are the bad guys. To neutralise them, we need to increase the number of antioxidants (the good guys) by eating more of the foods that contain the ACE vitamins. They're easy to spot because many of these vitamins are found in brightly coloured vegetables and fruit. Other chemical compounds in fruit and vegetables, known as flavanoids, also act as antioxidants. Flavanoids are found in red wine too. Some minerals, such as zinc and selenium, can also act as antioxidants.

So, make sure you eat a wide range of foods to get all the vitamins and minerals you need. If in doubt, consider taking a micronutrient supplement.

Reading nutrition labels

Nowadays we are fortunate that most food products we buy contain lots of useful information on the nutrition label. This provides us with a breakdown of their nutritional content as well as the number of calories and amount of fat. To simplify matters, as far as weight control is concerned, the two key things to look at are *energy* and *fat*.

The figure relating to 'energy' tells you the number of calories in 100g of the product (you can ignore the kJ figure – just look at the kcal one). You then need to calculate how much of the product you will actually be eating to work out the number of calories per portion.

NUTRITIONAL INFORMATION	
	Per 100g
ENERGY	172 kJ/40 kcal
PROTEIN	1.8g
CARBOHYDRATE	8.0g
(of which sugars)	(2.0g)
FAT	0.2g
(of which saturates)	(Trace)
FIBRE	1.5g
SODIUM	0.3g

The fat content may be broken down into polyunsaturates and saturates but, for anyone on a weight-reducing diet, this is not significant. It is the total fat content per 100g that is relevant in our calculations. I make the general and simple rule that my dieters should only select foods where the label shows the fat content as 4g or less fat per 100g of product, i.e. 4 per cent or less fat. I believe the actual amount of fat per portion is of lesser importance. If you follow the simple 4 per cent rule and restrict your calorie intake to around 1,400–1,600 calories a day for women and 1,700–2,500 calories a day for men, the fat content of your food will look after itself. The only exceptions to this rule are lean cuts of meat such as beef, lamb and pork, which may be just over the 4 per cent yardstick, and oily fish such as salmon and mackerel, which may yield as much as 10 per cent fat. I make these exceptions because these foods contain important nutrients. Vegetarians may use the occasional drop of oil in the preparation of their food.

Designing a diet plan

In very simple terms, a healthy low-fat, weight-reducing diet plan might look like the one below. Men can increase the quantities by 25 per cent and have one extra unit of alcohol each day. There are three bonus drinks per week, too, for both men and women. Remember, do not use any butter, margarine or oil.

DAILY ALLOWANCE
3/4 pint (450ml) skimmed or semi-skimmed milk
1 unit of alcohol for women, 2 for men

Throughout the day
Tea and coffee with milk from allowance
Low-calorie drinks and water

BREAKFAST
2oz (50g) bran cereal
Semi-skimmed milk from allowance
1 teaspoon sugar
1/4 pint (150ml) orange juice

LUNCH
2 slices of wholemeal bread made into a
    sandwich with 2oz (50g) chicken or tuna (in
    water or brine) plus salad
Low-fat salad dressing
1 piece of fresh fruit

DINNER
4oz (100g) red meat, 6oz (175g) poultry or 8oz
    (225g) white fish
6oz (175g) potatoes/pasta/rice (cooked
    weight)
12oz (350g) vegetables
Low-fat sauce or gravy
1 glass of wine
Fresh fruit with low-fat yogurt

Making the diet work for you

The right eating plan for you is the one that *works* for you. If you want to have your main meal at lunchtime, that's fine. If you want to save some calories from breakfast and lunch and have a three- or four-course banquet at night, that's fine too. Try to avoid skipping meals completely, or you'll only be tempted to start snacking later.

I don't think it's that crucial if you eat late at night, so long as it's not a large meal. Breakfast is a must, though, even if you don't eat it until 10am. Eating breakfast kick-starts your metabolism and gets things moving in your body.

During the night your body is a digesting-and-mending machine. Imagine it has a day and a night shift. The night shift workers come on duty when you go to bed, and carry out lots of repairs and maintenance while you are asleep. All the day's food is broken down and the nutrients distributed where they are needed. By the morning, the work is complete, so by getting up and having a fresh delivery of food (breakfast) you give the signal to the maintenance night shift to leave and rest while the day shift workers, the energy makers, wake up and take over. Their job is to ensure that the energy value of the foods you eat during the day are available as and when you need them. This is why breakfast is so important.

DO
Eat three meals a day
Drink ¾ pint (450ml) milk a day
Eat 1,400 calories a day if you're a woman, 1,700 calories a day if you're a man
Drink plenty of water
Eat fruit and vegetables every day – at least 5 helpings in any combination
Remove all fat and skin from any meat or poultry you eat
Cook and serve food without any added fat
Make exercise part of your lifestyle

AND SOME DON'Ts
Don't skip meals
Don't eat too few calories
Don't eat all your calories in one meal
Don't starve yourself if you've overindulged – just return to the diet without penalty
Don't become a diet bore!

Questions and answers

Each day I receive a vast mailbag of letters from readers. In these letters, a number of questions crop up again and again. I have included some of the most common ones here.

I have lost three stone on your low-fat diet and am now at my goal. How do I stay at this weight?

Look at the metabolic rate charts on pages 21–26 and check what your daily calorie expenditure is likely to be (that is the figure alongside your weight and in the column that best describes your activity level). This is how many calories you can eat in order to keep your weight constant. You may not need to count calories, since you may find that just sticking to healthy, low-fat meals is sufficient to keep your weight constant. If you occasionally indulge in foods you know are high in fat and calories, just enjoy them and then cut back a little the next day. This way, your body will quickly burn up those extra calories. Weigh yourself once a week (or at least once a month) and correct any small weight gains before they become a big problem.

My husband is overweight but will not stick to a diet. Any suggestions?

It's easy to feed men low-fat food, without their even noticing. Try using low-fat dressings instead of butter in sandwiches. Switch to semi-skimmed milk and make delicious low-fat menus. I've known many wives slim their husbands effectively in this way. Serve up the occasional plate of chips so that he doesn't miss them too much and offer him a luscious but low-fat dessert. I suggest you don't give him yogurt for dessert unless he really enjoys it. Yogurt is so widely regarded as a diet food that you might let out your secret!

I dine out regularly as part of my job. Any suggestions for keeping my weight under control?

Look at eating out as a treat, an occasion when you can select foods you wouldn't think of preparing at home. I always plan to balance my day so that if I'm out for lunch and dinner I'll just have fruit for breakfast. Then for lunch and dinner, I'll just have two courses from the menu, making sure one of the courses I choose is very light. Since I don't cook fish at home very often, I take the opportunity to have it when dining out. It keeps the calories down and gives me a treat. I just ask for it to be cooked without fat and for the vegetables to be served without butter. I ask for any sauce to be served separately so that I'm in control of how much I eat.

If someone's taking you out for a really special treat in the evening and you know you're likely to eat three or four courses, then just be extra careful throughout that day and cut back a little the day after. Perhaps one of the best tips I can give you is to drink loads of sparking water before, during and after your meal. It is a great filler. Also, always counter a really great meal with some extra exercise the next day.

I am not a vegetarian, though occasionally I do enjoy a vegetarian dish. I notice that in some of your vegetarian recipes you allow a little oil to make up for the lack of fat from meat. Can I cook them as your recipe states?

Yes, you can, as the amount of oil per serving is pretty minimal, although you can leave it out if you prefer. It's a matter of personal taste.

I have a medical condition that prevents me from exercising. Can I still lose weight?

Yes. On a diet of 1,400 calories a day you can still lose 1–1$\frac{1}{2}$lb (0.45–0.7kg) per week, although your rate of weight loss may be a little slower than that of someone who exercises regularly. If you stick very strictly to the diet, it definitely will work.

I have lost weight on your diet and hope to start a family soon. Can I still eat low fat when I'm pregnant?

Pregnancy is not a time to try and lose weight, but you should make sure your weight gain is controlled and not excessive, or it will be difficult to lose it later. An unborn baby is like a parasite and will take every nutrient it needs from its mother. This leaves the mother vulnerable, so she needs to ensure she gets sufficient nutrients both for her and her baby. A strict low-fat diet is not recommended but nor is a high-fat one!

You should drink a pint (600ml) of milk a day, have lots of fresh fruit and vegetables (as many as you like), plus lean meat, fish, poultry, eggs and low-fat cheese. Avoid soft cheese, uncooked eggs and liver during pregnancy, and do take a folic acid supplement for at least the first 12 weeks. This has proved to be important in preventing birth defects.

As you prepare to start your family, eat for health, and exercise regularly. Don't overdo it, though. Aim to do 25–30 minutes of moderate exercise three times a week. Once you are pregnant, follow the advice of your GP.

I have an overweight child. Should I put her on a diet?

I have quite definite views about children and their weight. I believe all children should be encouraged to exercise from an early age – from playing games in the garden to joining a sports club when they get older. Children who are active are rarely overweight. Heavier children should be encouraged to eat healthily, along with the rest of the family. Serve up low-fat meals and lots of fresh fruit and vegetables to give them energy and fill them up. This way, there's no need to put children on a weight-loss diet, but just allow them to grow into their weight as they get taller.

A word of warning here to parents. Please do not comment on your child's weight. It is such a sensitive issue, particularly these days. Some dads think it's funny to describe their daughter as tubby. She may be a little heavier than her friends, but commenting on it will only make her self-conscious and possibly paranoid, which could ultimately manifest itself in an eating disorder.

Does the alcohol used in your recipes have to come out of my daily allowance?

Thankfully, no. The quantities of alcohol used in my recipes amount to very little per actual serving.

What is the best time of day to exercise? For instance, is it better to exercise in the morning or evening?

The best time for you to exercise is whatever time you can actually do it. Your lifestyle dictates when that might be, but the most important thing is that you do it regularly. Make sure you have plenty of water to hand, so that you can take sips at regular intervals as you work out. This will prevent you from becoming dehydrated which will only make you feel fatigued sooner.

If you want to work out early in the morning, have a glass of fruit juice 30 minutes or so beforehand to give you some energy after a night's sleep. Also, if you work out hard, eat some carbohydrate within 90 minutes of finishing. This replenishes your energy stores and prevents you from feeling exhausted. Any food you eat, though, should come from your daily allowance and not be in addition to it!

Cooking the low fat way

When the idea was first put to me to write a cookbook, I immediately thought of Delia Smith's Complete Cookery Course. Delia, with all her expertise and experience, had put together a manual showing everyone how to cook – whether you were an expert or a complete novice. What everyone needs now, I thought to myself, is a 'How to cook low fat cookbook'. Delia is known for her fabulously rich recipes, so I wanted to come up with some ideas for low-fat ones. Readers would then be able to leap from one book to the other and balance their eating habits.

Because of Delia's comprehensive and skilled teaching of how to cook, I do not propose to do that in this book, only to show you how to cook low fat and what equipment you need.

Think of your family's favourite recipes and then look in here to see if we've come up with a low-fat version. It may be as simple as roast beef with Yorkshire pudding and roast potatoes, or even tiramisu. We've tried to think of everything, but there will doubtless be some we couldn't remember. Also there are some we just could not replicate. Low-fat 'death by chocolate' or 'sticky toffee pudding' sadly are not within the realms of this book. If you absolutely adore such dishes, then treat yourself to the real thing occasionally! The only recipes I have included are those that I believe taste just as good as their full-fat alternatives. Once you've become used to eating low fat you'll be amazed at how your taste buds change. Believe me, oily or fatty foods quickly lose their appeal and become quite unpalatable.

I have selected a few recipes from some of my earlier books that have proved immensely popular with readers, plus ones that have appeared in the entertaining section of my Diet & Fitness Magazine. I have also included many of the recipes I have demonstrated on my television cookery programme. All these, plus many, many new ones, make up this comprehensive book.

For easy reference and for your interest, I have listed the calorie and fat content per serving for each recipe. If you are trying to lose weight, it is up to you to select which recipes you include as part of your daily calorie allowance. If you simply want to maintain your existing weight, remember to look on the charts on pages 21–26 to check what your total daily calorie output is likely to be. Once you realise that you can eat really well and maintain your new weight, your confidence in food will increase.

Equipment you will need

Utensils

At one time, non-stick surfaces used to have a very short lifespan before becoming scratched and worn. Fortunately, in recent years great progress been made with non-stick pans, although the old adage 'you get what you pay for' still holds firm. Buy a cheap non-stick pan, and the first time you slightly burn the pan, the surface begins to peel.

It is worth investing in a top-quality non-stick wok and a non-stick frying pan, both with lids. I use these two pans more than anything else in my kitchen. The lid is crucial, since this allows the contents of the pan to steam which adds moisture to the dish.

Non-stick saucepans are useful, too, for cooking sauces, porridge, scrambled eggs and other foods that tend to stick easily. Lids are essential for these too. Also, treat yourself to a set of non-stick baking tins and trays. Cakes, Yorkshire puddings, scones, and lots more can all be cooked the low fat way.

Non-scratch implements

Wooden spoons and spatulas, Teflon (or similar) coated tools and others marked as suitable for use with non-stick surfaces are a must. If you continue to use metal forks, spoons and spatulas, you will scratch and spoil the non-stick surface of pans. Treat the surfaces kindly, and good non-stick pans will last for years.

Cleaning a non-stick pan

Always soak the pan first to loosen any food that is still inside, then wash with a non-abrasive sponge or cloth. Any brush or gentle scourer used carefully will do the trick of cleaning away every particle without effort and without damage to the surface. Allowing pans to boil dry is the biggest danger for non-stick pans, so when cooking vegetables, keep on eye on the water levels!

Other equipment

You will no doubt already have many of the items listed below, but there are some you may not have, such as baking parchment, which I find indispensable in a low-fat kitchen. I have therefore made the list as comprehensive as possible, including the things I use most often.

Aluminium foil
Baking parchment
Cling film
Kitchen paper
Chopping boards (1 small, 1 medium, 1 large)
Measuring jugs (1 × 2 pint/1.2 litre, plus 1 × 1 pint/$\frac{1}{2}$ litre)
Kitchen scales that weigh small amounts accurately
Mixing bowls (1 × 2 pint/1.2 litre, 1 × 4 pint/2 litre, 1 × 8 pint/4 litre)
Food processor
Juicer
Steamer

Fish kettle (this can be stainless steel)
Ovenproof dishes
Plastic containers with lids
Ramekin dishes
A good quality can opener
Set of sharp knives (all sizes)
Palette knife
Vegetable peeler
Potato masher (non-scratch)
Pasta spoon (non-scratch)
Slotted spoon (non-scratch)
Wire rack
Pizza cutter
Multi-surface grater
Lemon squeezer
Zester
Melon baller
Sieve (1 small and 1 large)
Colander (1 small and 1 large)
Rolling pin
Flour shaker
Garlic press
Pastry brush
Whisk (balloon type)
Pepper mill
Scissors

Store cupboard

There are many items that are very useful to have in stock. Build up your store cupboard over a period of time to avoid a marathon shopping trip!

Arrowroot

Cornflour

Plain flour

Self-raising flour

Gelatine

Marmite

Bovril

Dried herbs

Tomato ketchup

HP sauce

Fruity sauce

Barbecue sauce

Reduced oil salad dressing

Balsamic vinegar

White wine vinegar

Black peppercorns

Salt

White pepper

Vegetable stock cubes

Chicken stock cubes

Beef stock cubes

Lamb stock cubes

Pork stock cubes

Long-grain easy cook rice

Basmati Rice

Pasta

Oats

Tabasco sauce

Soy sauce

Worcestershire sauce

Caster sugar

Brown sugar

Artificial sweetener

fresh items

Garlic

Fresh herbs

Lemons

Oranges

Tomatoes

Eggs

Low-fat cooking techniques

Dry-frying meat and poultry

I haven't used oil or butter in my frying for 12 years, yet I fry all the time. The secret of dry-frying is to have your non-stick pan over the correct heat. If it's too hot, the pan will dry out too soon and the contents will burn. If the heat is too low, you lose the crispness recommended for a stir-fry. Practice makes perfect and a simple rule is to preheat the empty pan until it is quite hot (but not too hot!) before adding any of the ingredients. Test if the pan is hot enough by adding a piece of meat or poultry. The pan is at the right temperature if the meat sizzles on contact. Once the meat or poultry is sealed on all sides (when it changes colour) you can reduce the heat a little as you add any other ingredients.

Cooking meat and poultry is simple, as the natural fat and juices run out almost immediately, providing plenty of moisture to prevent burning.

When cooking mince, I dry-fry it first and place it in a colander to drain away any fat that has emerged. I wipe out the pan with kitchen paper to remove any fatty residue, then return the meat to the pan to continue cooking my shepherd's pie or bolognese sauce.

Dry-frying vegetables

Vegetables contain their own juices and soon release them when they become hot, so dry-frying works just as well for vegetables as it does for meat and poultry. Perhaps the most impressive results are with onions. When they are dry-fried, after a few minutes they go from being raw to translucent and soft and then on to become brown and caramelised. They taste superb and look all the world like fried onions but taste so much better without all that fat.

When dry-frying vegetables, it's important not to overcook them. They should be crisp and colourful so that they retain their flavour and most of their nutrients.

Good results are also obtained when dry-frying large quantities of mushrooms, as they 'sweat' and make lots of liquid. Using just a few mushrooms produces a less satisfactory result unless you are stir-frying them with lots of other vegetables. If you are using a small quantity, therefore, you may find it preferable to cook them in vegetable stock.

Alternatives to frying with fat

Wine, water, soy sauce, wine vinegar, balsamic vinegar, and even fresh lemon juice all provide liquid in which food can be cooked. Some thicker types of sauces can dry out too fast if added early on in cooking, but these can be added later when there is more moisture in the pan.

When using wine or water, make sure the pan is hot before adding the other ingredients so that they sizzle in the hot pan.

Flavour enhancers

Low-fat cooking can be bland and dry, so it's important to add moisture and/or extra flavour to compensate for the lack of fat.

I have found that adding freshly ground black pepper to just about any savoury dish is a real flavour enhancer. You need a good pepper mill and you should buy your peppercorns whole and in large quantities. Ready ground black pepper is nowhere near as good. Sometimes it has other things mixed with the ground pepper, so give this one a miss.

When cooking rice, pasta and vegetables I always add a vegetable stock cube to the cooking water. Although the stock cube does contain a little fat, the amount that is absorbed by the food is negligible and the benefit in flavour is very noticeable. I always save the water I've used to cook vegetables to make soups, gravy and sauces. Again, the fat from the stock cube that will be contained in a single serving is very small.

When making sandwiches, spread sauces such as Branston, mustard, horseradish and low-fat or fat-free dressings straight onto the bread. This helps the inside of the sandwich to stay 'put' and, because these sauces or dressings are quite highly flavoured, you won't miss the butter. Make sure you use fresh bread for maximum taste.

Here is a quick reference list of ingredients or cooking methods that can be substituted for traditional high-fat ones.

Cheese sauces Use small amounts of low-fat Cheddar, a little made-up mustard and skimmed milk with cornflour.

Custard Use custard powder and follow the instructions on the packet, using skimmed milk and artificial sweetener in place of sugar to save calories.

Cream Instead of double cream or whipping cream, use 0% fat Greek yogurt or fromage frais. Do not boil. For single cream, substitute natural or vanilla-flavoured yogurt or fromage frais.

Cream cheese Use quark (skimmed soft cheese).

Creamed potatoes Mash the potatoes in the normal way and add fromage frais in place of butter or cream. Season well.

French dressing Use two parts apple juice to one part wine vinegar, and add a teaspoon of Dijon mustard (see also recipes on pages 405–410).

Mayonnaise Use fromage frais mixed with two parts cider vinegar to one part lemon juice, plus a little turmeric and sugar (see recipe on page 407).

Marie Rose dressing Use reduced oil salad dressing mixed with yogurt, tomato ketchup and a dash of Tabasco sauce and black pepper (see recipe on page 410).

Porridge Cook with water and make to a sloppy consistency. Cover and leave overnight. Reheat before serving and serve with cold milk and sugar or honey.

Roux Make a low-fat roux by adding dry plain flour to a pan containing the other ingredients and 'cooking off' the flour. Then add liquid to thicken. Alternatively, use cornflour mixed with cold water or milk. Bring to the boil and cook for 2–3 minutes.

Thickening for sweet sauces Arrowroot, slaked in cold water or juice, is good because it becomes translucent when cooked.

Herbs

Herbs are fine fragrant plants that have been used to enhance and flavour food since the development of the art of cookery.

As well as adding the finishing touches to a dish, many are attributed with hidden medicinal strengths that contribute to our wellbeing. Never before has there been such a wide variety of herbs introduced to our palate from Mediterranean influences and worldwide cultures. You can buy them fresh, freeze-dried or dried, or make your own, and all have an important role to play. Since dried herbs have a stronger flavour, they should be used more sparingly than fresh ones.

Fresh herbs fall into two categories: hard wood and soft leaf. Generally, hard wood herbs, such as rosemary, thyme and bay, are added at the beginning of a recipe in order to allow the herbs to soften and release their flavours. Soft leaf herbs, such as parsley, chervil, and basil, have more delicate flavours and are added near the end of cooking time so that they retain their shape.

Fines herbes

This is a French blend of sweet, aromatic herbs that complement each other and is used as a complete flavour enhancer. The most common blend consists of parsley, chervil, chives, and tarragon, which is ideal for fish and salads, egg dishes (especially omelettes), poached chicken, and sauces.

Bouquet garni

A fresh bouquet garni is a small bundle of selected herbs such as parsley stalks and thyme, wrapped in bay leaves. Sometimes a celery stalk or the green part of the leek is also included.

A bouquet garni can also contain dried herbs. Commercially produced ones come in sachets that look rather like tea bags and usually contain equal quantities of dried thyme, bay and parsley. You can make your own by placing a selection of dried herbs in a small square of muslin and tying with a piece of string.

A bouquet garni is used to flavour soups, stews and casseroles and other dishes that need considerable cooking. It should be removed from the dish before serving.

Lemon grass

This sharp woody grass herb, commonly used in East Asian cooking, is unlike any other herb and has the appearance of a dried iris stem. Before using, the outer leaves are removed so that the softer core can be finely chopped. As its name implies, it has a strong lemon fragrance, and it can also be bought dried and chopped.

Fennel

This strong robust plant with sturdy dark green foliage has an anise flavour. Both the leaf and seeds are commonly used in cooking. The seeds are crushed or used whole in curries and casseroles or as a topping for breads.

Bay leaves

These green waxy leaves of the bay tree or Mediterranean laurel have a strong, spicy flavour. They are commonly used in soups and stews, and to flavour infusions of milk in sauces such as bread sauce.

Mint

There are many varieties of mint, from spearmint to applemint and fruit mint. The most aromatic of all herbs, mint is particularly known for its affinity with lamb. Spearmint or garden mint is the one most commonly used in cooking. You can use it to make mint sauce, serve with roast lamb, and add to the cooking water for vegetables such as new potatoes and peas. Mint is also ideal for decorating desserts and puddings. Freshly chopped mint has a strong aroma with which dried mint cannot compare.

Basil

This Mediterranean leaf with its pungent taste and aromatic scent can be used in salads and is perfect with tomatoes. Its main use is in pesto – a paste made with basil, garlic, olive oil and pine nuts. You can make low-fat pesto by omitting the pine nuts and substituting lemon juice for the olive oil.

Marjoram and oregano

These two plants are very similar (oregano is a member of the marjoram family), with small round leaves on woody stems. Marjoram has a more gentle flavour than oregano and is good in stuffings, egg dishes and on roasts. Oregano is commonly used in Italian dishes such as pizza. Both marjoram and oregano are available fresh or dried.

Chives

A member of the onion family, these long green strands have a light onion flavour. When in flower they hold a purple ball of tiny flowers at the pinnacle of the stem. The flowers can be finely snipped and used in salads and dressings and to garnish soups. Choose ones that have dark green and dry firm stems. Avoid yellow tinged ones, as these may be old.

Dill

This is a wispy dark green, feather-like plant. Both the leaves and seeds are cultivated. Fresh leaves are traditionally used with cured salmon such as Gravlax. The seeds are crushed or left whole to impart an anise flavour. Dried dill has a particularly concentrated flavour – use sparingly.

Chervil

This green leafy herb is very similar in appearance to parsley but is a much finer, delicate plant with a light flavour of aniseed. It is used a great deal in French cuisine. Freeze-dried chervil is excellent.

Tarragon

There are two types of tarragon: French and Russian. Russian has a more pungent taste. This large ganglion plant has long, thin greyish green leaves and is used to flavour vinegar and sauces.

Coriander

A member of the carrot family, this pretty plant is probably the most used herb throughout the world. The plant yields both leaf and seed for culinary use. The seeds are crushed or used whole and have a sweet, almost orange zest flavour. Coriander is used as a component in pickling spice and also sold in ground form. The leaf is very delicate with a distinctive flavour that is considered an acquired taste. Both the seeds and leaf are used for flavouring Indian curries and many Moroccan and Mexican dishes.

Parsley

There are two types: curly and flat leaf, and both are full of vitamins and minerals. Flat leaf parsley is better for cooking, as it has a stronger flavour than the curly leaf. Curly parsley, with its strong keeping qualities, is used as a garnish. The leaves can be chopped and sprinkled on many savoury dishes and vegetables, whereas the stalks are ideal for use in soups and stocks.

Rosemary

This hard wood herb has silver grey needle-like leaves and is widely used in Mediterranean cookery. It is used for marinades and spiking lamb or roasting with fish. This versatile herb can also be used with strongly flavoured vegetables, jams and jellies.

Sage

A strong and powerful herb which is used in stuffings and to add flavour to sausages. It can also be used to flavour casseroles and meat dishes (especially pork), but use sparingly.

Thyme

It is believed that there are about 100 different varieties of thyme. This special herb flavours a dish without overpowering it. It is used in soups and casseroles to add depth and a light flavour.

Herbes de Provence

This mixture of southern French herbs, which usually includes oregano, rosemary, marjoram, savory, basil, bay and thyme, is used in stews and is good with pizza, tomatoes and sauces.

Spices

Spices were originally used to disguise ill-flavoured meat and sour foods as a result of insufficient means of chilled storage. Mainly derived from distant shores such as Sri Lanka and the East Indies, spices have over the years developed into flavour-enhancing additions. Today, they are appreciated for their aroma, colour and ability to blend together to give unique flavours.

Since spices are made from seeds, they are quite high in fat. However, because of the relatively small quantities used in recipes, their fat content is insignificant.

Spices can be kept longer than herbs, although once opened they will deteriorate. Keep out of direct sun and seal well after use.

The strongest flavours are achieved by grinding fresh seeds or whole spices as opposed to buying them already ground.

Always add spices at the beginning of a recipe, as they need to be allowed to 'cook out' to allow the flavour to develop fully. Berries such as juniper need to be crushed before cooking to release their flavours, whereas some spices such as fennel or cumin seeds benefit from being toasted in a non-stick pan.

The best way is to experiment with different spices, adding them in tiny quantities, to give a unique flavour to your cookery.

Garlic

Garlic is a fundamental ingredient in many savoury dishes. Once native to the Mediterranean, China and Central Asia it is now grown all over the world, varying in size, colour and flavour.

A bulb or head of garlic contains several cloves, each covered with a thin film of skin and all held together by an outer thicker skin. The most common garlic is the white-skinned type, followed by pink-skinned, which is much stronger in flavour. Then there is Elephant garlic with its giant cloves that are much milder in strength and flavour.

A member of the onion family, garlic, like most vegetables, is seasonal. Fresh pungent bulbs are harvested in late spring and then hung and stored in cool, well-ventilated dark rooms.

In its raw state, garlic is strong and fiery. Cooking with garlic is very much a matter of personal taste. The longer it is cooked, the sweeter and more mellow the flavour. Crushed or chopped garlic can be dry-fried at the beginning of a recipe to release its flavour. However, do not allow it to burn or it will add a bitter flavour to the finished dish.

If you only like a little garlic, try rubbing the inside of a cooking pan or casserole dish with a peeled clove. This will impart a hint of garlic flavour.

Stocks

Any restaurant chef will tell you that the secret of a good sauce relies on a very good stock. Home-made stock is very time-consuming to make but well worth the effort, as the final flavours are quite different from any convenient stock cube alternatives. If you do decide to make your own stock, be sure to chill it completely. This allows the fat to set, making it easy to remove and discard before adding the stock to your cooking.

There are four basic stocks which are used as a base for many dishes. White stock is pale and light and made from meat and poultry. Unbrowned beef and chicken are excellent for this purpose, while lamb, pork and duck contain much higher levels of fat. Brown stock is made by browning the meat or bones first, you can either dry-fry the meat in a non-stick pan or roast in a hot oven (the latter method gives a darker colour). Both white and brown stock are then flavoured with root vegetables such as carrot, celery, onion and leek and left to simmer in plenty of water for $1\frac{1}{2}$–2 hours. A brown stock may be coloured with tomato purée or gravy browning for a deep finish.

Fish stock is quite different and needs careful cooking – the stock should not be allowed to simmer for more than 20 minutes, as the bones will make the stock bitter. You can use the bones, heads, skin and tails of any white fish such as sole, brill, plaice. Avoid fatty fish such as mackerel, which will make the stock oily.

Vegetable stock can be made easily by simmering a wide selection of fresh vegetables, taking care not to overpower the flavour with one particular ingredient. You can add tomato purée for additional colour.

The majority of recipes in this book use stock cubes for convenience and it is well worth spending a little extra on the better quality ones. Generally, one stock cube will make up with 1 pint (600ml) water.

Food facts Meat

Meat is a valuable source of protein and also contains a variety of vitamins and minerals. Fortunately, in recent years, meat producers have managed to reduce the fat content of much of the meat we buy. According to the Meat and Livestock Commission in the United Kingdom, cattle are now about 25 per cent leaner than they were 30 years ago, and pork has an even more impressive track record with a 50 per cent reduction in fat. Meat is one category of food where I am not too strict on my 4 per cent rule, and any meat with a fat content of up to 6 per cent is acceptable on my diets.

You can buy meat where much of the fat has already been trimmed off, but, before cooking, you should remove any remaining white strands of fat that are still visible. Meat can be cooked by using either dry heat methods such as roasting, baking, grilling or dry-frying or by using moist heat methods such as poaching, braising and steaming. While it is safe to serve beef and lamb undercooked or 'rare', pork on the other hand must be cooked thoroughly.

When grilling or roasting meat, make sure the grill or oven is preheated so that once the meat is placed under the heat the juices can be sealed quickly. Likewise, when dry-frying, make sure the pan is hot before adding the meat.

When roasting, I always use foil to cover the joint, placing it so that it completely covers the edges of the roasting tin. This allows a certain amount of steam to be retained, which results in a moister joint at the end. Twenty minutes before the end of cooking I remove the foil to allow the joint to crispen. It is important not to overcook beef, otherwise it will go dry. To check that pork is thoroughly cooked, insert a skewer into the thickest part to check that any juices running out are clear and not pink.

The fat content of meat can vary, according to the cut. For instance, belly pork and neck of lamb are much fattier than fillet. With beef, topside, rump, sirloin and fillet are among the leanest cuts. While veal is low in fat, I am vehemently opposed to its production methods, so I never use it in recipes or include it in my diets. Extra lean minced beef is now widely available in food stores and supermarkets, but it can be much more expensive than ordinary lean mince, although there is less waste. However, I find that if I dry-fry lean mince and drain off all the fat that emerges during cooking, I am left with very lean mince. As always, it is the removal of the fat that is important. Minced turkey or chicken make good alternatives to minced beef, since they are very lean and do add a different flavour to some standard dishes.

Whether you are barbecuing, grilling, dry-frying, roasting, braising, pot roasting or even just stewing, never add any oil, fat or butter. If you are able to make a casserole in advance, allow it to cool and then skim off the fat. Reheat thoroughly before serving. There are many kinds of marinades, glazes and stocks that will enable your meat to be full of flavour and moisture.

Glazes

You can glaze chops, steaks and joints to add extra flavour and create an attractive appearance. Spread the glaze over joints 20 minutes before the end of cooking, or brush over the surface of chops or steaks prior to grilling. Try the following.

Beef
Honey, ginger and orange juice
Mustard and honey
Garlic, root ginger and honey

Pork
Honey, soy sauce, garlic and pineapple juice
Plum jam, tomato ketchup and Worcestershire
   sauce
Maple syrup, orange juice and cinnamon

Lamb
Wholegrain mustard and brown sugar
Redcurrant jelly, garlic and fresh mint
Lemon juice, honey and fresh ginger

Gammon
Honey or brown sugar and ginger or cinnamon
Orange marmalade and orange liqueur
Plum jam and apple juice

Marinades

Marinating adds flavour and helps to tenderise meats. To ensure the flavours are absorbed successfully, you should leave meat to marinate overnight, or for at least four hours, covered and in the refrigerator. Try combining some of the following flavours or make up your own.

Beef
Fresh herbs and lots of garlic
Soy sauce, lemon juice, garlic, sherry and sesame
    seeds
Horseradish, mustard and red wine
Soy sauce, sherry, garlic and ginger

Pork
White wine, orange rind and juice and fresh
    coriander
Honey, orange juice and cinnamon
Pineapple juice, soy sauce and fresh ginger
Cider vinegar, apple juice and fresh sage

Lamb
Lemon juice, garlic and dried mixed herbs
Rosemary and garlic
Redcurrant jelly, red wine and fresh herbs
Yogurt, fresh mint and garlic
Yogurt, coriander and cumin

More flavour enhancers

Joints can be studded, spiked or covered with a crust to add extra flavour and/or texture. Try the following ways to add flavour:

- Stud or spike with fresh rosemary sprigs and garlic slivers.
- Stud or spike with finely chopped garlic and crushed black peppercorns.
- Sprinkle with a creole mixture of black peppercorns, paprika and dried mixed herbs.
- Twenty minutes before the end of cooking, spread the joint with a mixture of parsley and mustard then sprinkle with breadcrumbs.

Offal

Offal includes heart, liver and kidneys, although nowadays heart is rarely used in cooking.

Liver is a particularly good source of iron and, like meat, the iron in liver is more easily absorbed by the body than iron from sources such as bread, fortified breakfast cereals, dried fruits and eggs. Liver is not recommended for pregnant women because of its high vitamin A content. Too much vitamin A during pregnancy could cause problems for the foetus.

Liver provides 137 calories and 6.2g fat per 100g. Since it is high in fat, you are advised not to eat more than two portions a week. You can choose from ox's, pig's, or lamb's liver, although lamb's liver is considered to be the most tender. To tenderise liver, leave it to soak in skimmed milk for a minimum of 30 minutes. The most satisfactory low-fat way of cooking liver is to dry-fry it quickly in a non-stick pan.

Kidneys provide 91 calories and 2.6g fat per 100g and are used primarily in casseroles but can also be dry-fried or grilled. You should remove all the fat prior to cooking, then slice the kidneys lengthways and remove any membrane and the tough centre core. Quickly dry-fry the kidneys, or, alternatively, lay each one flat and skewer with two cocktail sticks at right angles to each other (this will help hold the kidneys flat), then place under a grill until cooked.

Poultry

Chicken is probably more popular than ever before. With the controversy surrounding beef and the fact that chicken is plentiful and cheap, low in fat and versatile, it is ideal for inclusion in a low-fat diet. The main thing to understand about chicken is that most of the fat is in the skin. A chicken breast weighing 100g grilled with the skin on will provide 173 calories and 6.4 per cent fat compared with 148 calories and only 2.2 per cent fat if grilled without the skin. So, next time you consider eating the skin off your roast chicken, remember that 100g of chicken meat with skin will give you 218 calories and 12.5g fat compared to 164 calories and 7.2g fat if you eat just the flesh.

The key is to buy skinless chicken breasts to keep in your freezer for stir-fries, casseroles, and so on, and when roasting whole chickens make sure you remove the fat found around the neck before cooking and remove the skin before serving. Roasting a chicken on a wire rack will enable all the fat from it to drip below the bird and keep it as low fat as possible. This has the same effect as spit roasting or grilling. When I'm roasting chicken I always cover it with foil for the first three-quarters of the cooking time and then remove it at the end to crispen the chicken for an attractive end result.

If you are using a frozen chicken, it is important to allow it to thaw out slowly, ideally in a refrigerator, before cooking. Always make sure chicken is thoroughly cooked before you eat it. To test this, pierce it with a skewer in the fleshiest part of the leg, and if the liquid that pours out is

CALORIE AND FAT CONTENT OF CHICKEN, DUCK AND TURKEY		
	kcal per 100g	fat grams per 100g
Roast chicken with skin	218	12.5
Roast chicken without skin	164	7.2
Roast duck meat with skin	423	38.1
Roast duck without skin	195	10.4
Turkey mince, stewed	176	6.8

clear, the chicken is cooked, but if the liquid is still pink, the chicken is not cooked.

Interestingly, skinless chicken or turkey breast has more protein than fatty steak but only about one-tenth the fat and half the calories. Even the flesh of fattier poultry such as goose or duck still contains substantially less fat than fatty red meat. It is always a good idea to buy smaller, younger birds as these are less fatty than older ones. Minced chicken or turkey is a useful alternative in certain dishes where beef mince would normally be used.

Game

The term game applies to wild birds or animals hunted and then hung to tenderise before being prepared for cooking. In Britain there is a close season for most game when hunting is forbidden. Only rabbits, pigeon and quail are not protected and are available throughout the year.

Most game sold through licensed poulterers and fishmongers has been hung to tenderise and allow the meat to develop its gamey flavour, and most game is low in fat.

Venison

This is the meat of young male deer between 18 months and two years old. It is a dense, dark meat, very lean and close grained and is usually sold in joints. Leg and saddle are the prime roasting joints. Other cuts can be braised. The season for venison is June to January.

Pheasant

Pheasant is usually sold as a brace – one hen bird and one cock bird. The hen bird is considered the tastiest and will serve three people, while a cock bird serves four. You can roast it or use it in a casserole. The season for pheasant is 1 October to 31 January.

Partridge

There are two species of partridge: English or grey partridge, or the rarer French partridge. It is a sweet-flavoured, lean bird. The season for partridge is 1 September to 31 January. You can roast, grill or poach it, or use it in a casserole. Serve half a bird per person.

Quail

A much smaller bird than the pheasant with a slightly less gamey flavour. It is available all year round. It is usually roasted whole. Serve one bird per person.

Hare

There are two species of hare: English brown and Scottish blue. A young hare weighs approximately 6–7lb (2.75–3kg). Hare is best stewed or used in a casserole. The season for hare is 1 August to 31 March.

Rabbit

Rabbit is a very lean white meat, slightly stronger than chicken, and is available all year round. You can braise or roast it or dice it and use in a casserole.

Fish

Rich in protein, minerals and vitamins A and D, fish is one of the most nutritious foods we can eat. Oily fish such as salmon and kippers contain essential fatty acids that are beneficial for health. For this reason, you may ignore the 4 per cent rule as far as oily fish is concerned, but avoid ones canned in oil. Try to eat some at least once a week, but no more than three times a week.

Fish falls into various categories but is simply classed as white fish or oily fish. White fish includes fish such as cod, halibut, skate, sole, and so on, and oily fish includes herrings, salmon, anchovies, mackerel and sardines. The reason I allow oily fish on my low-fat diets is because it contains a unique group of polyunsaturated fatty acids called omega-3. Not only do these omega-3 fatty acids decrease the levels of the artery-choking LDL (low density lipoprotein) cholesterol, but it is believed they also raise the levels of artery-clearing HDL (high density lipoprotein) cholesterol.

Many studies have shown that in communities where increased amounts of fish were eaten, the incidence of heart disease has decreased. Fish oil is also known to help prevent hardening of the arteries by thinning the blood and is also effective in reducing the likelihood of blood clots. Furthermore, salmon and sardines are particularly rich sources of calcium. Try to eat the soft bones they contain to bolster your calcium intake.

Tuna contains less fat than oily fish such as salmon but more fat than white fish. Although it is not a particularly rich source of fish oils, it forms a good alternative to meat.

Shellfish are reasonably low in fat, although the fat they contain is high in cholesterol. However, it is now recognised that high blood cholesterol is made worse by a high-fat diet rather than by cholesterol itself. This is good news for low-fat dieters, since prawns, crab and lobster can add a delightful variation to a salad or sandwich. However, as with oily fish, limit your intake to three servings a week maximum.

Fish can be cooked in many ways, and we have tried to include some interesting and varied recipes in this book. Remember, white fish is so low in fat and calories that you can have a large portion yet still keep within your calorie allowance.

Grilling

Fish does not take long to cook. Placing it on some foil on the grill pan will keep any smell away from food cooked later and also make it easier to move the fish around. Moisten the flesh with lemon or lime juice or any other sauce, according to the recipe you are using. Do not allow the fish to dry out and don't forget to serve it with a low-fat sauce.

Microwaving

Microwaving is ideal for fish, because sealing fish in cling film retains all the moisture while ensuring the fish is cooked thoroughly. Season well before cooking.

Poaching

Poaching is a satisfactory way of cooking large white fish. It keeps the fish moist and encourages it to take on the flavourings of the sauce in which you are poaching it. You can use fish stock, milk, water or wine and add whatever flavours you choose such as lemon or herbs. Always add plenty of freshly ground black pepper. Since fish cooks quickly, allow just 10–15 minutes. Just keep it on a gentle heat to simmer, and avoid any furious boiling.

A fish kettle is one of those utensils you might use only two or three times a year, but on those occasions when you do use it, it is worth its weight in gold. Cooking a whole salmon is almost impossible without one, so next time you wonder what to put on your Christmas list, I suggest you ask for one.

Baking

When baking fish in the oven, it's best to place it in aluminium foil parcels or in a covered ovenproof dish. Make sure there is some liquid surrounding the fish to encourage it to stay moist. You can use any liquid left after cooking to add to a sauce.

CALORIE AND FAT CONTENT OF WHITE FISH

	kcal per 100g	fat grams per 100g
White fish, grilled	95	1.3
White fish, coated in breadcrumbs and fried	235	14.3
White fish, coated in batter and fried	247	15.4

CALORIE AND FAT CONTENT OF SHELLFISH

	kcal per 100g	fat grams per 100g
Prawns, boiled	99	0.9
Crab, boiled	126	5.5
Lobster, boiled	103	1.6

CALORIE AND FAT CONTENT OF OILY FISH

	kcal per 100g	fat grams per 100g
Salmon, grilled	215	13.1
Mackerel, grilled	239	17.3
Herrings, grilled	181	11.2
Sardines, grilled	195	10.4

Fish in curries and casseroles

Depending on the recipe you are using, it may be appropriate to add the fish towards the end of the cooking time. For instance, when cooking a curry or casserole, if you add the fish too early, you may find it has disintegrated into almost invisible strands by the time you come to serve it.

Pulses

Kidney beans, lentils, chick peas, black beans, haricot beans, baked beans are all different types of pulses. Nowadays, pulses are available dried or, much more conveniently, ready to use in a can.

Pulses provide more protein than any other plant food. They are low in fat and are a valuable source of soluble fibre, which can help to reduce blood cholesterol. Also rich in B vitamins and the minerals iron, zinc, and copper, pulses are an extremely nutritious food for vegetarians and non-vegetarians alike and make a great low-calorie but satisfying option for dieters.

Great care must be taken during the preparation and cooking of dried pulses. So, follow the three steps below.

Cleaning

Pick over the beans, peas or lentils carefully, removing any sediment or unwanted extras.

Soaking

Most pulses need rehydrating after the ripening and drying process. Immerse in water, then remove and discard any that float to the top. Rinse and top up with fresh boiling water and leave to soak for eight hours.

Cooking

Place in a saucepan of cold water, using three parts water to one part beans, peas or lentils. Bring the water slowly to the boil and skim off the starchy scum that rises to the surface. Boil until tender (this may take an hour or more). During the initial stages of cooking, it is very important that pulses are boiled vigorously to destroy their lectins (these are toxins that can cause gastrointestinal distress). Most dried pulses should be boiled vigorously for at least ten minutes, but two to three minutes is sufficient for lentils and split peas.

Eggs

Basically a protein food, eggs offer many and varied nutrients. They are extremely versatile, forming a delicious meal on their own or as a vital ingredient to a recipe. As far as fat is concerned, the white is the good guy and the yolk is the bad guy. The white is high in protein yet very low in fat. For this reason, I use it widely in sorbets, meringues, mousses, and so on. The white of an egg contains 11 calories and zero fat. The yolk, on the other hand, is high in calories (61 calories per yolk), relatively high in fat (5.49g), and high in cholesterol. For this reason I recommend that non-vegetarians consume just two egg yolks per week, while vegetarians may have three because of the absence of meat in their diet.

Egg yolk is a rich source of iron which will be absorbed more efficiently if the egg is eaten at the same meal as a food containing vitamin C. This is why, throughout my diets, I always include either a glass of orange juice or half a grapefruit when I suggest an egg for breakfast.

Eggs used in recipes do not need to be counted in your weekly allowance, since the proportion of egg per serving is minimal. It's important to remember that young children, the elderly, and pregnant women should not eat slightly cooked or soft boiled eggs because of the risk of salmonella.

Butter, margarines and low-fat spreads

Butter contains 80 per cent fat, margarines approximately 70 per cent fat, and spreads that are labelled 'low fat' can contain as much as 60 per cent fat! Of all the spreads I know, Tesco's low-fat spread has the lowest fat content, at five per cent fat, and so is acceptable in small quantities if you find you really cannot live without having some spread on your bread. The only good thing about low-fat spreads, to my mind, is that, generally, they taste so awful that you wouldn't want to spread much on your bread anyway!

There is much confusion among the general public about whether polyunsaturated fats are beneficial for health. The confusion arises between those who have high blood cholesterol or a heart problem and those who need to reduce their weight. For someone who is slim but needs to eat a low-cholesterol diet because of a heart problem, then polyunsaturated margarine is a better choice than saturated fat such as butter. If, however, a heart patient is overweight, then it is better to eat a low-fat diet and avoid polyunsaturated margarines in order to lose weight. At 9 calories per gram, fat offers more than twice as many calories as protein or carbohydrate, weight for weight. If you need to lose weight, then you need to reduce your fat intake dramatically. The amount of fat necessary for good helath is very small indeed and will be provided by other foods, without the need to eat butter or mayonnaise.

Even if you have lost weight successfully and are just seeking to maintain your new weight, I do not recommend you start reintroducing low-fat spreads into your diet. There is no question that butter tastes better than low-fat spreads and, once you get the taste for fat again, you may find yourself on a very slippery slope and slide back into your old eating habits. But if you never start re-introducing it, then your new lifestyle habit will stay a lifetime habit – and so will your figure!

Cheese

Most hard cheeses contain 30 per cent fat and eating them is one of the surest ways to trap you into consuming more fat and calories than you realise. I know regular hard cheese tastes terrific, but it is high in fat, high in sodium, high in cholesterol and high in fattening power, so if you want to have a great body, this is one sacrifice you have to make.

So if you are trying to lose weight, hard cheese is off the menu, I'm afraid, but once you reach your goal weight, you may consume reduced-fat hard cheeses occasionally.

Cottage cheese, on the other hand, is high in nutrients and low in fat. I used to detest it. Strangely, though, as soon as I stopped eating high-fat Cheddar, I grew to like cottage cheese, and now I adore it. I eat it with fruit, I make delicious sandwiches by spreading Marmite onto the bread and filling it with cottage cheese – try it, it's delicious – and I'm very happy to have it on a jacket potato or in a salad.

You can substitute quark for full-fat cream cheese in many recipes and you won't even notice the difference when you come to eat the finished dish.

If you do need to keep cheese in your fridge for the rest of the family, then keep it wrapped in foil and out of sight. It is probably the single most dangerous food to have in your fridge to tempt you. If it's in a see-through plastic container, begging you to slice off a chunk each time you go to the fridge, then it's not surprising the weight loss on the scales is disappointing.

Milk

Milk is an extremely valuable source of nutrients. It provides high-quality protein as well as many minerals and vitamins. While the fat-soluble vitamins A and D which are found in whole milk are removed when the fat is removed from whole milk, they are often added to skimmed milk, so no loss is suffered. Milk also contains the B vitamins and a small amount of vitamin C. By far the most important mineral found in milk is calcium, but other minerals include phosphorous, potassium and a very small but easily absorbed amount of iron, as well as magnesium and copper.

CALORIE AND FAT CONTENT OF CHEESE		
	kcal per 100g	*fat grams per 100g*
Cheddar	103	8.6
Cheddar (reduced fat)	65	3.7
Cottage cheese (full fat)	25	0.9
Cottage cheese (reduced fat)	20	0.3

Semi-skimmed milk has about half the fat content of whole milk. Skimmed milk has almost no fat and yields only half the number of calories of whole milk. The drawback with skimmed milk, in my view, is that it is so unpalatable – it looks and tastes watery. Whether you choose skimmed or semi-skimmed milk, though, is entirely up to you. Both supply as much calcium as whole milk, because the calcium contained in milk is not in the fatty bit. We are likely to get most of our calcium requirements through the milk we drink.

Not everyone can tolerate milk because of its lactose content. Such problems arise when the digestive enzyme lactase, which helps to break down lactose into its component sugars, is produced in insufficient amounts by the body. If you have a lactose intolerance, try consuming cultured milk products such as live cultured yogurt. You can also buy milk products that have been treated with lactase, or you can buy lactase and add it to dairy products at home. If you do not consume any milk or dairy products it is important that you take a calcium supplement or eat significant quantities of calcium rich non-dairy products such as green leafy vegetables. A good intake of calcium is essential to build and maintain strong bones and to reduce the risk of osteoporosis in later life.

Yogurt, fromage frais and cream

Yogurt is simply milk that has been fermented by several strains of bacteria such as Lactobacillus acidophilus and Bifidobacteria bifidum. The bacteria curdle the milk by converting the milk sugar to lactic acid. Yogurt is made from a skimmed milk base with added skimmed milk powder. The milk is pasteurised, cooled and special bacteria are added to cause fermentation. The milk is then incubated in large tanks at a constant temperature until it thickens, after which it is cooled.

One of the main nutritional benefits of yogurt is to reinforce additional 'friendly' bacteria in the intestines, promoting the growth of beneficial intestinal flora. The bacteria of the intestinal flora aid digestion and absorption of food, produce B vitamins and prevent the growth of pathogenic bacteria (such as candida) which cause disease. These bacteria also promote a healthy intestinal acidity. In this respect, yogurt is especially beneficial for people who are taking antibiotics, and for those who eat a lot of sugary products or who drink chlorinated water, all of which deplete friendly bacteria. Yogurt also helps to synthesise vitamin K, preventing internal haemorrhages, and it lowers cholesterol levels and reduces the risk of colon cancer.

Yogurt is a good source of high-quality protein, vitamins and minerals. It contains vitamins A, B complex, D and E, and is an excellent source of easily absorbed calcium, potassium and phosphorus, with just a modest sodium content.

Yogurt is easily digestible – in fact most of its protein is digested within an hour. It also has a valuable role in the treatment of gastro-enteritis, colitis, constipation, bilious disorders, flatulence, bad breath, high cholesterol, migraine and nervous fatigue. Moreover, yogurt can often be tolerated by people who are unable to consume other forms of milk due to lactose intolerance.

Yogurt is more widely available now than ever before. Most yogurt produced in the UK is low in fat. If you find natural yogurt too acidic for your taste, you can add fruit, fruit juice, muesli, honey or any other flavourings you like.

Unless yogurt is pasteurised after preparation (it will say on the label), it will contain 'live' bacteria which remain dormant while kept cool. If the yogurt is not kept in the refrigerator or a similarly cool place, the bacteria

CALORIE AND FAT CONTENT OF CREAM, YOGURT AND FROMAGE FRAIS

CREAM	kcal per 100g	fat grams per 100g	kcal per 15ml tablespoon	fat grams per 15ml tablespoon
Double	449	48	134	14
Single	198	19.1	29	2.8
Soured	205	19.9	62	5.9
Clotted	586	63.5	263	28.5
Whipping	373	39.3	167	17.6

YOGURT	kcal per 100g	fat grams per 100g	kcal per average portion (150g)	fat grams per average portion (150g)
Low-calorie	41	0.2	51	0.25
Low-fat flavoured	90	0.9	135	1.35
Low-fat fruit	90	0.7	135	1.05
Low-fat plain	56	0.8	84	1.2
Soya	72	4.2	86	5.04

FROMAGE FRAIS	kcal per 100g	fat grams per 100g	kcal per 15ml tablespoon	fat grams per 15ml tablespoon
Fruit	131	5.8	59	2.61
Plain	113	7.1	51	3.19
Very low fat	58	0.2	29	0.1

will become active again and produce more acid until the yogurt eventually separates.

You can buy commercially frozen yogurt or freeze your own, using home-made or shop-bought flavoured yogurt, providing it contains sugar.

Low-fat yogurt is just as valuable a source of protein, calcium and other nutrients as the full-fat brands, and forms an invaluable part of a low-fat diet. The use of artificial sweeteners or artificial sweetening agents in certain brands means there is a wide variety of low-calorie ones to choose from. Find a brand you enjoy, but do check the fat content and the total number of calories per pot before purchasing. Many yogurts which are virtually fat free offer 180 calories per pot. Why use up so many calories on one pot of yogurt when you can buy another of the same size that yields only 60 calories? For the same number of calories, you could have a sandwich as well as the pot of yogurt!

Yogurt is extremely versatile and a useful substitution for cream. Eat it with fruit, or use it to dress a dessert. Try the low-fat sherry trifle on page 369, where vanilla-flavoured yogurt is used instead of cream. There is no sacrifice here for having a low-fat alternative. A pot of yogurt is also ideal to include in the children's packed lunch for school.

Alternatives to cream
All cream, whether single, whipping, double, soured, or crème fraîche, is extremely high in fat and therefore high in calories. It has no place on a low-fat diet, but fortunately, there are some great alternatives. Yogurt (plain or flavoured) is a good alternative to single cream, while low-fat fromage frais, 0% fat Greek yogurt and set bio yogurts are excellent alternatives to the thicker varieties of cream.

Cream is high in cholesterol and very high in fattening power, but if we're used to eating it, then we like the taste. It takes time for our taste buds to adjust to eating the low-fat alternatives, but, given time, you will be amazed how you find you come to dislike the taste of cream and grow to love the taste of these healthier options.

The golden rule to remember when using yogurt or fromage frais in cooking is never to boil them. If they become too hot, they will curdle, so add them at the end of cooking when the dish has been removed from the heat, for example as in the recipe for beef stroganoff on page 132.

Ice cream and sorbets

The fat content of ice cream varies enormously, from being quite modest for an almost synthetic product to being high fat when made with real cream and butter. It is, however, a versatile and often quite nutritious dessert and certainly one of my favourites! When buying branded ice creams, remember to look at the nutrition label. As well as checking the fat content, look at the number of calories too and make sure they fit into your daily allowance. Wall's and Weight

Watchers from Heinz offer some excellent low-fat iced desserts which taste every bit as good as the real thing. You could also try yogurt-based ice cream as an alternative.

Sorbets are naturally low in fat and make a delicious dessert to follow any meal. Check out the ones in your local supermarket – Marks & Spencer has a particularly good range, and you'll find plenty of recipes in this book.

Potatoes

Potatoes play an invaluable role in a low-fat diet. They are cheap, versatile, low in calories and virtually fat free. You can create a whole meal around this humble vegetable. Baked or 'jacket' potatoes are a firm favourite, and baby new potatoes can honour the most lavish dinner party menu.

Potatoes provide just 25 calories per ounce (25g) and are a carbohydrate food, which means the calories are not easily stored as fat on the body but are easily burned as energy. It was once thought that potatoes were fattening, but this was only because most people used to eat them with lots of added fat. Now that we've learned ways of cooking and eating them without fat, they are a real friend of the dieter because they are so filling. They contain valuable nutrients such as folic acid and thiamine as well as vitamin C. In fact, until relatively recently when fruit and vegetables became more popular, Britain's population used to acquire most of its vitamin C intake through potatoes, simply because we ate them so much.

Potatoes can be boiled with or without their skins, dry-roasted (see my recipe on page 134), or mashed with yogurt or fromage frais instead of

CALORIE AND FAT CONTENT OF POTATOES

Type	kcal per 100g	fat grams per 100g
New potatoes, boiled	75	0.3
Old potatoes, boiled	72	0.1
Potatoes, dry-roasted	72	0.2
Potatoes, roasted with fat	149	4.5
Instant potato powder made up with water	57	0.1
Chips, home fried	189	6.7
Chips, crinkle-cut, fried in corn oil	290	16.7
Frozen oven chips, baked	162	4.2
Frozen oven chips, microwaved	221	9.6

butter. You can even buy ready-made oven chips with a fat content of less than four per cent. It's interesting to note that a serving of regular chips has three times the number of calories and 12 times the amount of fat of boiled potatoes. If you must have chips occasionally, make sure you go for thick-cut ones and not the small crinkle-cut varieties which have a greater surface area to absorb the fat.

Bread

I could devote half this book to the different kinds of breads and the differences between them. For simplicity's sake, I recommend you always check the fat content on the packaging before purchasing. Almost all bread requires some form of fat to make it into a finished loaf. The fat can be anything from olive oil to butter, margarine, and so on. Some of the newer 'fancy' breads in the supermarkets today contain surprisingly large amounts of fat. Watch out, too, for those with added high-fat ingredients such as olives, cheese or sun-dried tomatoes.

Wholemeal bread contains flour which is less processed than that used for white bread and thereby retains more natural ingredients. With white bread, most of the fibre and the wholegrain has been removed, although in the UK it is fortified with many nutrients and, fibre content aside, is just as healthy as wholemeal. In fact, white bread contains more calcium than brown bread. Brown bread doesn't necessarily

mean that it's wholemeal, so do check the label to ensure that it meets your particular requirements. If you want a high-fibre loaf, then choose a wholegrain one or one with added fibre – this will be stated on the packaging.

On average, bread provides 70 calories per ounce (25g) and its fat content can vary enormously. Freshly baked bread tastes superb without any fat spread on it and can become a firm favourite on a low-fat diet. You have probably eaten butter or margarine on bread for many years and it comes as a shock to start eating bread without a greasy layer. Give yourself 30 days to get used to having marmalade spread directly onto dry toast and mustard or low-fat dressing spread directly onto bread for sandwiches. As long as there's some moisture there, you won't miss the butter or margarine. If you're eating bread prior to a meal

CALORIE AND FAT CONTENT OF BREAD			
Type	Portion	kcal	fat grams
Brown	average slice	78	0.7
Granary	average slice	84	0.9
Wheatgerm	average slice	83	0.9
White	average slice	84	0.9
Wholemeal	average slice	77	0.9
Garlic	$1/3$ baguette	290	15.8
Naan	1 naan	469	13
Pitta	1 pitta	163	
Ciabatta	$1/6$ ciabatta	108	1.6
Soda	40g	92	0.8

in a restaurant, a good restaurant will bring you hot rolls, and these taste delicious on their own.

Bread is a carbohydrate and is easily burned by the body. Some people are intolerant to wheat and may need to follow a gluten-free diet. You can purchase gluten-free bread in cans from many high street chemists or from healthfood shops. Rice cakes are a good alternative for anyone who has an allergy to wheat flour.

Pasta

Pasta is a carbohydrate and, as such, is burned easily as energy by the body. Pasta is made from wheat flour and can be home-made or purchased fresh or dried. There are many varieties and shapes and sizes available, some made with just flour and water and some with added egg. On a low-fat diet, obviously, it is preferable to choose the egg-free varieties. Dried pasta is convenient to have in the store cupboard. Cooked properly, it tastes excellent, and it can be used in lunch and dinner menus.

Pasta adds variety to a low-fat diet, forming a delicious high-carbohydrate, low-fat

accompaniment to many dishes. Dry pasta yields 80 calories per ounce (25g). One ounce of dry pasta when boiled will weigh almost 3oz (75g) and, providing you add no butter or oil to the finished pasta, you can make your calorie calculations based on 80 calories per ounce dry weight or 80 calories per 3oz (75g) cooked weight. When cooking pasta, I always add a vegetable stock cube to the water for extra flavour. Make sure there is plenty of water in the pan so that the pasta does not need to be rinsed after cooking. This will help retain the delicate flavour that has been absorbed from the stock cube. Cooked pasta can be saved in a covered dish and served on a later occasion.

Pasta can be served hot or cold with a variety of different sauces. Many children love it, and the small spirals and shell-shaped pasta are ideal to pack for school lunches.

One word of warning: it is easy to underestimate how much pasta you are eating. This is one of the first things I ask my dieters to check when they tell me their weight-loss progress is proving too slow. So, if this applies to you, do check your serving sizes.

CALORIE AND FAT CONTENT OF PASTA		
Type	kcal per 100g	fat grams per 100g
Dried egg pasta	358	3.5
Dried pasta without egg	345	2.0
Fresh egg pasta	279	3.6

Rice

Long grain, short grain, basmati, patna, wild – there are so many different types of rice to choose from. In each of the recipes in this book I have stated what type of rice should be used if a special one is needed. Otherwise, use long-grain rice for a savoury dish and short-grain rice for a sweet dish.

One ounce (25g) of dry weight rice yields 100 calories, and an ounce of dry weight rice weighs 2 1/2oz (65g) when cooked. On a low-fat eating plan, the simple message is to boil rice and never fry it. You can save many grams of fat and loads of calories simply by never frying rice. Rice is a carbohydrate and is easily burned by the body but the quantities are deceptive and a typical portion is surprisingly high in calories. Mixing boiled rice with boiled or steamed beansprouts is an excellent way of making the rice go further and help fill you up.

Rice can be eaten hot or cold in savoury and sweet dishes and is a highly absorbent substance. I always boil my rice in plenty of water with a vegetable stock cube and, providing I am using easy cook rice, I find no need to rinse the rice before serving. However, If you wish to cook rice for a cold dish or in advance for a dinner party, then rinse it and cool it right off with cold water. You can reheat rice easily by just pouring boiling water over it or reheating in a microwave. The key is not to overcook rice, as this makes it go soft and soggy. Rice is cooked when it doesn't taste grainy. It should be firm but soft. If you add a vegetable stock cube to the cooking water there is no need to add butter or oil, as the tiny amount of fat contained in the stock cube will ensure that the particles of rice stay separated. Cooked rice can be kept in a cupboard or refrigerator for up to two days and used hot or cold on a later occasion.

I always buy the easy cook variety of rice for everyday use, as it's so quick and easy to prepare. However, for dinner parties and special occasions I use basmati rice. Wild rice is very attractive and is also excellent for dinner parties.

Brown rice is rice with the husk still attached, which gives extra fibre, although it requires almost four times more cooking time than the easy cook or white varieties.

NUTRIENT VALUES OF RICE			
Type	*energy per 100g*	*protein per 100g*	*fat per 100g*
Brown rice, raw	357 kcal	6.7g	2.8g
White rice, easy cook, raw	383 kcal	7.3g	3.6g

Fruit and vegetables

Fruit and vegetables are a real friend of the low-fat dieter, but one of the greatest myths of low-fat eating is the belief that, because fruit is virtually fat free, you can eat it quite freely between meals, as if the calories disappeared into obscurity! Fruit contains more sugar and therefore more calories than vegetables. On average, fruit contains around 10 calories per ounce (25g) compared with vegetables, which have just 5 calories per ounce, with some exceptions such as potatoes, peas and sweetcorn.

Fruit and vegetables have a valuable role to play in the daily diet and should be consumed in generous quantities within your calorie allowance. Try to vary your choices so that you eat a wide range of different types and colours to gain maximum benefits from the vitamins and minerals they contain. Rather than stocking up on large amounts in one go, aim to buy smaller amounts regularly so that they don't become stale and lose some of their vitamin content. Fruit and vegetables eaten raw will yield a greater vitamin content than when cooked. In most of my diets I recommend you eat three portions of fruit and three portions of vegetables each day. One portion of fruit can be in the form of $\frac{1}{4}$ pint (150ml) fruit juice, or a piece of fruit, or 4oz (100g) of fruit such as strawberries, cherries, raspberries, blackberries, etc.

When cooking vegetables, never add any fat, although you can add a vegetable stock cube to the cooking water for extra flavour. If you do this, there is no need to add salt. Vegetables act as a great filler and are the only food that I suggest can be eaten between meals on my diets. Cucumber, cherry tomatoes, celery and carrot sticks all offer few calories yet have lots of munching and filling power. It's a good idea to create a nibble tray each morning and keep it in the refrigerator or take it to work so that if you feel peckish between meals you have an instant low-fat alternative to a chocolate bar.

Three vegetables which deserve a special mention here are mushrooms, onions and tomatoes. I use these a lot in my cooking, because they are cheap and also great for adding flavour and bulk to low-fat recipes, making a more satisfying meal without adding too many calories.

Mushrooms

Mushrooms come in many shapes, sizes and varieties, and the flavours between the different types vary enormously. Since they contain very few calories (2 calories per ounce/25g), they are a real friend of the low-fat dieter. They act as a useful filler as well as adding a special flavour to any low-fat recipe. When fried in any type of fat, mushrooms are like little sponges and their calorific value increases from 13 calories per 100g in their natural state to 157 calories per 100g when fried in oil or butter. The golden rule when using mushrooms in low-fat recipes is to avoid the use of fat and allow them to absorb moisture from flavoured sauces.

Mushrooms contain quite a lot of their own liquid, so if you slice and cook them in a non-stick frying pan with no added liquid, you will be surprised how much liquid they make. They also taste great when sliced and served raw in salads. You can buy dried mushrooms from the supermarket, which means you can have a supply of exotic ones to hand in the store cupboard ready for that special occasion when you need a different flavour.

Onions

Onions, like mushrooms, are low in calories in their natural state, but as soon as you put them near fat, they soak it up like a sponge. Onions yield only 36 calories and 0.2g fat per 100g, but, when fried, that figure bumps up to a massive 164 calories and 11.2g fat. The calorie and fat content is roughly the same for any type of onion, whether it be Spanish, cooking, red, spring, pickling or shallots.

Cooking onions offer the strongest flavour, followed by Spanish onions and then red onions, which makes the latter particularly suitable for salads. Onions are a great way to bulk up a low-fat recipe, add lots of flavour and bring moisture to the dish. Again, try cooking in stock for added flavour. They also dry-fry magnificently. All round, they are a useful ally for the low-fat dieter.

Tomatoes

Tomatoes are another vegetable full of flavour but with very few calories and virtually no fat, and they are a rich source of vitamin C. Available all year round and generally inexpensive, they are extremely versatile and can be used in many dishes, hot or cold. Tomato purée adds a richness to any sauce and a tin of chopped tomatoes takes all the hard work out of preparing a spaghetti bolognese sauce. There is no need to add butter or cream or oil to any tomato-based recipe, but the flavour of cooked tomato will be enhanced by allowing it to reduce and thicken. The end result is a sweeter, stronger-tasting tomato flavour.

Another useful tomato-based item is in the unlikely form of tomato ketchup. Although this contains some sugar, it is a useful low-fat addition to any store cupboard and can be mixed with reduced-oil salad dressing to make a low-fat Marie Rose dressing, or with cottage cheese to make a tasty topping for potatoes.

Sun-dried tomatoes have come into their own in recent years, but do avoid those canned or bottled in oil.

Sugar

Sugar is a simple carbohydrate offering what some nutritionists term empty calories. In other words, apart from energy-giving carbohydrate, there are no other nutrients in sugar, yet it has a very positive role to play in a low-fat diet. In the absence of high amounts of fat, the body will naturally yearn energy-giving foods, and by including a moderate amount of sugar in a low-fat diet, I firmly believe it is easier to hold our willpower intact. I do in fact advocate having a small teaspoon of sugar in tea or coffee, since I find this is one of the best ways to resist the temptation to eat biscuits or cakes between meals. Sugar taken in moderation is easily burned by the body as energy and is not easily stored, but you still need to count the calories.

This does not mean I am giving licence for everyone to eat a high-sugar diet. Certainly not. All I am suggesting is that sugar, in moderation, can still be included in a weight-reducing diet. Remember, though, that calories do count, but within a daily calorie allowance of 1,400 calories, I believe there is room for small amounts. Like fat, sugar is an acquired taste and if we decrease our liking for it, then it will be easier to moderate our intake. One of the easiest ways of cutting our sugar intake is to avoid high-sugar fizzy drinks, since these not only contain a high proportion of sugar offering unnecessarily high amounts of calories but can also be harmful to teeth. Substitute diet brands instead or, even better, try fizzy water. There are now many flavoured varieties available.

I am not a great advocate of sugary confectionery, as I believe it is habit forming and has no part in a healthy eating plan. I would prefer you to have a spoonful of sugar in your tea than have a packet of mints every other day. To make my point further, I suggest you look at your friends – who takes sugar in their tea and who doesn't. Often it's the overweight ones that don't and the slim ones that do. Be aware, also, that a lot of confectionery, such as chocolate or toffee, is high in fat as well as sugar.

I'm also not a great advocate of reduced-sugar brands of foods such as baked beans, as the difference in calories and fat between these and the ordinary varieties is minimal. Far better to go for the real thing and feel that you are not eating diet food.

Jams, marmalades, preserves and honey

In the absence of butter or margarine on your toast, marmalade, honey, jams and preserves come into their own. Offering easily released energy-giving carbohydrate as well as moisture,

CALORIE AND FAT CONTENT OF SUGAR		
Type	kcal	fat grams
White sugar, per 25g	99	Nil
White sugar, per 5ml teaspoon	24	Nil
Demerara sugar, per 25g	91	Nil
Demerara sugar, per 5ml teaspoon	24	Nil

they add a delightful taste to freshly toasted wholemeal bread. Again, be aware of the calories, so don't spread them onto your toast an inch thick! There is no need to buy reduced-sugar varieties of jams and preserves unless you find one that you prefer to the full-sugar version. Otherwise, the number of calories you save are at the expense of the flavour, and this will only leave you with a feeling of deprivation which, in turn, could lead to cheating. Better to have a teaspoon of the real thing than to go off the rails because you didn't enjoy a low-calorie alternative.

Sauces and dressings

When cooking and preparing everyday food without fat, sauces and dressings are important for adding flavour and taste. Today, we are spoilt for choice with the numerous varieties available on supermarket shelves, but do check the fat content before you buy. These are a convenient and helpful aid to anyone following a low-fat eating plan, but it can be quick and easy to make your own.

Experiment with different dressings when preparing salads or sandwiches. Soy sauce on a salad made of rice, beansprouts and mixed vegetables, or with grated raw beetroot or carrot tastes superb. Try mixing some ready-made mustard with balsamic vinegar, a little sugar and plenty of freshly ground black pepper for an instant dressing. You'll find a variety of low-fat salad dressings in this book. Try them, modifying them to suit your own taste if necessary, and soon they will become part of your everyday menu planning.

Breakfasts

Breakfast is a particularly important meal as it kick-starts your metabolism after an all-night fast, hence the name break-fast.

For breakfast, if you are trying to lose weight, I allow 250 calories for women and 350 for men. Those who just wish to maintain their weight can increase this allowance to 400 and 500 calories respectively.

Some people love a cooked breakfast; other people struggle to eat a couple of bananas. Some like to eat early, while others can't face anything before 10am. Frankly, so long as you are mindful of the calories and everything you eat is low in fat, you can have whatever you enjoy, but do try to eat by 10am at the latest.

Here are a few simple tips on preparing some favourite breakfast items.

Scrambled eggs

Cook slowly in a non-stick saucepan with a little skimmed or semi-skimmed milk from your $^3/_4$ pint (450ml) daily allowance. Season well with salt and freshly ground black pepper. Do not overcook or it will become too dry. Serve on dry toast or, alternatively, spread a little tomato ketchup or similar low-fat sauce on your toast.

Fried eggs

Cook in a non-stick frying pan over a moderate heat. When almost cooked, remove from the heat and cover with a lid. Leave for 30 to 60 seconds to allow the top of the yolk to change colour. Do not overcook.

Omelettes

A one-egg omelette is not very big so you need to fill it out with some ready-cooked vegetables or tomatoes and mushrooms.

Preheat a small non-stick frying pan. Whisk an egg with a little skimmed or semi-skimmed milk and season well with salt and freshly ground black pepper. Pour into the warm pan and keep tilting the pan to allow the omelette mixture to spread. Add sliced raw mushrooms and/or tomatoes and allow them to sink into the egg mixture.

For a lunch suggestion, you could add sweetcorn kernels, peas, chopped onions and peppers to the omelette mixture. These provide only a few extra calories but lots of flavour and bulk.

Sausages

As far as I am aware, Marks & Spencer makes the leanest sausage on the market, with just 3.8 per cent fat. It tastes excellent and is terrific hot or cold. Beware of other so-called low-fat sausages. They may be leaner than full-fat ones, but that doesn't mean they're less than 4 per cent fat. Pierce sausages before cooking to allow any fat to drip out and to prevent them splitting during cooking. Either grill sausages or roast them, uncovered, on a wire rack in the oven.

Bacon and turkey rashers

Lean back bacon, grilled, can be eaten on a low-fat diet, but do remove all the fat and rind BEFORE grilling or dry-frying.

Turkey rashers are very low in fat and provide an excellent alternative to bacon, with fewer calories and less fat. You can now buy flavoured varieties, which taste excellent. Turkey rashers can also be used in recipes in place of bacon.

Mushrooms

All kinds of wonderful mushrooms are available now and many are ideal for the breakfast table. The key is to keep them away from fat and butter. Grill or dry-fry them or cook them in vegetable stock. Serve on toast or with eggs, bacon or turkey rashers, or add them to omelettes.

Tomatoes

Tomatoes are low in fat and calories and can be added to any savoury dish to add flavour and colour as well as lots of vitamin C. Eat them any way you want – raw, grilled, baked, boiled or dry-fried – just so long as you don't add any fat. Tinned tomatoes are also acceptable. Serve on toast or with eggs, bacon or turkey rashers, or add to omelettes.

Toast

Toast is a great favourite for breakfast because it's quick and, if you're in a rush, you can eat it as you walk! Not good for your digestion but, nevertheless, a reality for many. Top your toast with marmalade, honey or preserve and you'll have a good carbohydrate fix to start you off for the day. You'll be amazed how quickly you get used to not having butter or spread on your toast.

Porridge

Porridge oats are very nutritious. They provide a small amount of beneficial fatty acids and a high level of soluble fibre which can help reduce cholesterol levels. Another special quality of porridge is that it releases its energy slowly and is therefore likely to keep you satisfied throughout the morning. Porridge definitely gets my seal of approval!

In its raw state, porridge yields about 8 per cent fat, but when made up with water, the fat content falls below the four per cent mark. Using water instead of milk keeps the calories down yet still gives you plenty of bulk. Serve with milk from your allowance and brown sugar (I think this tastes nicer than white sugar) or liquid honey. I find that if you pour the milk into the bowl first, and then add the cooked porridge, the porridge will float on top and you'll need less milk. Also, if you make your porridge the night before with plenty of water and allow it to stand, covered, overnight, it expands quite dramatically and makes a heftier helping!

Cereals

Cereals come in all shapes, sizes, colours and flavours. I'm not too worried which ones we give our children — any of them are healthier than a bag of crisps eaten on the school run. We take milk with cereal, which is a vital nutrient for all of us but particularly for children, so giving them cereal for breakfast is a good way of ensuring they obtain sufficient calcium from their daily diet.

I have found that a bran-based cereal is a great way to start the day. Cereals such as All-Bran, Sultana Bran and branflakes provide lots of iron and, if you take them with milk, you get lots of calcium too. Bran-based cereals contain fewer calories than corn-

or rice-based ones. This means you can eat a larger portion for the same number of calories. Sugar-coated cereals contain less fat than other varieties and require no additional sweetening, thereby saving you calories.

Muesli usually has a higher fat content than other cereals because of its oat and nut content. It is also quite dense, so you get very little in a 1oz (25g) serving. However, muesli supplies many useful nutrients and is a particularly good choice for vegetarians. Just be vigilant with the portion sizes, or you could be eating twice as much as you think.

The recipe for home-made muesli (opposite) is adapted from a recipe I discovered in the Austrian Alps. It is best made the day before you eat it. Take it from me, it's delicious!

Milkshakes

For those who really can't stomach a proper breakfast, a banana whizzed with milk in a food processor or blender makes a nutritious meal in a glass.

Fruit

If you're a fruit lover, or you just don't have time to eat before you leave for work, fruit for breakfast could be the answer. It provides many vitamins and minerals important for good health.

Have 4 bananas or a combination of any 4 fruits to suit your taste buds. But remember, don't graze on fruit throughout the day or eat it between meals unless you are already at your goal weight and are just seeking to maintain your weight.

Home-made muesli

SERVES 1
PER SERVING:
260 KCAL / 2.2G FAT

1 eating apple
$\frac{1}{2}$oz (15g) oats
$\frac{1}{2}$oz (15g) sultanas
2 teaspoons bran
skimmed or semi-skimmed milk
   or 75g (3oz) low-fat natural
   yogurt
honey to taste
$\frac{1}{2}$ banana

Peel and grate the apple. Place the grated apple, oats, sultanas and bran in a bowl. Stir in the milk or yogurt and add honey to taste. Place in the refrigerator and leave overnight.

Just before serving, chop the banana, add to the muesli and mix well.

Starters

Traditionally, a starter is meant to whet the appetite for the courses to follow. However, if you are watching your waistline, a starter can act as a useful filler so that you don't need to eat so much food later! There are a variety of delicious low-fat ingredients that can be used for this purpose. On a low-fat eating plan, salads and fresh fruit are simple and practical options, but in this chapter you'll find plenty more challenging ideas to tempt your taste buds. Many of these dishes are also suitable as a light lunch.

When choosing a starter, as a general rule, try to keep to a limit of 100 calories per portion. However, should you exceed this, then simply bear it in mind when selecting your main course and counterbalance the calories to fit in with your allowance.

Don't forget, also, that you may wish to serve bread or other accompaniments with your starter, so don't overdo it. Remember, it's only meant to be a taster, not a complete meal!

Parma ham with pink grapefruit

SERVES 4
PER SERVING:
81 KCAL/2.3G FAT

2 large pink grapefruit
4 large thin slices Parma ham
a little paprika

Cut the peel from both grapefruit and remove the segments with a small sharp knife. Divide the segments into 4 portions and arrange each portion in a fan on one side of each serving plate.

Remove any fat from the Parma ham slices. Wrinkle the slices and place on each plate opposite the grapefruit.

Sprinkle a little paprika on each portion of grapefruit and refrigerate until required.

Simple melon cocktail

SERVES 8
PER SERVING:
110 KCAL/0.4G FAT

1 galia melon
1 honeydew melon
1 ogen melon
1 egg white
a little caster sugar
6–8 small sprigs fresh mint
2 tablespoons Grand Marnier or
    Cointreau liqueur

Choose ripe but firm melons. If you wish, you can add a few segments of fresh orange for colour and texture.

Cut the melons in half and remove the seeds. Cut the melon flesh away from the skin with a melon baller, or cut into small chunks.

Place the prepared melon flesh in a large bowl and sprinkle with Grand Marnier or Cointreau. Leave to stand for 15 minutes (do not place in the refrigerator or it will flavour the other foods).

For the next stage you will need one wineglass per person. Place the egg white in a small dish and place the caster sugar in a separate small bowl. Take a wine glass and dip it upside down in the egg white, then twizzle the dampened glass, again inverted, in the caster sugar. Repeat with the other glasses. This gives a pretty frosting effect at the top of each glass.

When all the glasses are prepared, distribute the melon cocktail evenly in the glasses and decorate each with a sprig of fresh mint.

Lemon and caper
stuffed pears

Choose good round pears such as Williams or Comice de Guyenne.
They need to be firm but ripe for this dish to be at its best.

Peel the pears, cut each one in half and scoop out the cores with a
teaspoon or ball-cutter. Using the point of a small knife, ease out
the part going to the stalk. Brush the lemon juice all over the
pears.

Mix together the cottage cheese, capers and 1 tablespoon of
the chopped chives and place a good spoonful in the centre of
each pear.

Place a leaf or two of Lollo Rosso on 4 individual plates and
place 2 pear halves in the centre of each. Cover and refrigerate
until required.

Just before serving, sprinkle the crushed red peppercorns and
the remaining chopped chives over the top of the cottage cheese
mixture.

SERVES 4
PER SERVING:
132 KCAL/0.8G FAT

4 large ripe pears
2–3 tablespoons lemon juice
6oz (175g) low-fat cottage
   cheese
1 tablespoon capers
1–2 tablespoons chopped
   chives
1 small Lollo Rosso lettuce
1 teaspoon crushed red
   peppercorns
salt and freshly ground black
   pepper

Garlic and herb celery sticks

Quark is a good substitute for the usual cream cheese or other high-fat cheeses that are commonly used as fillings in party food. It tastes delicious and looks just like the real thing!

Cut each celery stick into 3 pieces.

Combine all the remaining ingredients to form a smooth paste. Place in a piping bag and pipe into the celery sticks.

Dust with additional paprika or chopped parsley.

SERVES 4
PER SERVING:
54 KCAL/0.3G FAT

4 celery sticks
8oz (225g) quark
1 garlic clove, crushed
1 tablespoon chopped fresh
    parsley
1 tablespoon chervil
1 teaspoon paprika
4 pieces sun-dried tomato, finely
    chopped
2 teaspoons lemon juice
salt and freshly ground black
    pepper

Italian bean salad

SERVES 6
PER SERVING:
75 KCAL/0.9G FAT

8oz (225g) broad beans
(weighed after shelling)
salt
8oz (225g) French beans
1 medium onion, finely chopped
1–2 garlic cloves, crushed
1 × 14oz (400g) can chopped
tomatoes
2–3 teaspoons lemon juice or to
taste
$\frac{1}{2}$ teaspoon caster sugar
salt and freshly ground black
pepper
1–2 tablespoons chopped fresh
basil to garnish

Cook the broad beans in boiling salted water for 10–15 minutes or until tender. Drain well and refresh under cold running water until completely cold. Drain well again. If the skins are tough, make a slit in each one and pop the beans out of the skins.

Top and tail the French beans and cut into short lengths. Cook in boiling salted water for 8–10 minutes then refresh in the same way as broad beans.

Place the onion and garlic in a pan. Add the tomatoes, lemon juice, sugar, a little salt and black pepper, bring to the boil and simmer until the onions are tender and the sauce has thickened slightly.

Purée the sauce in a food processor or liquidiser and then strain to remove the seeds of the tomatoes, or pass through a vegetable mill or sieve. Check the seasoning and add more lemon juice, sugar, salt or pepper as required. Leave until completely cold.

Pile the beans into the centre of a serving dish. Pour sufficient sauce over to cover most of the beans, leaving a few beans showing around the edge. Sprinkle the chopped basil over. Cover and refrigerate until required.

Prawn cocktail

Recreate this classic starter, using low-fat ingredients. The sauce can also be used on many other seafood dishes or served with cold crab or lobster.

Wash the prawns and drain well. Wash the lettuce leaves, drain well and finely shred. Place the shredded lettuce in the bottom of 4 wineglasses or small dishes and arrange the prawns on top.

Combine the tomato ketchup, yogurt and salad dressing in a small bowl, and season to taste with salt and pepper and a dash of Tabasco. Spoon the dressing over the prawns and sprinkle with paprika.

Garnish with the lemon wedges.

SERVES 4
PER SERVING
122 KCAL/1.2G FAT

12oz (350g) peeled and cooked
  prawns
1 crisp green lettuce
4 tablespoons tomato ketchup
4 tablespoons low-fat natural
  yogurt
2 tablespoons reduced-oil low-
  calorie salad dressing
dash of Tabasco sauce
salt and freshly ground black
  pepper
paprika
4 lemon wedges to garnish

Cucumber and tuna boats

These are also great to serve at children's parties. You will need 8 cocktail sticks to use as 'masts' for the cucumber sails!

Slice the whole cucumber in half lengthways (reserve the half cucumber). Scoop out the seeds with a teaspoon, and divide each half into 4 portions to resemble 'boats'.

Mix the tuna with the spring onions, sweetcorn, yogurt and parsley, season to taste, and combine well. Place a small amount of the mixture in each boat.

Using a vegetable peeler, take 8 long strips from the remaining cucumber. Thread each strip onto a cocktail stick and place one on each boat to represent a sail.

SERVES 8
PER SERVING:
46 KCAL/0.4G FAT

1½ large cucumbers
8oz (225g) canned tuna in brine, drained
2 spring onions, finely chopped
4oz (100g) canned sweetcorn, drained
2–3 tablespoons low-fat natural yogurt
1 tablespoon chopped fresh parsley
salt and freshly ground black pepper

Baked mushrooms

SERVES 4
PER SERVING:
112 KCAL/10.1G FAT

1lb (450g) bite-sized chestnut
    mushrooms
6 spring onions, finely chopped
1 garlic clove, crushed
4oz (100g) fresh brown
    breadcrumbs
zest and juice of 1 lemon
2 tablespoons chopped fresh
    parsley
2 tablespoons soy sauce
1 tablespoon chopped fresh
    oregano
salt and freshly ground black
    pepper

Preheat the oven to 180°C, 350°F, Gas Mark 4.

Wipe the mushrooms with a damp cloth. Choose 3–4 of the best even-sized ones and remove the stalks. Place the bodies on a baking sheet.

Chop the stalks and the remaining mushrooms and dry-fry in a non-stick frying pan for 1–2 minutes. Add the spring onions and garlic and cook for a further minute. Add the remaining ingredients and mix well.

Spoon the mixture into the mushroom bodies and bake in the oven for 15–20 minutes. Serve hot.

Marinated roast vegetables

These marinated roast vegetables are a perfect light starter. Serve them piping hot from the oven or chilled with salad leaves. Either way, the strong contrasting flavours make this such a tasty dish.

Prepare the vegetables by slicing into wedges about ¹/₂ in (1 cm) thick. Place in a roasting tin and season well with salt and black pepper.

Combine the lemon juice, soy sauce, lemon grass and marjoram in a small bowl. Pour over the vegetables and allow the vegetables to marinate for at least 30 minutes, turning occasionally.

Preheat the oven to 200°C, 400°F, Gas Mark 6.

Give the vegetables a final mix, sprinkle with the sesame seeds and place in the oven. Roast for 35–40 minutes until soft and tender with slight charring around the edges.

Serve with a sprinkling of fresh chopped parsley.

SERVES 4
PER SERVING:
79 KCAL / 2.6 G FAT

2 medium courgettes
1 aubergine
1 red and 1 yellow pepper, seeded
2 baby leeks
1 small bulb of fennel
1 red onion
4 tablespoons lemon juice
2 tablespoons light soy sauce
2 teaspoons finely chopped lemon grass
2 tablespoons chopped fresh marjoram
1 tablespoon sesame seeds
salt and freshly ground black pepper
chopped fresh parsley to garnish

Chicken liver pâté with brandy and green peppercorns

Wash the chicken livers and drain well.

In a non-stick frying pan, dry-fry the onion and mushrooms until soft. Add the garlic, bacon and chicken livers and season well. Cook over a medium heat for 3–4 minutes, turning the mixture well. Place into a food processor or liquidiser, add the tomato purée, mixed herbs and brandy. Blend until smooth. Spoon the mixture into a small loaf tin or individual pots, pressing it down well. Press the green peppercorns into the top of the pâté and sprinkle with the parsley.

To make the melba toast, toast the bread both sides, cut each slice in half horizontally and remove the crusts. Arrange on a grill tray, untoasted side-up, and brown under the grill.

Just before serving, cut the pâté into slices, garnish with lemon wedges and serve with salad.

SERVES 6
PER SERVING:
165 KCAL/4.4G FAT

8oz (225g) chicken livers
1 onion, finely chopped
4oz (100g) mushrooms, sliced
1 garlic clove, crushed
4 slices lean back bacon, chopped
1 tablespoon tomato purée
2 tablespoons chopped fresh mixed herbs
2 tablespoons brandy
1 tablespoon green peppercorns in brine
1 tablespoon chopped fresh parsley
salt and freshly ground black pepper
lemon wedges to garnish

for the melba toast
6 thin slices bread

Chicken liver salad

SERVES 4
PER SERVING:
83 KCAL/2.7G FAT

4oz (100g) chicken or duck livers
6 spring onions, finely chopped
2 rashers lean back bacon
$\frac{1}{2}$ slice white bread
2 tomatoes, cut into 8 chunks
1 × 2in (5cm) piece cucumber,
   finely chopped
freshly ground black pepper
a few salad leaves

for the dressing
1 teaspoon French mustard
3 tablespoons lemon juice
1 tablespoon orange juice
1 tablespoon wine vinegar
salt and freshly ground black
   pepper

This stunning salad bursts with flavour. Prepare it at the last minute and serve piping hot, since the chicken livers will continue to cook with the heat from the pan. You can store any leftover dressing in a jar in the refrigerator and use as a standard salad dressing.

Make the dressing by placing all the ingredients in a jar and shaking well.

Wash and trim the chicken or duck livers and dry-fry them, together with the spring onions, in a non-stick pan, seasoning them well with black pepper. Cook until the livers are brown on the outside and pink in the centre.

Trim all the fat from the bacon, grill well and chop into small pieces.

Toast the bread and cut into tiny squares.

Mix the tomato and cucumber together. Arrange the salad leaves on 4 individual dishes.

When the livers and spring onions are cooked, distribute the tomatoes and cucumber evenly between the 4 dishes, then top with the chopped hot bacon, chicken livers, spring onions and croutons. Pour the dressing over.

Roasted tomatoes with wilted chicken liver salad

Plum tomatoes are best for this dish. However, if these are too expensive you can use firm round tomatoes. Choose good red ones. Ready-prepared salads are ideal for this recipe because you get a good selection of different types of lettuce. If you prefer to make your own salad, try to add a little chicory frisée or radicchio. A little lamb's lettuce or some small spinach leaves will also provide a contrast in texture and flavour.

Preheat the oven to 200°C, 400°F, Gas Mark 6.

Toast the bread. Cut the garlic cloves in half and rub over both sides of each piece. Remove the crusts from the toast and cut the toast into neat cubes. Reserve until later.

Drain the chicken livers. Cut each liver into 2–3 pieces. Place on a plate, cover with cling film and refrigerate until required.

Wash and drain the salad leaves. Cut the tomatoes in half lengthways and place, cut-side up, in a non-stick roasting tin. Season well with salt and black pepper. Place in the oven for 25–30 minutes or until they are well browned on top. Keep hot.

Dry-fry the chicken livers in a hot non-stick frying pan until they are brown on the outside and pink in the centre.

While the chicken livers are cooking, arrange a little salad on 4 individual plates. Arrange the tomato halves around the outside of the lettuce.

When the livers are cooked, distribute them evenly between the 4 plates of salad.

Quickly add the balsamic vinegar to the pan, place over the heat and swill around. Pour the vinegar over the chicken livers and sprinkle the garlic croutons on top. Serve immediately.

SERVES 4
PER SERVING:
129 KCAL/2.2G FAT

2 slices white or wholemeal
    bread
2 large garlic cloves
8oz (225g) chicken livers
mixed green salad of your
    choice
8 medium tomatoes
salt and freshly ground black
    pepper
2–3 tablespoons balsamic
    vinegar

Smoked mackerel stuffed chicory leaves

Trim the ends off the chicory and separate the leaves. Place the leaves on a serving dish.

Skin the mackerel and remove any bones. Using a fork, break up the mackerel in a bowl. Add the cottage cheese and the remaining ingredients and mix well to combine the ingredients.

Spoon the mixture onto the chicory shells.

Chill until ready to serve.

SERVES 6
PER SERVING:
92 KCAL/6.1G FAT

3 heads chicory
4oz (100g) smoked mackerel
    fillets
4oz (100g) low-fat cottage
    cheese
4 spring onions, finely chopped
$\frac{1}{2}$ red pepper, seeded and finely
    chopped
2 teaspoons horseradish
2 teaspoons lemon juice
4oz (100g) canned sweetcorn,
    drained
1 tablespoon chopped fresh dill
salt and freshly ground black
    pepper

Mackerel with apples cooked in cider

SERVES 4
PER SERVING:
217 KCAL/12.3G FAT

12oz (350g) fresh mackerel
1 medium onion, finely chopped
2 sweet eating apples, peeled
    and finely sliced
1 teaspoon coriander seeds
2 bay leaves
2 tablespoons white wine
    vinegar
1/4 pint (150ml) dry cider
salt and freshly ground black
    pepper
a few sprigs fresh chervil or
    parsley to garnish

This dish is similar to roll mop herrings. The apple and cider impart a sweet flavour, leaving the mackerel moist and flavoursome.

Preheat the oven to 190°C, 375°F, Gas Mark 5.

Prepare the mackerel by removing the head with a sharp knife. Wash the fish under a running cold tap, opening the front of the fish with a knife. Place on a chopping board, face-side down, and press along the backbone to flatten the fish out. Turn the fish over and remove the backbone and any stray bones. Re-form the mackerel and slice into bite-sized pieces.

Place the mackerel on the base of an ovenproof dish, scatter the onion and apple over and season well. Add the coriander seeds, bay leaves, white wine vinegar and cider. Cover with a piece of greaseproof paper and place in the oven for 10–15 minutes. Allow to cool, then refrigerate until cold.

Garnish with a few sprigs of chervil or parsley before serving.

Moules marinière

At one time mussels could only be purchased when in season, from September to March, but now they are farmed all year round. They require careful preparation but are well worth the wait.

Scrape and wash the mussels well. Remove the beard on the side of the shell and any grit or sand. Discard any open mussels or those with broken shells, since these may be dead. If in doubt, tap the mussel on its side. If it remains open, discard it. If it closes, it's OK to use. Once they are thoroughly cleaned, check the mussels over, making sure there are no broken shells.

In a non-stick pan, dry-fry the shallots until soft, add the garlic and cook for a further 30 seconds. Add the mussels, wine, stock and peppercorns.

Squeeze out the juice from the lemon halves and squeeze over the mussels and stock. Add the lemon halves to the pan and cover with a tight-fitting lid. Cook over a high heat for 2–3 minutes or until the mussel shells are open.

Spoon the mussels into serving bowls, discarding any unopened shells. Sprinkle with the parsley.

Using a sieve, strain the cooking liquor over the mussels and serve immediately.

SERVES 4
PER SERVING:
222 KCAL/4.92G FAT

2¼lb (1kg) mussels
4oz (100g) shallots, finely chopped
3–4 garlic cloves, crushed
1 wineglass white wine
¼ pint (150ml) fish stock
6 whole black peppercorns
1 lemon, halved
2 tablespoons chopped fresh parsley

Thai rosti crab cakes with tomato and lime salsa

SERVES 4
PER SERVING:
138 KCAL / 2.7G FAT

1lb (450g) waxy potatoes,
    peeled
4 spring onions, finely chopped
1 teaspoon finely chopped fresh
    red chillies
1 teaspoon finely chopped
    lemon grass
1 tablespoon chopped fresh
    coriander
$2 \times 1^1/_2$oz (2×43g) cans
    dressed crab or 4oz (100g)
    fresh crab meat
salt and freshly ground black
    pepper
1 teaspoon vegetable oil

for the salsa
6 ripe tomatoes
1 lime
1 tablespoon finely chopped
    fresh parsley
1 tablespoon balsamic vinegar
salt and pepper

Using the coarse side of a cheese grater, grate the potatoes onto a clean tea towel. Draw the corners of the tea towel together and twist to enclose the potato. Squeeze well to remove as much liquid as possible. Transfer the potato to a mixing bowl and season with salt and pepper. Add the spring onions, chillies, lemon grass, coriander and crab meat and mix well with a fork. Using your hands, form the mixture into 8 equal balls.

Preheat a non-stick frying pan, add the oil, then wipe out the pan carefully with kitchen paper to remove most of the oil, taking care not to burn your fingers (wear an oven glove if necessary).

Lightly flatten the crab cakes with the palm of your hand and place in the frying pan. Cook for 4 minutes, until they are a golden brown colour. Remove from the pan and transfer to an ovenproof dish. Place in a low oven to keep warm.

To make the salsa, skin the tomatoes by plunging them in boiling water for just 10 seconds, remove and submerge in ice cold water. The skins should peel away easily. Slice each tomato in half and scoop out the seeds with a teaspoon. Rinse well to remove any stray seeds. Chop the tomatoes into $^1/_2$in (1cm) dice and place in a bowl.

Using a zester, remove thin strips of zest from the lime and place in the bowl. Add the lime juice, parsley and balsamic vinegar and season well with salt and pepper. Mix well and serve with the crab cakes.

Crab mousse
with asparagus

These crab mousses can be made the day before they are required,
providing the crab has been bought that day. Store in the coldest
part of the refrigerator until required, but do not deep freeze. A
prepared dressed crab yields about 6¹/₂–7oz (185–200g) crab
meat which is sufficient for this dish. If buying crab meat loose or
frozen, then buy 8oz (225g) as some meat will inevitably be left
clinging to the wrapping paper.

Place $6 \times 3^{1}/_{2}$oz (90g) ramekins in a deep freeze or in the ice box
of the refrigerator for 1–2 hours to chill well.

Dissolve the aspic crystals in $^{1}/_{4}$ pint (300ml) boiling water.
Leave until on the point of setting, then pour some into each
ramekin and swirl around so that the base and sides are lightly
covered. Pour any excess aspic into the bowl or jug containing the
remaining aspic and stand it in hot water until the aspic has just
melted again.

Lightly trim the ends from the asparagus. Place in a steamer
over boiling water and steam for 4–5 minutes until just tender.
Remove from the heat and sprinkle with a little salt. Leave until
cold.

Trim the green tips from the top of each piece of asparagus.
Dip each piece into the liquid aspic and place 4 pieces in each
ramekin, with the points in the centre. If the asparagus pieces are
rather thick, cut the tips in half lengthways and place, cut-side up,
in the ramekins. Pour a teaspoon of liquid aspic over the tips to set
them in place, then refrigerate until required. Cut the remainder
of the asparagus into $^{1}/_{2}$in (1cm) lengths and reserve.

Purée the cottage cheese, fromage frais and milk in a food
processor or liquidiser. Add the crab meat and mix until smooth.
Turn out into a large bowl.

Pour 2 tablespoons of water and the lemon juice into a
heatproof or microwave-proof bowl. Sprinkle the gelatine into the
bowl and place it over hot water or in a microwave to dissolve the

SERVES 6
PER SERVING (INCLUDING
THE HONEY AND ORANGE
DRESSING):
78 KCAL/2.2G FAT

$^{1}/_{2}$oz (15g) aspic crystals
4oz (100g) small asparagus tips
4oz (100g) low-fat cottage
   cheese
2oz (50g) low-fat fromage frais
2 tablespoons skimmed milk
1 dressed crab or 8oz (225g)
   crab meat
1×11g sachet gelatine
1 tablespoon lemon juice
1 egg white
salt and white pepper
Honey and orange dressing
   (see recipe, page 407)

gelatine. Allow to cool slightly. Pour into the crab mixture, mix well and season to taste with salt and white pepper. Leave until on the point of setting.

At this stage whisk the egg white until it stands in stiff peaks. Stir a small spoonful into the crab mixture to loosen the mixture then carefully fold in the rest. Pour into the prepared ramekins and refrigerate until required.

To serve, dip each ramekin into hot water for a moment or two and turn each mousse out onto an individual dish.

Sprinkle the reserved chopped asparagus around each mousse and spoon a little of the Honey and Orange Dressing over it. Keep refrigerated until required.

Tomato cups with smoked salmon pâté

Quark is a soft curd cheese made from skimmed milk. It is virtually fat free, making it an ideal filler for pâtés and cooked cheese recipes.

Place the smoked salmon trimmings, the quark or cottage cheese and the parsley in a food processor or liquidiser and purée until smooth. Add a little lemon juice and white pepper to taste.

Blanch the tomatoes in boiling water for 10 seconds, then plunge them into ice cold water to prevent the flesh from going soft. Remove the skins. Cut the tomatoes in half through the middle and remove the seeds and flesh. Sprinkle the insides lightly with salt and leave until required.

Using a piping bag with a large star pipe, pipe the smoked salmon pâté into the tomato cups. If you don't have a piping bag, you can spoon the pâté into the cups.

Cut the grapes in half, remove any pips and place a grape half on the top of each filled cup. Arrange the lettuce leaves on 4 individual plates and place 2 tomato cups in the centre of each. Chill until required.

SERVES 4
PER SERVING:
68 KCAL/1.3G FAT

4oz (100g) smoked salmon
    trimmings
4oz (100g) quark or low-fat
    cottage cheese
1 tablespoon chopped fresh
    parsley
a little lemon juice
4 medium tomatoes
salt and white pepper
4 black grapes
a few lettuce leaves

Quick tuna pâté

SERVES 4
PER SERVING:
69 KCAL/0.7G FAT

8oz (200g) canned tuna in brine
3oz (75g) low-fat yogurt
2 tablespoons reduced-oil salad
   dressing
2 teaspoons lemon juice
1 teaspoon chopped fresh or
   freeze-dried dill
$1/4$ teaspoon cayenne pepper
4 lemon slices
salt and freshly ground black
   pepper

This quick, tasty pâté is always a good standby for unexpected guests. Many of the ingredients can be stocked in the larder or refrigerator ready for a quick assemble.

Drain the tuna well and place in a bowl. Add the yogurt, reduced-oil dressing and lemon juice. Mash with a fork until well combined. Add the fresh dill and cayenne pepper and season well with salt and pepper. Mix well.

Spoon the mixture into 4 small ramekin dishes and place a slice of lemon on the top of each one. Refrigerate for at least 2 hours before serving.

Serve with French bread and a few celery sticks.

Potted smoked trout

A wonderful fish starter with a tangy mustard flavour. Ideal for entertaining, this dish is easy to prepare and forms a stunning start to any meal.

Using a fork, break the trout fillets in a small bowl. Add the mustard, quark, and parsley. Mix well, and season with salt and pepper.

Press the mixture into 4 small ramekin dishes and smooth the tops over with a knife.

Refrigerate until ready to serve. Serve with a watercress salad.

SERVES 4
PER SERVING:
96 KCAL/3.2G FAT

8oz (225g) fresh trout fillets
1 tablespoon Dijon mustard
4oz (100g) quark
1 tablespoon chopped fresh parsley
salt and freshly ground black pepper
1 bunch watercress

Rabbit and pork terrine with juniper

SERVES 10
PER SERVING:
155 KCAL / 7.6G FAT

1 lb (450g) diced rabbit
1 lb (450g) lean minced pork
8 oz (225g) lean smoked bacon,
    finely chopped
2 tablespoons gin
6 juniper berries, crushed
2 tablespoons chopped fresh
    mixed herbs (e.g. parsley,
    thyme, marjoram)
salt and freshly ground black
    pepper

Rabbit is a very lean meat and is readily available in supermarkets. Mixing it with lean pork and smoked bacon produces a rich and tasty terrine.

Preheat the oven to 180°C, 350°F, Gas Mark 4.

Mix all the ingredients together in a large bowl. Season well with salt and pepper. Press the mixture into a 2lb (1kg) terrine mould or individual ramekins. Stand the mould or ramekins in a roasting tin and pour sufficient water around to come halfway up the sides of the mould or ramekins.

Cover with foil and bake in the oven for 1–1½ hours. Allow to cool, then refrigerate overnight.

Serve with salad leaves and lemon wedges.

Turkey, pheasant and cranberry terrine

Preheat the oven to 180°C, 350°F, Gas Mark 4. Line a 2lb (1kg) loaf tin with greaseproof paper.

Using a sharp knife, cut the breasts from the pheasant and remove the skin. Cut the visible meat from the carcass, removing any fat.

Slice the pheasant breasts into long thin strips and reserve. Mince or finely chop the remaining pheasant meat and mix with the minced turkey in a large bowl. Add the thyme, mace, garlic, lemon, wine and parsley and mix well. Season with salt and plenty of freshly ground black pepper.

Place a small amount of the minced meat mixture in the prepared loaf tin, just enough to cover the base. Add a layer of cranberry sauce then a layer of the reserved strips of pheasant breast. Continue with additional layers, ending up with a layer of the minced mixture.

Place the loaf tin into a roasting tin, and pour sufficient water into the roasting tin so that it comes halfway up the side of the loaf tin. Cover with foil and place in the oven for $1-1\frac{1}{2}$ hours.

Allow to cool, then refrigerate overnight.

To serve, slice thinly and serve with additional cranberry sauce.

SERVES 10
PER SERVING:
220 KCAL/8G FAT

1 pheasant
1lb (450g) minced turkey
1 tablespoon chopped fresh thyme
1 teaspoon ground mace
1 garlic clove, crushed
fine zest and juice of 1 lemon
¼ pint (150ml) dry white wine
2 tablespoons chopped fresh parsley
1 × 12oz (350g) jar cranberry sauce
salt and freshly ground black pepper

Garlic bread

SERVES 8
PER SERVING:
185 KCAL/2.4G FAT

4oz (100g) very low-fat spread
  (maximum 5% fat)
4 garlic cloves, crushed
1 teaspoon lemon juice
2 tablespoons chopped fresh
  parsley
1 French stick
salt

I try not to use low-fat spreads in my recipes, since it can be hard to resist temptation once you have a knife and some bread in your hands. If you require just a small quantity of garlic bread, then adjust the recipe accordingly and use the spread sparingly.

Preheat the oven to 220°C, 425°F, Gas Mark 7.

Mix the very low-fat spread with the garlic, lemon juice and parsley.

Cut the loaf into ¾in (2cm) slices, slanting the knife diagonally across the loaf. Spread each slice with the garlic mixture, re-form the loaf and sprinkle a little salt across the top. Wrap in foil and place in the oven for 10 minutes.

Serve immediately.

Crudités

Crudités and dips are ideal for serving with pre-dinner drinks. You can use any selection of raw vegetables. Prepare the vegetables as indicated below, arrange on a large plate and serve with any of the dips in this chapter.

Carrots: cut into batons

Celery: cut into batons

Courgettes: cut into batons

Red or green peppers: core, seed and cut into strips

Spring onions: slice down through the green part 4 or 5 times and place in iced water for 1 hour to form 'tassels'

Radishes: round ones can be cut through almost to the base 6–8 times and put into iced water until they open up

White button mushrooms: cut small ones into quarters and larger ones into slices. Pierce with cocktail sticks

Chicory: separate the individual spears and rinse quickly in water (don't leave to soak or they will become bitter)

Canned artichoke hearts: drain and rinse well. Cut into quarters and pierce with cocktail sticks

Small canned corn on the cob: drain and rinse

Broccoli and cauliflower: cut into small florets

Cocktail dip

Mix the fromage frais or yogurt with sufficient tomato ketchup to colour and flavour. Season to taste with Tabasco sauce, salt and freshly ground black pepper. Spoon into a small serving dish.

SERVES 8
PER SERVING:
27 KCAL/0.07G FAT

4–5 tablespoons low-fat
    fromage frais or yogurt
3–4 tablespoons tomato
    ketchup
a few drops Tabasco sauce
salt and freshly ground black
    pepper

Tuna dip

Drain the tuna and place in a bowl. Flake into small pieces with two forks. Mix together with the quark and salad dressing. Season to taste with horseradish relish, salt, white pepper and chervil.

SERVES 12
PER SERVING:
19 KCAL/0.3G FAT

1 small can tuna in brine
4oz (100g) quark
2 tablespoons low-fat salad
    dressing
$1/2$ teaspoon horseradish relish
    or to taste
1 tablespoon chopped fresh
    chervil

Garlic and caper dip

SERVES 8
PER SERVING:
11 KCAL/0.1G FAT

2 garlic cloves, crushed
1 tablespoon capers, finely
     chopped
1 spring onion, finely chopped
1 tablespoon chopped fresh
     parsley
5oz (150g) low-fat fromage frais
     or yogurt
salt and freshly ground black
     pepper

Mix all the ingredients together and season to taste with salt and black pepper.

Prawn and ginger dip

SERVES 12
PER SERVING:
26 KCAL/0.1G FAT

6oz (175g) peeled and cooked
     prawns
4oz (100g) quark
2 teaspoons lemon juice or to
     taste
1–1½ teaspoons grated fresh
     ginger
1–2 tablespoons low-fat
     fromage frais or yogurt
salt and white pepper
chopped fresh chives to garnish

Place the prawns in a food processor or liquidiser and blend until finely chopped, or chop finely by hand.

Mix the quark with the lemon juice and grated ginger. Add the prawns. Adjust the consistency of the dip with the fromage frais or yogurt. Season with salt and white pepper. Sprinkle the chives on top.

Soups

Delicious home-made soup is welcome at any time of year and tastes far better than any commercially produced brand. Today we are lucky to have access to a wide range of fresh ingredients to tempt our cooking pots.

Good home-made soup gives a feeling of comfort and warmth at any family meal, and ladled from a tureen, hot or chilled, it can grace any dinner party table as a first course.

Low-fat soup doesn't have to mean thin, tasteless soup. In this section I have included some of my all-time favourite recipes, full of flavour and bursting with nutrition. The thickness of soup is a matter of personal choice and it can easily be adjusted to suit your own preference.

When serving soup as a first course, be careful not to give too generous a helping, as this can spoil the appetite for subsequent courses.

Allow $\frac{1}{3}$ pint (200ml) soup per serving.

Bortsch

SERVES 4
PER SERVING:
165 KCAL / 1.2G FAT

2½lb (1.2kg) raw baby beetroot
3 medium onions, finely
   chopped
2 pints (1.2 litres) vegetable
   stock
6 tablespoons dry sherry
2 tablespoons lemon juice
salt and freshly ground black
   pepper
2 tablespoons low-fat yogurt
a few chopped chives to garnish

Beetroot gives this traditional Russian soup an almost ruby red velvet appearance. The soup can be left with fine dice of vegetables or blended as in this recipe. Either way, it makes a spectacular start to any meal.

Wash the beetroot well and place in a saucepan. Barely cover the beetroot with water, bring to the boil and cook until tender. Allow to cool, then remove the outer skin. This should come away quite easily by rubbing it with your fingers or with the back of a knife. Trim the tops and bottoms with a knife and chop into fine dice.

Dry-fry the onion in a non-stick saucepan until soft. Add the beetroot and the vegetable stock and simmer for 20 minutes. Pour into a food processor or liquidiser and blend until smooth. Return the soup to the pan, add the sherry and lemon juice and season well with salt and freshly ground black pepper. Leave to cool and chill in the refrigerator.

Just before serving, swirl the yogurt on top and sprinkle with chopped chives. Serve well chilled.

Carrot and coriander soup

This flavoursome soup really benefits from being made the day before you eat it and stored in the refrigerator. Choose young, crisp carrots, as these tend to be sweet and you may find that they don't need peeling.

Place the onion, garlic and carrots in a large saucepan. Add the stock and the ground coriander and bring to the boil. Reduce the heat and simmer for 30 minutes. Pour into a liquidiser or food processor and purée until smooth. Return the soup to the pan, add the fresh coriander and orange juice, and season to taste with salt and pepper.

Just before serving, garnish with fresh orange slices and a few sprigs of fresh coriander.

SERVES 6
PER SERVING:
87 KCAL/0.9G FAT

3 medium onions, chopped
1 garlic clove, crushed
1 lb (450g) carrots, diced
1 pint (600ml) vegetable stock
1 tablespoon ground coriander
2 tablespoons chopped fresh
    coriander
juice of 1 orange
salt and freshly ground black
    pepper
orange slices and coriander
    sprigs to garnish

Leek and potato soup

SERVES 6
PER SERVING:
169 KCAL/1.1G FAT

3 large leeks, sliced

1 large onion, diced

2 garlic cloves, crushed

$\frac{1}{2}$ pint (300ml) vegetable stock

2 tablespoons flour

4 large potatoes, scrubbed and diced

1 pint (600ml) skimmed milk

1 bouquet garni

2 tablespoons chopped fresh parsley

salt and freshly ground black pepper

This strong-flavoured traditional soup is almost a meal in itself. Make sure you wash the leeks thoroughly under a running tap, as they tend to harbour soil and grit. You can serve this soup for lunch with a slice of wholemeal bread, or serve it as a first course and then choose a light main course to follow in order to balance the calories.

In a large saucepan, sweat the leeks, onion and garlic in 3 tablespoons of the stock for 2–3 minutes. Sprinkle the flour over and mix well with a wooden spoon. Cook for a further 1 minute in order to 'cook out' the flour.

Gradually add the rest of the stock, stirring continuously. Add the potatoes, milk and bouquet garni and simmer gently for 20 minutes until the potatoes are tender and the soup has thickened. Season to taste with salt and freshly ground black pepper.

Just before serving, stir in the parsley.

Gazpacho

This iced soup originates from Spain where ripe tomatoes, garlic and peppers are grown in abundance. It forms the perfect refreshment on a summer's evening. If you wish, you can add a small quantity of gelatine to the soup before you chill it and then serve it slightly jellied, or try adding a little sparkling wine just before serving to lightly fizz the finished soup.

Cut the cucumber in half. Peel one piece of the cucumber. Cut the other piece in half lengthways, remove the seeds with a teaspoon and discard. Chop the tomato, green and red peppers, onion and seeded cucumber into small dice.

Place the breadcrumbs and a little of the tomato juice into a liquidiser or food processor and purée until smooth. Scrape out the mixture into a bowl.

Place the peeled piece of cucumber, half the chopped onion, half the diced green pepper, and the garlic, lemon juice and 4–5 tablespoons of the tomato juice into the liquidiser or food processor and purée until smooth.

Add the puréed vegetable mixture to the breadcrumb mix and stir in the remainder of the tomato juice. Season to taste with salt and black pepper and a little sugar as desired.

Stir in the reserved diced tomatoes, onion, cucumber and green and red peppers. Check the seasoning again and stir in half the basil. Cover and chill in the refrigerator for at least 2–3 hours or overnight.

Just before serving, check the consistency and seasoning of the soup. If left overnight, the soup will thicken, so add a little chicken stock or more tomato juice as necessary and adjust the seasoning.

Pour into a soup tureen or individual bowls and sprinkle with the remainder of the chopped basil. Garnish with a basil leaf.

SERVES 4–6
PER SERVING:
75 KCAL/0.5G FAT

1 × 4oz (100g) piece cucumber
6 large ripe tomatoes, skinned and seeded
1 green pepper, seeded
1 red pepper, seeded
$\frac{1}{2}$ small onion, finely chopped
2oz (50g) fresh white breadcrumbs
$1\frac{1}{4}$ pints (750ml) tomato juice
1 large garlic clove, crushed
$1\frac{1}{2}$ tablespoons lemon juice
a little caster sugar
1 tablespoon finely chopped fresh basil
extra tomato juice or a little chicken stock if desired
salt and freshly ground black pepper
1 basil leaf to garnish

Watercress soup

SERVES 4
PER SERVING:
108 KCAL / 1.3G FAT

1 medium onion, finely diced
1 garlic clove, crushed
8oz (225g) potatoes, peeled and
    diced
1 pint (600ml) vegetable stock
4 bunches fresh watercress
½ pint (300ml) skimmed milk
5oz (150g) low-fat natural
    yogurt
salt and freshly ground black
    pepper

To obtain a beautiful green soup, the secret is not to cook the watercress but just add it to the hot stock and blend together. The heat of the stock will wilt it sufficiently and produce a wonderful colourful result.

Dry-fry the onion and garlic in a non-stick saucepan until soft. Add the potatoes and the vegetable stock and simmer for 10 minutes until the potatoes are tender.

Add the watercress and the milk. Remove from the heat, pour into a liquidiser or food processor and blend until smooth. Return to the pan and season well with salt and black pepper.

Just before serving, stir in the yogurt.

French onion soup

This tasty low-fat recipe is a great alternative to the usual high-fat version. The onions cook well without fat, and the flour thickens the soup to make it quite substantial.

Place the onions in a large pan with a little vegetable stock. Sweat the onions until soft. Add the garlic and thyme. Sprinkle the flour over and mix well. Season to taste, and cook for a moment or two to 'cook out' the flour. Gradually add the remaining stock, bring to the boil and simmer for 10 minutes.

Just before serving, sprinkle with the parsley and toasted croutons.

SERVES 8
PER SERVING:
95 KCAL/1.2G FAT

1 ½lb (675g) large onions, sliced
2 pints (1.2 litres) vegetable stock
2 garlic cloves, crushed
1 tablespoon chopped fresh thyme
2 tablespoons plain flour
salt and freshly ground black pepper
2 tablespoons chopped fresh parsley
2 slices bread, toasted and cut into croutons

Cream of mushroom and lemon soup

SERVES 4
PER SERVING:
100 KCAL / 1.1G FAT

3 medium onions, finely
     chopped
2 garlic cloves, crushed
12oz (350g) chestnut
     mushrooms
1 lemon, finely zested and
     segmented
1 tablespoon flour
1 tablespoon light soy sauce
1 pint (600ml) vegetable stock
$^1/_2$ pint (300ml) skimmed milk
1 teaspoon chopped fresh dill
salt and freshly ground black
     pepper
lemon wedges to garnish

Lemon has a real affinity with mushrooms, giving this classic cream soup a bitter twist. If you cannot get chestnut mushrooms, button ones will suffice, although these do not have such a strong flavour.

In a large non-stick saucepan, dry-fry the onions, garlic and mushrooms for 2–3 minutes, seasoning well, until the onions are soft and the mushrooms cook down. Add the lemon zest, flour and soy sauce and cook for a further minute to 'cook out' the flour. Gradually stir in the stock and skimmed milk. Bring to the boil, stirring continuously, then reduce the heat and simmer for 20 minutes.

   Season with salt and freshly ground black pepper.

   Just before serving, stir in the fresh dill and garnish with the lemon wedges.

Italian vegetable soup

This soup is thickened with pasta. Choose small pasta shapes or, alternatively, break spaghetti into ¹/₂in (1cm) pieces. The easiest way to do this is to wrap the spaghetti in a tea towel and run it over the edge of the work top, adding a little pressure. Unfold the tea towel and shoot the spaghetti pieces into the soup.

Place all the vegetables and the chopped tomatoes in a large saucepan. Add the garlic, bay leaf and vegetable stock. Bring to the boil and simmer for 40 minutes until the vegetables are tender. Twenty minutes before the end of the cooking time, add the pasta shapes and oregano.

When cooked, remove the bay leaf and season to taste with salt and pepper.

SERVES 6
PER SERVING:
84 KCAL / 1.3G FAT

2 carrots, thinly sliced
2 leeks, thinly sliced
1 red pepper, seeded and cut
   into ¹/₄in (5mm) dice
1–2 celery sticks, thinly sliced
1 medium onion, thinly sliced
a few dark Savoy cabbage
   leaves, finely shredded
1 × 14oz (400g) can chopped
   tomatoes
2 garlic cloves, crushed
1 bay leaf
2 pints (1.2 litres) vegetable
   stock
2oz (50g) small pasta shapes
1 tablespoon chopped fresh
   oregano
salt and freshly ground black
   pepper

Beef and roasted tomato soup

SERVES 6
PER SERVING:
92 KCAL/1.5G FAT

3lb (1.5kg) ripe tomatoes
1 tablespoon chopped fresh
    rosemary
2 garlic cloves, crushed
2 medium onions, finely
    chopped
1 celery stick, chopped
1 pint (600ml) strong beef stock
3 tablespoons tomato purée
salt and freshly ground black
    pepper

This recipe is a great way to use up over-ripe tomatoes. You can also use canned tomatoes – choose the ones with mixed herbs for additional flavour.

Preheat the oven to 200°C, 400°F, Gas Mark 6.

Cut the tomatoes in half, and place, cut-side up, in a large roasting tin. Season well with salt and black pepper. Sprinkle with the rosemary and crushed garlic. Place in the oven for 35–40 minutes until the tomatoes have softened and started to roast.

In a large non-stick saucepan dry-fry the onions and celery until soft. Add the tomatoes and their juices, and stir in the beef stock and tomato purée. Simmer for 10–15 minutes. Pour into a liquidiser or food processor and blend until smooth.

Strain the soup through a metal sieve into a saucepan to remove the tomato seeds. Reheat the soup, adjust the seasoning and serve hot.

Roasted garlic and green pea soup

This soup requires a little forward thinking. The garlic needs to be roasted for approximately 45 minutes before you make the soup. Roasting the garlic gives it a much mellower flavour than usual, so it's a good idea to roast a couple of whole heads together while you have the oven on. You can wrap roasted garlic in foil and keep in the refrigerator for up to one week.

Preheat the oven to 200°C, 400°F, Gas Mark 6.

Remove the outer skin from the garlic bulb or slice the top off. Place in a square of foil and wrap the foil around to form a parcel. Place in the oven for 45 minutes until soft.

Place the peas and chopped onion in a large saucepan, barely cover with salted water and boil for 20 minutes. Pour into a liquidiser or food processor and purée until smooth.

Squeeze out the garlic purée from the roasted bulbs and place in a food processor. Add the mint and the vegetable stock and blend again until smooth. Return to the saucepan and reheat. Season to taste with salt and pepper.

Just before serving, stir in the fromage frais.

SERVES 4
PER SERVING:
85 KCAL/1.7G FAT

1 whole head garlic
1 lb (450g) frozen petits pois
1 medium onion, finely chopped
8 fresh mint leaves
1 pint (600ml) vegetable stock
1 tablespoon virtually fat-free fromage frais
salt and freshly ground black pepper

Parsnip and cognac soup

SERVES 6
PER SERVING:
98 KCAL / 1.7G FAT

1½lb (675g) parsnips
1 large onion, chopped
2 garlic cloves, crushed
1 celery stick, chopped
2½ pints (1.5 litres) vegetable
    stock
1 bouquet garni
1oz (25g) skimmed milk powder
½ wineglass brandy
salt and freshly ground black
    pepper

Parsnips are a sweet and comforting vegetable with a natural thickening starch. Combined with brandy, they make this a rich, thick and creamy soup. This soup benefits from being made in advance to allow all the flavours to come together and blend. Store in the refrigerator until ready to use.

Peel and chop the parsnips and place in a large saucepan. Add the onion, garlic and celery. Pour the stock in the pan and add the bouquet garni. Bring to the boil and simmer until the vegetables are tender.

Dissolve the milk powder in a little cold water and stir into the soup. Place the soup in a food processor or liquidiser and purée until smooth. Adjust the seasoning.

Reheat the soup and, just before serving, stir in the brandy.

Double soup of red and yellow peppers

Bring together two vibrant colours in this stunning soup. Use only firm, fresh peppers as these will give a stronger colour to the finished soup. This recipe is excellent for freezing or can be made in advance and stored in the refrigerator for up to two days.

Using two separate pans, place the red peppers in one and the yellow peppers in the other. Divide all the other ingredients, except the parsley or fromage frais, in half and place half in each pan. Cover with a lid and simmer for 20–25 minutes or until soft.

Remove the bay leaf from each pan and pour one mixture into a liquidiser or food processor. Blend until smooth, then pour into a clean pan to reheat. Rinse out the liquidiser or food processor and repeat with the second mixture, pouring it into a separate pan when blended.

To serve, pour equal quantities of each soup into 2 separate jugs. Holding a jug in each hand at either side of a soup bowl, pour both soups into the bowl.

Garnish with a sprig of parsley or a swirl of fromage frais.

SERVES 4
PER SERVING:
194 KCAL/2.3G FAT

6 red peppers, seeded and
    chopped
6 yellow peppers, seeded and
    chopped
2 large onions, chopped
2 garlic cloves, crushed
2 teaspoons chopped fresh
    thyme
2 celery sticks, chopped
4 pints (2.5 litres) vegetable
    stock
2 bay leaves
salt and freshly ground black
    pepper
sprig of parsley or a little
    fromage frais to garnish

Red lentil and cumin soup

This soup is easy to prepare and provides many nutrients, which makes it a perfect winter warming lunch that is suitable for vegetarians. It tends to thicken considerably if left overnight in the refrigerator. If it does, thin it down with a little stock when you reheat it.

In a large saucepan, dry-fry the onion, leeks and celery for 3–4 minutes. Add the carrots, cumin, lentils and vegetable stock. Bring to the boil, add the bouquet garni, bay leaves and cayenne pepper. Reduce the heat and simmer for 30 minutes until the lentils and vegetables are tender.

Stir in the tomato purée and season well with salt and pepper.

SERVES 6
PER SERVING:
193 KCAL／1.9G FAT

2 onions, chopped
8oz (225g) leeks, diced
3–4 celery sticks, diced
8oz (225g) carrots, diced
1 tablespoon ground cumin
6oz (175g) [dry weight] red
     lentils, rinsed
2 pints (1.2 litres) vegetable
     stock
1 bouquet garni
2 bay leaves
$\frac{1}{2}$ teaspoon cayenne pepper
2 tablespoons tomato purée
salt and freshly ground black
     pepper

Pumpkin and ginger soup

SERVES 8
PER SERVING:
36 KCAL/0.5G FAT

2 medium onions, diced
2 garlic cloves, crushed
1 lb (450g) pumpkin, peeled and
    seeds removed
2 tablespoons chopped fresh
    ginger
1 tablespoon chopped fresh
    thyme
2$\frac{1}{2}$ pints (1.5 litres) chicken
    stock
2 tablespoons tomato purée
salt and freshly ground black
    pepper
low-fat natural yogurt and
    chopped fresh parsley to
    garnish

Pumpkin makes a superb sweet creamy soup, full of body and flavour. Fresh ginger is readily available in supermarkets and will keep covered in the refrigerator for up to one month. The roots are usually quite knobbly in appearance and need to be peeled before use. The easiest way to peel fresh ginger is to use a teaspoon to scrape the skin away.

Dry-fry the onion and garlic in a non-stick saucepan until soft. Add the pumpkin and ginger and cook for a further 2–3 minutes, taking care not to allow the ginger to brown. Add the thyme and stock. Bring to the boil and simmer for 25–30 minutes until tender.

Place the soup in a liquidiser or food processor and blend until smooth. Return to the saucepan and stir in the tomato purée. Season with salt and freshly ground black pepper. Adjust the consistency with a little stock or skimmed milk.

Just before serving, garnish with a swirl of yogurt and a little chopped parsley.

Crab bisque

Bring the flavour of the British seaside to your table with this light yet rich crab bisque. For that extra bite, try adding a dash of Tabasco sauce just before serving.

In a large saucepan, soften the onions and celery in a little fish stock. Add the flour and cook for 1 minute to 'cook out' the flour. Stir in the remaining stock, the white wine and the lemon juice. Simmer for 2–3 minutes until the soup thickens. Add the crab meat, anchovy paste and tomato purée and cook for a further 2–3 minutes. If the soup becomes too thick, thin it down with a little skimmed milk.

Heat the brandy in the ladle over a low flame. Tilt the ladle and ignite. Allow the alcohol to burn off the brandy, then pour the brandy into the soup.

Season to taste. Remove from the heat and stir in the yogurt. Just before serving, garnish with chopped parsley.

SERVES 6
PER SERVING:
113 KCAL / 1G FAT

2 medium onions, finely chopped
1 celery stick, finely chopped
1 pint (600ml) fish stock
2 tablespoons flour
$1/4$ pint (150ml) white wine
juice of 1 lemon
meat from 1 cooked crab or 8oz (225g) frozen or canned crab meat
1 teaspoon anchovy paste
1 tablespoon tomato purée
$1/2$ ladle brandy
5oz (150g) low-fat natural yogurt
salt and freshly ground black pepper
chopped fresh parsley to garnish

Chicken consommé

A consommé is a strong-flavoured, clear soup. You can garnish it with tiny cooked vegetables or a couple of finely diced tomatoes for an attractive touch.

Place the chicken carcass or drumsticks in a large saucepan. Add the vegetables, stock herbs and peppercorns. Bring to the boil, cover and simmer gently for 1$\frac{1}{2}$–2 hours. Taste for flavouring, and add another stock cube if necessary. Season to taste with salt and pepper.

Strain the soup through a colander. Allow to cool, then store in the refrigerator. The fat will then separate and rise to the surface. When the soup is quite cold, remove all the solidified fat from the top and discard. Reheat the soup and serve.

SERVES 6
PER SERVING:
124 KCAL / 1.9G FAT

1 chicken carcass or 6 skinless
    chicken drumsticks
2 large carrots, chopped
2 large onions, chopped
2–3 celery sticks, chopped
2 garlic cloves, crushed
2 pints (1.2 litres) chicken stock
    plus an extra chicken stock
    cube
1 tablespoon herbes de
    Provence
2 bay leaves
6 whole black peppercorns
salt and freshly ground black
    pepper

Duck and white bean soup

SERVES 6
PER SERVING:
189 KCAL/3.2G FAT

4oz (100g) white haricot beans
2 medium onions, finely
    chopped
2 garlic cloves, crushed
2 celery sticks, finely chopped
1 tablespoon chopped fresh
    thyme
1 vegetable stock cube
2 lean skinless duck breasts
1 pint (600ml) chicken stock
$\frac{1}{2}$ pint (300ml) skimmed milk
1 tablespoon cornflour
salt and freshly ground black
    pepper
2 tablespoons toasted brown
    breadcrumbs

This meaty soup is based on the classic French dish, Cassoulet, which combines duck with beans and garlic. The crunchy breadcrumb topping adds to the authenticity. You can serve this soup as a lunch, or serve as a first course and then choose a light main course to follow in order to balance the calories.

Soak the beans overnight in plenty of cold water.

Rinse the soaked beans well and place in a saucepan. Add the onion, garlic, celery, thyme and vegetable stock cube. Cover with water and bring to the boil. Reduce the heat and simmer for $1\frac{1}{2}$ hours until the beans are tender.

Prepare the duck breasts by slicing into thin strips. Place in a preheated non-stick frying pan and dry-fry over a high heat, seasoning well with salt and black pepper. Using a slotted spoon, remove the duck from the pan and add to soup pan. Add the chicken stock and skimmed milk and simmer gently for 10 minutes to allow the flavours to combine. Slake the cornflour with a little cold water and add to the soup. Check the seasoning.

Just before serving sprinkle with the toasted breadcrumbs.

Smoked fish and corn chowder

This luxurious soup is ideal for a lunch, or you could serve it as a starter, providing you choose a light main course to follow.

A chowder is a thick, usually fish, soup thickened with potato and flour. Since smoked fish can sometimes be quite salty, you may need to make your fish stock weak and then add more seasoning once you have added the fish. As a variation, you could add a few cooked prawns to this soup.

Place the fish in a saucepan. Add 1 pint (600ml) of water and simmer for 10 minutes until tender. Drain, reserving the liquid. Flake the fish coarsely, discarding any skin and bones.

Dry-fry the onions in a large non-stick pan until soft. Add 3 tablespoons of the reserved liquid, sprinkle the flour over and beat well with a wooden spoon. Cook for 1 minute in order to 'cook out' the flour. Gradually add the rest of the reserved liquid, stirring continuously. Add the mustard powder, sweetcorn and potatoes, stock and milk. Bring to the boil, reduce the heat and simmer for 10 minutes until the vegetables are tender. Stir in the flaked fish and the parsley. Taste, and adjust the seasoning with a fish stock cube if necessary and salt and freshly ground black pepper.

Just before serving, stir in the fromage frais. Serve piping hot.

SERVES 4
PER SERVING:
252 KCAL/2.04G FAT

1 lb (450g) smoked haddock or cod
2 onions, chopped
2 tablespoons flour
2 teaspoons English mustard powder
8oz (225g) canned sweetcorn, drained
8oz (225g) potatoes, peeled and cut into $\frac{1}{2}$in (1cm) dice
1 pint (600ml) fish stock
$\frac{1}{2}$ pint (300ml) skimmed milk
2 tablespoons chopped fresh parsley
2 tablespoons virtually fat-free fromage frais
salt and freshly ground black pepper

Beef

Here is a wide selection of beef recipes which can be enjoyed on a variety of occasions – from a simple supper to an extravagant dinner party. You can even enjoy traditional roast beef with Yorkshire pudding.

Beef is still considered a luxury meat and, providing you select lean cuts, it is perfectly acceptable on a low-fat diet. Remember, the golden rule when cooking low fat is to remove the fat from meat before cooking, not afterwards.

Peppered steaks

SERVES 2
PER SERVING:
200 KCAL/4.5G FAT

Guidelines for cooking steak
rare: 4–5 minutes
medium rare: 5–7 minutes
well done: 10–12 minutes

2 × 4oz (2 × 100g) rump or
    sirloin steaks
2 tablespoons Madeira wine
2 spring onions, thinly sliced
    (including the green)
course grain mustard to season
1 teaspoon mixed peppercorns
1 beef stock cube
2 tablespoons low-fat fromage
    frais
1 tablespoon chopped fresh
    parsley
salt and coarsely ground black
    pepper

In the traditional recipe, the steak is coated in a creamy pepper sauce usually made with lashings of cream or butter. Try this alternative.

Trim the steaks, removing all the fat. Generously cover the steaks with coarse black pepper and a little salt. Place under a preheated hot grill and cook to your individual preference (see left).

To make the sauce, pour a little of the Madeira wine into a wok or non-stick pan, add the spring onions and cook for approximately 2 minutes until softened.

Add the rest of the Madeira, coarse grain mustard to taste, peppercorns, stock cube and fromage frais. Turn down the heat and cook gently until the sauce has thickened. If the sauce is too thick, thin it down with a little water. Stir in the parsley and pour the sauce over the steaks. Serve with new boiled potatoes and fresh vegetables.

Beef stroganoff

Traditionally, beef stroganoff is a luxurious creamy dish packed with butter and cream. In this recipe we replace the butter and cream with low-fat natural yogurt to give an excellent creamy alternative.

It is very important to 'cook out' the flour for at least 1 minute in the initial cooking stages. This releases the starch which thickens the sauce without a floury taste.

Preheat a non-stick wok or frying pan. Dry-fry the onion until soft. Add the garlic and the beef, season well and cook until sealed.

Sprinkle the flour over the beef. Stir well and cook for 1 minute to 'cook out' the flour.

Add the white wine and the stock and mix well. Stir in the mustard and mushrooms and simmer for 2–3 minutes until the sauce thickens.

Remove the pan from the heat and stir in the yogurt and parsley. Check the seasoning.

Just before serving, dust with paprika. Serve with boiled rice.

SERVES 6
PER SERVING:
217 KCAL/7.2G FAT

1 medium onion, finely chopped
2 garlic cloves, crushed
1½lb (675g) lean beef fillet, sliced
1 tablespoon flour
1 wineglass white wine
¼ pint (150ml) beef stock
1 tablespoon Dijon mustard
8oz (225g) button mushrooms, sliced
½ pint (300ml) low-fat natural yogurt
2 tablespoons chopped fresh parsley
salt and freshly ground black pepper
pinch of paprika

Provençale beef olive platter

SERVES 4
PER SERVING:
202 KCAL/5.2G FAT

4 x 3oz (75g) thin slices topside
   or skirt of beef
4oz (100g) lean minced pork
2 tablespoons soft white or
   brown breadcrumbs
2 tablespoons chopped fresh
   parsley
$\frac{1}{2}$ teaspoon mixed dried herbs
   or herbes de Provence
4oz (100g) carrots, cut into $\frac{1}{2}$in
   (1cm) slices
4oz (100g) onions, sliced
2 garlic cloves, crushed
$\frac{1}{2}$ pint (300ml) tomato passata
$\frac{1}{2}$ pint (300ml) red wine or beef
   stock
salt and freshly ground black
   pepper
extra chopped parsley to
   garnish

Preheat the oven to 180°C, 350°F, Gas Mark 4.

Trim the slices of beef, removing all the fat.

Mix the pork with the breadcrumbs, parsley and dried herbs or herbes de Provence, and season well with salt and black pepper. Divide the mixture into 4 and place an equal amount on each slice of beef. Fold the edges of each slice over the stuffing, then roll up neatly so that the stuffing is completely enclosed. Secure the flap with a cocktail stick.

Dry-fry the beef olives in a non-stick frying pan over a good heat until they change colour. Transfer to an ovenproof dish and add the carrots, onion and garlic.

Place the tomato passata in the pan and mix in the red wine or beef stock. Bring to the boil, taking care to mix in all the meat juices which may have caramelised in the pan. Season to taste and pour the tomato sauce over the meat and vegetables. Cook in the oven for $1\frac{1}{2}$–2 hours until tender.

Transfer the beef olives to a hot serving dish and remove the cocktail sticks. Keep hot. Check the seasoning and pour the sauce over the meat. Just before serving, sprinkle with chopped parsley.

Roast beef with Yorkshire pudding, dry-roast potatoes and parsnips

Preheat the oven to 180°C, 350°F, Gas Mark 4.

Prepare the beef by removing as much fat as possible. Place the onion, carrot, celery and herbs in the bottom of a roasting tin or ovenproof dish, sit the beef on top and pour ¼ pint (300ml) water around. Place in the oven. Allow 15 minutes per 1lb (450g), plus 15 minutes over for rare beef, 20minutes per 1lb (450g), plus 20 minutes over for medium rare, and 25 minutes per 1lb (450g) plus 30 minutes over if you like your beef well done.

Cook the potatoes and parsnips separately in boiling water. Drain and place in a non-stick roasting tin. Place in the top of the oven for 35–40 minutes until golden brown. You can baste the vegetables with the diluted soy sauce if they appear to dry out.

Forty minutes before the beef is ready, make the batter by blending the flour with the egg and a little milk to a smooth paste. Add the salt and whisk in the remaining milk until smooth. Preheat a 6-hole, non-stick Yorkshire pudding tin for 2 minutes in the oven. Remove and half-fill each mould with batter. Increase the oven temperature to 200°C, 400°F, Gas Mark 6, place the pudding batter in the oven and cook for 35–40 minutes.

When the beef is cooked, remove it from the roasting tin and wrap in foil to keep warm. Allow it to rest for 5–10 minutes. Meanwhile, add the beef stock to the pan juices, slake the cornflour with a little water and add to the pan. Stir well as the gravy thickens and add 1–2 drops of gravy browning as required.

To serve, carve the beef thinly. Serve with the Yorkshire puddings, dry-roast potatoes and parsnips, gravy and seasonal vegetables.

SERVES 6
PER SERVING:
BEEF: 218 KCAL/8.3G FAT
DRY-ROAST POTATOES AND PARSNIPS: 106 KCAL/0.9 FAT
YORKSHIRE PUDDING: 79 KCAL/1.3G FAT

1 × 2lb (1kg) joint lean beef (topside)
1 onion, finely diced
1 carrot, diced
1 celery stick, diced
2 teaspoons mixed dried herbs
1 pint (600ml) beef stock
1 tablespoon cornflour
1–2 drops gravy browning

for the dry-roast potatoes and parsnips
1lb (450g) potatoes, peeled and cut in half
8 medium parsnips, peeled and left whole
1 tablespoon soy sauce diluted in 2 tablespoons water (optional)

for the Yorkshire pudding batter
4oz (100g) plain flour
1 egg
pinch of salt
¼ pint (150ml) skimmed milk

Winter casserole

SERVES 4
PER SERVING:
438 KCAL/11.7G FAT

1lb (450g) braising steak

2 lean back bacon rashers

1 onion, thinly sliced

2 celery sticks, thinly sliced

½ small Swede, peeled and chopped

2 carrots, chopped

10oz (275g) old potatoes, peeled and cut into chunks

8oz (225g) large button mushrooms, halved

1 × 7oz (200g) can butter or red kidney beans, drained and rinsed

1 pint (600ml) beef stock

¼ pint (150ml) dry cider

1 teaspoon ground cinnamon

1 teaspoon ground nutmeg

1 teaspoon garlic salt

1 teaspoon dried thyme

2 bay leaves

2 tablespoons fruit chutney

2 tablespoons soy sauce

1 tablespoon cornflour

salt and freshly ground black pepper

In this truly heartwarming recipe, the cinnamon and nutmeg add just enough spice to complement the dish.

Preheat the oven to 190°C, 375°F, Gas Mark 5.

Trim all the fat from the meat, and cut the meat into 1 in (2.5cm) cubes and place in a large flameproof casserole dish.

Trim the rind and fat from the bacon, chop the bacon and place in the casserole dish.

Add all the remaining ingredients except the cornflour and season with salt and pepper. Place over the heat, bring to the boil and simmer gently for 5 minutes. Cover and place in the oven for 1–1½ hours or until meat is tender.

Remove the casserole from the oven. Mix the cornflour with a little cold water and stir into the casserole. Stir over a gentle heat until the sauce thickens.

Serve with additional potatoes and fresh vegetables if desired.

Beef and pepper skewers with teriyaki sauce

This dish works equally well with chicken or lamb.

Cut the steaks into thin strips, then thread the strips, concertina-style, onto 4 large skewers, placing a chunk of green pepper between each strip.

To make the sauce, place all the ingredients in a small pan and heat gently until simmering, stirring occasionally. Allow the sauce to simmer gently while you cook the meat.

Place the skewers on a grill pan and brush a little sauce over the meat and peppers. Cook under a preheated grill for 5–8 minutes, basting occasionally with a little more of the sauce.

When cooked, arrange the skewers on a plate and pour the remaining sauce over the meat.

SERVES 4
PER SERVING:
147 KCAL/4.6G FAT

12oz (350g) extra thin beef
   steaks
1 green pepper, seeded and cut
   into chunks

for the sauce
4 tablespoons soy sauce
4 tablespoons dry sherry
1 garlic clove, crushed
1 teaspoon ground ginger
1 teaspoon dark Muscovado
   sugar

Steak and kidney pie

Preheat the oven to 180°C, 350°F, Gas Mark 4.

Trim the steak, removing all the fat, then cut the steak into cubes. Preheat a non-stick frying pan. Dry-fry the cubes of beef steak and kidneys until well browned. Place in a 12 × 8in (30 × 20cm) pie dish. Dry-fry the onion until soft and add this to the meat in the pie dish.

Place ¹/₂ pint (300ml) water in the pan. Add the wine and stock cubes and bring to the boil. Mix the gravy powder with a little cold water and add to the boiling stock in the pan, stirring continuously. The gravy should be quite thick. Add more gravy powder mixed with a little water as necessary. Pour the gravy over the meat in the pie dish.

Boil the potatoes and drain. Mash the potatoes with the yogurt and sufficient skimmed milk to make the consistency quite soft. Season to taste. Using a fork or a piping bag with a star nozzle, carefully spoon or pipe the potato on top of the meat and gravy, spreading the potato so that it covers the meat completely.

Place in the oven and cook for 30–40 minutes, or until crisp and brown on top.

SERVES 4
PER SERVING:
355 KCAL/6.8G FAT

8oz (225g) lean rump or sirloin steak
8oz (225g) kidneys, cut into bite-sized pieces
2 medium onions, chopped
1 wineglass red wine
2 beef stock cubes
1 tablespoon gravy powder
2lb (900g) potatoes, peeled
2 tablespoons low-fat natural yogurt
4–5 tablespoons skimmed milk
salt and freshly ground black pepper

Neapolitan beef

SERVES 4
PER SERVING:
402 KCAL / 10.2G FAT

1 ½lb (675g) lean braising
   steak, cubed
2 onions, chopped
1 clove garlic, crushed
1 × 14oz (400g) can chopped
   tomatoes
½ pint (300ml) red wine or
   stock
2 tablespoons chopped fresh
   mixed herbs
1 tablespoon tomato ketchup
1 red pepper, seeded and cubed
1 courgette, sliced
1 small aubergine, cut into
   chunks
salt and black pepper

Preheat the oven to 170°C, 325°F, Gas Mark 3.

Place the meat, onions and garlic in an ovenproof casserole.
Add the tomatoes, wine or stock, herbs, ketchup and seasoning.
Cover and cook in the oven for 1½ hours.

Remove the casserole from the oven and stir in the red
pepper, courgette and aubergine. Cover and return to the oven for
a further 30 minutes, stirring once.

Serve with pasta shells and seasonal green vegetables.

Cottage pie with leek and potato topping

This recipe also works well using minced lamb or pork instead of beef.

Preheat the oven to 190°C, 375°F, Gas Mark 5.

Boil the potatoes until softened, adding the leeks 5 minutes before the end of cooking.

Meanwhile, dry-fry the mince for 3–4 minutes in a non-stick frying pan. Remove the mince from the pan and drain. Discard the liquid and put the meat to one side. Wipe out the pan. Return the meat to the pan. Add the onion and carrots and stir in the flour. Gradually add the stock, tomato purée and dried herbs. Bring to the boil and stir until thickened. Season with salt and black pepper. Transfer to an ovenproof dish.

Drain the potatoes and leeks and mash with a little milk and half the cheese (if using). Season to taste. Place on top of the mince mixture. Sprinkle with the remaining cheese (if using).

Bake in the oven for 25 minutes until golden.

SERVES 4
PER SERVING:
WITH CHEESE:
359 KCAL / 8G FAT
WITHOUT CHEESE:
327 KCAL / 6.2G FAT

1 lb (450g) lean minced beef
1 onion, chopped
2 carrots, chopped
2 tablespoons plain flour
$\frac{1}{2}$ pint (300ml) stock
1 tablespoon tomato purée
1 tablespoon mixed dried herbs
salt and freshly ground black
    pepper

for the topping
1$\frac{1}{2}$lb (675g) potatoes, peeled
    and chopped
2 leeks, sliced
2 tablespoons skimmed milk
2oz (50g) low-fat Cheddar
    cheese, grated (optional)
salt and freshly ground black
    pepper

Beef goulash

This dish can be enjoyed all year round. Paprika, a traditional Hungarian pepper spice, gives this dish its reddish colour.

Preheat the oven to 180°C, 350°F, Gas Mark 4.

In a non-stick pan or casserole, dry-fry the onion until soft, add the beef and cook until browned. Season well with salt and black pepper. Add the carrots and celery and cook for a further minute. Sprinkle with the flour and paprika and cook for a further minute. Gradually add the stock, stirring well to prevent any lumps forming. Add the thyme, bay leaves and tomato purée.

Cover the casserole and cook in the oven for approximately 2 hours or until the meat is tender.

Just before serving, swirl the yogurt on top and sprinkle with chopped mint and parsley. Serve with potatoes and fresh vegetables.

SERVES 4
PER SERVING:
429 KCAL/15.7G FAT

2 large onions, chopped
1½lb (675g) lean stewing steak
2 carrots, diced
2 celery sticks, chopped
1 tablespoon plain flour
1½ tablespoons mild paprika
1 pint (600ml) beef stock
1 tablespoon chopped fresh thyme
2 bay leaves
2 tablespoons tomato purée
salt and freshly ground black pepper
4 tablespoons low-fat natural yogurt
chopped fresh mint and parsley to garnish

Quick beef curry

SERVES 4
PER SERVING:
206 KCAL/5.4G FAT

1 onion, finely chopped
2 garlic cloves, crushed
1lb (450g) lean beef rump, cut
 into thin strips
2 tablespoons Madras curry
 powder or paste
2 courgettes, diced
2 × 14oz (2 × 400g) cans
 chopped tomatoes
salt and freshly ground black
 pepper
2 tablespoons chopped fresh
 coriander
2 tablespoons low-fat natural
 yogurt

This beef curry is great when you are pushed for time, although the flavour will be much improved if you leave it to simmer for an hour.

Heat a non-stick wok or large frying-pan. Dry-fry the onion for 2–3 minutes until soft. Add the garlic and the beef and cook for a further 2–3 minutes until the beef is browned.

Add the curry powder or paste and cook for a further minute, stirring well. Add the courgettes and tomatoes and season well. Simmer for 3–4 minutes until the sauce thickens. Remove from the heat, stir in the coriander and yogurt and serve immediately.

Serve with boiled rice.

Beef and mushroom stir-fry

Choose good quality beef for this recipe. If you wish, you can mix the strips of beef with crushed garlic. This will help to tenderise the meat.

Remove any fat from the beef. Cut the beef into thin strips and season well with salt and pepper.

Mix together all the marinade ingredients in large bowl. Add the beef, cover and leave for 20 minutes.

Using a slotted spoon, remove the meat from the marinade. Heat a wok. Add the beef and stir-fry quickly for 3–4 minutes until browned. Add the mushrooms, celery and beansprouts and cook for a further 2–3 minutes. Pour the marinade into the wok and bring to the boil.

Serve immediately with rice and Chinese noodles.

SERVES 4
PER SERVING:
242 KCAL / 6.8G FAT

1lb (450g) lean beef steak or
    frying beef
1lb (450g) mushrooms (e.g.
    chestnut, shiitake, button,
    oyster), chopped
2 celery sticks, cut into strips
4oz (100g) fresh beansprouts
salt and freshly ground black
    pepper

for the marinade
8 tablespoons dry sherry
4 tablespoons dark soy sauce
2 tablespoons clear honey
2 tablespoons tomato purée
1 × 1in (2.5cm) piece fresh root
    ginger, peeled and finely
    chopped
1 teaspoon cornflour

Moroccan beef
with orange

SERVES 4
PER SERVING:
217 KCAL/5.8G FAT

1 large onion, diced

1 lb (450g) lean diced beef

2 garlic cloves, crushed

2 tablespoons plain flour

$^1/_2$ pint (300ml) beef stock

1 tablespoon chopped fresh
    marjoram

1 teaspoon coriander seeds

1 teaspoon ground cumin

1 teaspoon ground cinnamon

$^1/_2$ teaspoon cayenne pepper

6 cardamom pods, crushed

1 × 14oz (400g) can chopped
    tomatoes

2 pieces orange peel

$^1/_4$ pint (150ml) orange juice

salt and freshly ground black
    pepper

*The colourful array of herbs and spices tenderises and flavours this
beef dish beyond belief. A real taste of Tunisia!*

In a non-stick frying pan, dry-fry the onion until soft. Add the beef
and garlic and cook until sealed.

Add the flour, coating the beef well, and cook for 1 minute.
Gradually mix in the stock. Add the herbs and spices, and the
tomatoes, orange peel and orange juice.

Cover and simmer for 40 minutes or until tender. Season to
taste.

Beef with green vegetables stir-fry

Fresh crunchy vegetables with a lemon dressing add texture and plenty of iron and vitamin C to this stir-fry.

Prepare the vegetables by slicing them into fine strips.

In a non-stick wok or frying pan, dry-fry the beef and garlic for 3–4 minutes. Add the vegetables and cook for a further 4–5 minutes.

Stir in the Hoisin sauce, lemon juice and sherry. Bring to the boil and sprinkle with parsley.

Serve immediately with boiled rice or noodles.

SERVES 4
PER SERVING:
178 KCAL/4.8G FAT

2 celery sticks
4oz (100g) fine green beans
4oz (100g) courgettes
4oz (100g) broccoli florets
4oz (100g) asparagus
1lb (450g) lean beef rump, cut into thin strips
2 garlic cloves, crushed
4 tablespoons Hoisin sauce
2 tablespoons lemon juice
2 tablespoons dry sherry
1 tablespoon chopped fresh parsley

Herby meat loaf with onion sauce

SERVES 4
PER SERVING:
341 KCAL/11.8G FAT

2 onions, finely chopped
1lb (450g) lean minced beef
3oz (75g) fresh breadcrumbs
1 garlic clove, crushed
1 teaspoon paprika
4 tablespoons tomato purée
2 tablespoons chopped fresh
    mixed herbs (rosemary,
    thyme, oregano, parsley)
1 egg, beaten
$\frac{1}{2}$ pint (300ml) skimmed milk
1–1$\frac{1}{2}$ tablespoons cornflour
1 tablespoon Dijon mustard
salt and freshly ground black
    pepper

This tasty meat loaf is ideal for all the family. Adding mustard to the sauce makes it look luxuriously creamy.

Preheat the oven to 150°C, 300°F, Gas Mark 2. Lightly grease and line a 2lb (900g) loaf tin.

In a non-stick frying pan, dry-fry half the chopped onion until soft, add the beef and continue cooking for 3–4 minutes. Add the breadcrumbs, garlic, paprika, tomato purée and herbs, and mix well. Remove from the heat, beat in the egg and season well.

Spoon the mixture into the loaf tin and place the loaf tin in a roasting tin. Pour sufficient water around to come halfway up the loaf tin, cover with foil and place in the oven for 1–1$\frac{1}{2}$ hours.

Meanwhile, dry-fry the remaining onion until soft. Pour in the milk and bring to the boil. Slake the cornflour with a little water and whisk into the sauce with the mustard. Simmer until thickened and season to taste.

Serve the meat loaf with the onion sauce and potatoes and seasonal vegetables.

Chilli con carne tortillas

Tortilla is a soft, flat bread, which makes it ideal to fold in half and fill with this savoury mixture with added spice. If you do not like your chilli too hot, omit one of the chillies, or add an extra one if you like it hot!

In a large, shallow non-stick frying pan, dry-fry the onions, garlic and chilli. Cook until transparent but do not brown. Add the minced steak and tomatoes, kidney beans, wine, stock cube, tomato purée and paprika. Mix together and simmer on a low heat for approximately 1 hour.

When the beef chilli is almost cooked, place the tortillas on a baking tray, and place in a low oven at 180°C, 350°F, Gas Mark 4 for 10 minutes to warm through. Cup the tortillas in a clean tea towel. Place some red onion, white cabbage and tomato in the bottom of each one, and fill with the beef mixture.

Serve with a crisp green salad and yogurt dressing.

SERVES 4
PER SERVING:
418 KCAL/7.8G FAT

1 large onion, finely chopped
2 garlic cloves, finely chopped
2 red chillies, seeded and chopped finely
1 lb (450g) very lean mince steak
1 × 14oz (400g) can chopped tomatoes
1 × 14oz (400g) can red kidney beans, drained
2 wineglasses red wine
1 beef stock cube
2 tablespoons tomato purée
1 teaspoon paprika
4 flour tortillas
1 red onion, finely sliced
$\frac{1}{2}$ small white cabbage, finely sliced
4 tomatoes, sliced

Super low-fat burgers

SERVES 4
PER SERVING:
413 KCAL/10G FAT

6oz (175g) bulgar wheat
12oz (350g) lean minced steak
1 small onion, finely chopped
1 tablespoon brown fruity sauce
$\frac{1}{2}$ teaspoon dried mixed herbs
salt and freshly ground black
    pepper
4 small sesame seed baps
a few lettuce leaves
2 tomatoes, sliced
1 red onion, sliced

These healthy burgers are really easy to make. You could make up several at once, separate them with greaseproof paper and then freeze until required.

Place the bulgar wheat in a mixing bowl and cover with boiling water. Allow to stand for 20 minutes until the grains have softened and swelled. Drain, then rinse under cold water until cold, and drain well again.

Mix together the bulgar wheat, minced steak, onion, brown sauce, herbs and seasoning until well combined. Divide the mixture into 4 and form into burger shapes, each about $\frac{1}{2}$in (1cm) thick. Chill for 20 minutes.

Cook the burgers under a preheated grill or in a ridged grill pan for 5 minutes each side. Take care not to break the burgers when turning them.

Toast the sesame seed baps. Place a burger in each bap and top with lettuce, tomatoes and onion.

Lamb

is a wonderfully tasty meat and is perfect for using in a number of dishes with different herbs, spices and other flavourings. In this section you'll find a variety of recipes, from simple stews, hot pots, or kebabs to exotic curries or more ambitious recipes such as lamb with crusty garlic topping. Always choose lean cuts of lamb and ensure that chops are trimmed of fat before cooking.

Lancashire hot pot

SERVES 4
PER SERVING:
415 KCAL/10.1G FAT

1½lb (675g) boneless lean neck of lamb, cubed

4 lamb's kidneys, cored and chopped

2 onions, sliced

2 teaspoons cornflour

¾ pint (450ml) beef stock

1 teaspoon Worcestershire sauce

1 tablespoon chopped fresh thyme

2lb (1kg) potatoes, peeled and thinly sliced

salt and freshly ground black pepper

2 tablespoons chopped fresh parsley to garnish

Make sure you choose lean lamb, as the fat content can vary tremendously. This dish can be made in advance and reheated.

Preheat the oven to 170°C, 325°F, Gas Mark 3.

Dry-fry the lamb and kidneys briskly in a non-stick frying pan until the meat is well browned. Using a slotted spoon, transfer the lamb and kidneys to a shallow casserole dish.

Wipe out the frying pan with kitchen paper. Reduce the heat in the pan a little and dry-fry the onions until soft and light brown. Blend the cornflour with 2 tablespoons of water. Gradually stir the beef stock, blended cornflour, Worcestershire sauce and thyme into the pan. Bring to the boil, stirring continuously.

Season well and pour the mixture over the contents of the casserole. Top with a layer of seasoned potato slices. Cover and bake in the oven for 2 hours.

Remove the lid from the casserole. Increase the oven temperature to 220°C, 425°F, Gas Mark 7 and continue to cook for a further 30–35 minutes until the potatoes are crisp and brown.

Just before serving, sprinkle with chopped parsley.

Lamb with crusty garlic topping

You should find boned legs or shoulders of lamb in your local supermarket. Ready boned joints may appear more expensive per 1lb/kg than ones with the bone left in, but when you take into account the weight of the bone you will find that the price ratio for edible meat is about the same. They are ideal for entertaining as they are so easy to carve at the table. I have used leg of lamb in this recipe because it is leaner than the shoulder cut, but you could use a boned shoulder if you wish. However, take care to cut out all the visible fat from the inside and also the fat and most of the skin from the outside so that no fat or skin is rolled inside the joint when you tie it. It is rather difficult to stuff a half shoulder because of its shape, but you can always use a full shoulder and make more stuffing. Then, after you have stuffed and tied the shoulder, you can cut it in half and deep freeze the extra piece for another time, providing the meat has not been frozen previously.

Preheat the oven to 220°C, 425°F, Gas Mark 7.

Mix the garlic, breadcrumbs and parsley in a bowl and season with salt and black pepper.

Cut away any surplus fat from the lamb and place about half the breadcrumb mixture in the cavity. Tie and skewer to a neat shape and place in a roasting tin. Estimate the cooking time at 20 minutes per 1lb (450g). Cook for 20 minutes in a preheated oven then reduce the oven temperature to 180°C, 350°F, Gas Mark 4 for the remainder of the cooking time.

Twenty minutes before the end of the cooking time, remove the joint from the oven, remove the string and, using a small sharp knife, slit the skin, peel it off and discard. Pour off any fat and wipe the roasting tin clean but leave any caramelised juices.

Place the joint in the roasting tin, spread the French mustard over the skin-free surface and pat the rest of the breadcrumb mixture on top. Return to the oven for the remainder of the cooking time or until the top is golden brown and crusty.

SERVES 6
PER SERVING:
404 KCAL/16.2G FAT

2–3 garlic cloves, crushed
5 tablespoons fresh breadcrumbs (white or wholemeal)
2 tablespoons chopped fresh parsley
1/2 boned leg of lamb (approximately 3lb/1.5kg)
2 tablespoons French mustard
1/4 pint (150ml) red wine
1/4 pint (150ml) stock
1 teaspoon arrowroot or 2 teaspoons low-fat gravy granules
salt and freshly ground black pepper
fresh parsley to garnish (optional)

Remove the meat from the oven and place on a hot serving dish. Keep hot. Pour the wine and stock into the roasting tin and place over a gentle heat. Stir well to mix in the juices and any mustard or stuffing which has fallen from the joint. Bring to the boil and remove any scum which rises to the surface since this will be fat.

Mix the arrowroot (if using) with a little water and stir it into the boiling liquid, or, alternatively, pour some of the boiling liquid onto the gravy granules. Stir well and return to the roasting tin. Bring the gravy back to the boil, stirring all the time. Whisk the gravy well with a balloon whisk to incorporate any bits of stuffing. Check the seasoning and add more salt and black pepper if desired and adjust the consistency of the gravy if necessary by adding more water or thickening as required. Pour into a sauce boat.

Garnish the meat with the parsley, if using, and cut the joint into moderately thick slices at the table.

Lamb tagine

A tagine is a Moroccan stew cooked very slowly for a long time. It is often served with couscous.

Place the lamb in a non-stick saucepan, season and gently dry-fry for 5 minutes, stirring occasionally. Add the onion, fennel, potatoes, ginger, saffron and orange peel. Sweat for 3–4 minutes, then add the stock. Bring to the boil then reduce the heat to a gentle simmer and cook for 40–45 minutes.

Stir in the mange tout and apricots and cook for a further 2–3 minutes. Add the tomato purée and stir well until thickened. Stir in the lemon juice and adjust the seasoning.

Garnish with the mint leaves and serve with rice or potatoes and vegetables.

SERVES 4
PER SERVING:
302 KCAL / 9.4G FAT

1lb (450g) lamb fillet, trimmed
 and cubed
1 medium onion, sliced
1 medium head fennel, roughly
 chopped
12oz (350g) potatoes, peeled
 and roughly diced
1/2 teaspoon ground ginger
pinch of saffron diffused in a
 little hot water
1 strip orange peel
14fl oz (400ml) chicken stock
4oz (100g) mange tout, topped
 and tailed
4oz (100g) canned apricot
 halves in natural juice,
 drained and quartered
2 tablespoons tomato purée
1 tablespoon lemon juice
salt and freshly ground black
 pepper
fresh mint leaves to garnish

Lamb and pineapple curry

SERVES 4
PER SERVING:
193 KCAL/7.4G FAT

1 large onion, sliced
1 garlic clove, crushed
1 tablespoon plain flour
1–2 tablespoons Madras curry
   powder
12oz (350g) lean lamb, cubed
1 tablespoon tomato purée
1 pint (600ml) beef stock
4oz (100g) canned pineapple
   cubes in natural juice, drained
salt and freshly ground black
   pepper

Most of the ingredients for this simple recipe come straight from the store cupboard. You can make it even more fruity by adding a few sultanas or a diced dessert apple.

If you prefer a mild curry, use less curry powder or a milder one.

Preheat the oven to 180°C, 350°F, Gas Mark 4.

Dry-fry the onion and garlic in a non-stick pan until soft. Place in a casserole dish.

Mix the flour and curry powder together. Toss the lamb in this mixture then dry-fry until brown. Place in a casserole dish.

Stir the remaining flour and curry mixture into the hot pan and cook for a minute. Add the tomato purée and a little stock, stirring well to loosen any mixture from the base of the pan. Gradually add the rest of the stock, stirring continuously, and bring to the boil.

Pour the sauce over the lamb. Stir the pineapple cubes into the lamb curry and season to taste. Cover and cook in the oven for 1 hour or until the lamb is tender.

Check the seasoning and adjust if necessary. Serve with boiled rice.

Lamb steaks boulangère

This classic French dish is easy to prepare yet full of flavour. Serve straight from the oven with plenty of seasonal vegetables. Choose potatoes suitable for baking. The waxy, firm type such as red Desirée is the best, as these will hold their shape and not break up during baking.

Preheat the oven to 180°C, 350°F, Gas Mark 4.

Remove any fat from the lamb. Season each lamb steak on both sides, then dry-fry in a non-stick frying pan until sealed. Place in an ovenproof dish.

Cover the steaks with the garlic and onion. Sprinkle the herbs on top and cover with the sliced potatoes. Season well with salt and pepper. Add the lamb stock and cook in the oven for 1 hour.

When the lamb is cooked, blend the cornflour with a little water and use to thicken the stock. Serve immediately.

SERVES 4
PER SERVING:
296 KCAL/8.1G FAT

4 lean lamb steaks
2 medium onions, sliced
2 garlic cloves, crushed
1 tablespoon herbes de
  Provence
1lb (450g) potatoes, peeled and
  finely sliced
2 pints (1.2 litres) lamb stock
1 tablespoon cornflour
salt and freshly ground black
  pepper

Lamb dhansak

Traditionally this dish is made by frying the onion and meat in ghee or oil. In this low-fat version the lentils act as a thickening agent to give a thick, rich sauce tinged with tomato.

Dry-fry the onion in a non-stick pan until soft. Add the garlic and the lamb. Cook for 5–6 minutes until the meat is sealed.

Add the spices, chillies and lentils and cook for a further minute.

Stir in the stock and tomato purée. Season well. Cover and simmer for 35–40 minutes.

Serve with boiled rice.

SERVES 4
PER SERVING:
221 KCAL/7.9G FAT

2 medium onions, chopped
2 garlic cloves, crushed
1lb (450g) lean lamb, diced
1 teaspoon ground coriander
1 teaspoon fennel seeds
1 teaspoon ground cumin
2 fresh green chillies, seeded
  and chopped
4oz (100g) [dry weight] red
  lentils
1 pint (600ml) lamb stock
3 tablespoons tomato purée
salt and freshly ground black
  pepper

Balti mince

SERVES 4
PER SERVING:
243 KCAL/14.1G FAT

1lb (450g) lean minced lamb
1 onion, chopped
1 garlic clove, crushed
1 × 14oz (400g) can chopped
    tomatoes
6oz (175g) frozen spinach,
    thawed and squeezed
4oz (100g) mushrooms, sliced
1 tablespoon medium curry
    powder
salt and freshly ground black
    pepper
2 teaspoons chopped fresh
    coriander

In a large non-stick wok or saucepan, dry-fry the mince until browned. Remove from the pan and drain. Discard the liquid and put meat to one side. Wipe out the pan with kitchen paper.

Return the meat to the pan. Add the onion and garlic and cook for 1–2 minutes. Add the chopped tomatoes, spinach, mushrooms, curry powder and season to taste. Bring to the boil, cover and simmer for 8–10 minutes. Stir in the coriander.

Serve with rice and poppadoms (cooked under the grill or in the microwave).

Spiced lamb with couscous

In a large non-stick saucepan, dry-fry the meat, onion and garlic until the meat is browned. Add the cumin, apricots and stock and season to taste. Simmer uncovered for 10 minutes.

Soak the couscous in boiling water for 5 minutes. Drain the couscous and stir the couscous and mint into the lamb mixture. Cover with a lid.

Serve with a selection of seasonal vegetables.

SERVES 2
PER SERVING:
354 KCAL/9.7G FAT

8oz (225g) lean lamb steak, diced
1 onion, chopped
1 garlic clove, crushed
$\frac{1}{2}$ teaspoon ground cumin
2oz (50g) 'no soak' dried apricots, diced
$\frac{1}{4}$ pint (150ml) stock
4oz (100g) [dry weight] couscous
1 tablespoon chopped fresh mint
salt and freshly ground black pepper

Cranberry and cinnamon-glazed lamb kebabs

SERVES 4
PER SERVING:
317 KCAL / 8.4G FAT

1 small red onion, finely
    chopped
¼ pint (150ml) white wine
¼ pint (150ml) lamb stock
4oz (100g) [dry weight]
    couscous
(1lb) 450g lean lamb, cubed
1 baby courgette, halved, or
    ½ large courgette, cut into
    wedges
1 red pepper, seeded and cut
    into quarters
1 baby aubergine or ½ large
    aubergine, sliced
salt and freshly ground black
    pepper

for the glaze
4 tablespoons cranberry sauce
4 tablespoons port *or* cranberry
    juice *or* orange juice
pinch of cinnamon

Place the onion, wine and stock in a small saucepan and bring to the boil. Add the couscous, remove the pan from the heat, season with salt and pepper and stir well. Cover and leave for approximately 10 minutes until all the liquid is absorbed.

Thread the lamb onto 4 large skewers. Cook under a preheated grill for approximately 6 minutes each side.

Meanwhile, make the glaze. Place all ingredients in a small saucepan, bring to the boil and simmer for 3–4 minutes. Brush the kebabs with the glaze and grill for a further 1–2 minutes. Turn the kebabs and repeat.

Five minutes before the end of the cooking time, place the vegetables under the grill with the kebabs, turning them once during cooking.

Serve the kebabs with the couscous and grilled vegetables.

Lamb cobbler

The topping on this dish is somewhere between a scone and a dumpling. It transforms a simple dish into something quite special.

Preheat the oven to 200°C, 400°F, Gas Mark 6.

In a large non-stick saucepan dry-fry the lamb mince until browned. Season with salt and pepper. Remove from pan and drain. Discard the liquid and put the meat to one side. Wipe out the pan with kitchen paper.

Add the onion and mushroom to the pan and dry-fry until soft. Add the cooked meat. Sprinkle with the flour and cook for 1 minute to 'cook out' the flour. Gradually add the stock, stirring well to prevent any lumps forming. Add the gravy browning and the herbs, cover and simmer gently for 30 minutes.

Make the topping by sieving the flour and salt into a large bowl. Rub in the quark with your fingertips until the mixture resembles breadcrumbs. Stir in the mint and the mustard powder. Add the milk and mix well with a knife. You may need to add a little extra milk to bind the mixture into a soft dough.

Divide the cobbler mixture into 8 small balls and flatten them slightly with the back of your hand.

Pour the minced lamb mixture into an ovenproof dish and dot the cobbler dumplings on top. Cook in the oven for 30 minutes.

Serve with new potatoes and plenty of fresh vegetables.

SERVES 4
PER SERVING:
458 KCAL/9.3G FAT

1 lb (450g) lean minced lamb
1 onion, finely chopped
8oz (225g) button mushrooms, finely sliced
1 tablespoon plain flour
$\frac{1}{2}$ pint (300ml) lamb stock
$\frac{1}{2}$ teaspoon gravy browning
1 tablespoon chopped fresh rosemary
1 tablespoon chopped fresh parsley
salt and freshly ground black pepper

for the cobbler topping
12oz (350g) self-raising flour
pinch of salt
3oz (75g) quark
1 tablespoon chopped fresh mint
1 teaspoon mustard powder
4fl oz (120ml) skimmed milk

Lamb with rosemary and horseradish crumble

SERVES 4
PER SERVING:
463 KCAL/14.4G FAT

4 trimmed lamb chops
5oz (150g) wholemeal
    breadcrumbs
2 onions, thinly sliced
2 leeks, sliced
1 small onion, finely chopped
2 tablespoons chopped fresh
    parsley
2 tablespoons chopped fresh
    rosemary
2 tablespoons horseradish sauce
8fl oz (250ml) red wine
8fl oz (250ml) lamb stock
2 sprigs rosemary
salt and freshly ground black
    pepper

Choose horseradish sauce rather than creamed horseradish since the latter is higher in fat. If you don't like horseradish you can substitute wholegrain mustard.

Preheat the oven to 180°C, 350°F, Gas Mark 4.

Dry-fry the chops in a non-stick frying pan until browned on both sides. Place in a casserole dish and season with salt and pepper.

Dry-fry the sliced onions for 15 minutes until they begin to colour. Add the leeks and cook for a further 5 minutes. Place a quarter of the mixture on each chop.

Meanwhile dry-fry the chopped onion until soft. Place in a mixing bowl. Add the breadcrumbs, parsley, rosemary, and horseradish sauce and season to taste.

Pile the breadcrumb mixture on top of chops. Pour the wine and the stock around the chops. Add the rosemary sprigs.

Bake in the oven for 20–30 minutes or until the meat is tender.

Serve with wilted spinach and new potatoes.

Moussaka

Traditional moussaka uses a heavy quota of oil. The sauce is usually started by frying the onion and meat, then the aubergine slices are individually fried in oil, and this is all topped with a rich cheese sauce. This low-fat alternative is a treat for any palate. If you wish, you can prepare the aubergine in advance and store in a container in the refrigerator.

Preheat the oven to 180°C, 350°F, Gas Mark 4.

Dry-fry the onion in a non-stick frying pan until soft. Add the garlic and the lamb. Cook quickly until the meat is well sealed.

Add the thyme, tomatoes and tomato purée. Simmer gently and season with salt and black pepper.

Cut the aubergine into thin slices. Place on a non-stick baking sheet. Season with plenty of salt and pepper. Grill for 2–3 minutes on each side until golden .

Place alternate layers of the lamb mixture and aubergine in an ovenproof dish. Combine the yogurt with the beaten egg and the mustard, season well, and pour over the lamb.

Bake in the oven for 30–35 minutes or until golden brown.

Serve with a crisp green salad.

SERVES 6
PER SERVING:
258 KCAL/10G FAT

1 large onion, chopped

2 garlic cloves, crushed

1 lb (450g) lean minced lamb

1 tablespoon chopped fresh thyme

1 × 14oz (400g) can chopped tomatoes

1 tablespoon tomato purée

1 large aubergine

½ pint (300ml) low-fat natural yogurt

1 egg, beaten

1 teaspoon English mustard powder

salt and freshly ground black pepper

Pan-fried liver with onions and balsamic vinegar

This quick and delicious meal takes just minutes to prepare. Cook the liver to your personal taste. The pinker it is, the softer the texture and the more moist the centre – it's a case of trial and error.

SERVES 4
PER SERVING:
177 KCAL/6.4G FAT

1 teaspoon vegetable oil
1 tablespoon plain flour
1 lb (450g) lamb's liver
1 medium onion, finely diced
1 teaspoon ground coriander
3 tablespoons balsamic vinegar
$\frac{1}{4}$ pint (150ml) lamb stock
salt and freshly ground black
   pepper

Place the oil in a non-stick frying pan and heat the pan. Wipe out the pan with kitchen paper, taking care not to burn your fingers (wear an oven glove if necessary).

Season the flour with salt and pepper and toss the liver in it so that it is well coated. Place the liver in the hot pan to seal on both sides (this will take about 1–2 minutes each side depending on how thick the slices are).

Remove the liver from pan and place in a low oven (150°C, 300°F, Gas Mark 2) to continue cooking. Place the onion and coriander in the frying pan and dry-fry until the onion softens. Add the balsamic vinegar.

To de-glaze the pan, stir in the stock, scraping any residue from the pan. Just before serving, return the liver to the pan to coat with the sauce.

Dijon-style kidneys

SERVES 4
PER SERVING:
253 KCAL/10.7G FAT

10–12 lamb's kidneys
6oz (175g) mushrooms
6fl oz (175ml) red wine
4 tablespoons beef or lamb
   stock
1 heaped teaspoon arrowroot
3oz (75g) low-fat natural yogurt
   or quark
1 1/2 teaspoons Dijon mustard
salt and freshly ground black
   pepper
chopped fresh parsley to garnish

Skin the kidneys, cut them in half and remove the cores. Soak in cold salted water for 20 minutes. Drain well and dry on kitchen paper.

Wash, trim and slice the mushrooms. Place in a saucepan and season lightly with salt and black pepper. Add the red wine and stock and cook gently for 7–8 minutes until tender.

Meanwhile, dry-fry the kidneys in a non-stick frying pan until tender but still slightly pink in the centre. Place on a hot dish and cover to keep hot.

Mix the arrowroot with a little water and add to the mushrooms, red wine and stock. Bring to the boil, stirring all the time. Whisk in the yogurt or quark and the mustard a little at a time. Reheat without boiling. Check the seasoning and add more salt and freshly ground black pepper if necessary.

Add the kidneys to the sauce. Pour into a hot dish and, just before serving, sprinkle with chopped fresh parsley. Serve hot.

Lamb's liver with orange sauce

Liver and orange is a delightful combination. You could also try them together on kebabs with smoked bacon.

Remove any membrane or veins from the liver. Place the liver in a bowl and cover with the milk. Leave to stand for 1–2 hours. This will remove any bitter flavours and keep the liver moist during cooking.

Remove the liver from the milk. Dry-fry the liver in a preheated non-stick frying pan, seasoning it well with salt and black pepper as you turn it over. Continue to dry-fry the liver until it is cooked but still slightly pink in the centre, then remove from the pan and keep warm.

Add the onion to the pan and dry-fry for 1 minute, scraping up any residue from the liver. Pour in the orange juice and add the thyme. Mix the arrowroot with a little cold water to form a paste. Pour this into the pan, stirring well, and simmer until the sauce thickens. Return the liver to the pan, turning it well to coat it with the sauce.

Transfer to individual plates. Garnish with orange slices and parsley and serve immediately with potatoes and seasonal vegetables of your choice.

SERVES 4
PER SERVING:
177 KCAL/6.4G FAT

1 lb (450g) lamb's liver
$\frac{1}{4}$ pint (150ml) skimmed milk
1 onion, finely chopped
$\frac{1}{2}$ pint (300ml) orange juice
1 teaspoon chopped fresh thyme
1 teaspoon arrowroot
salt and freshly ground black pepper
orange slices and fresh parsley to garnish

Pork

Great advancements have been made in recent years to breed leaner pigs, with the result that pork is now lower in fat than ever before. In fact, some extra lean pork is now almost as low in fat as chicken, which makes it ideal for inclusion in a low-fat diet. While pork flesh is pale in colour, it is nevertheless classed as a red meat.

The recipes in this section range from roasts, stir-fries, casseroles to barbecue dishes and burgers. Remember to trim off all the fat before cooking to prevent it from penetrating the meat – and also to avoid the temptation of nibbling on the pork crackling which could stretch your willpower to its limits!

Barbecued pork chops

SERVES 4
PER SERVING:
220 KCAL/6.8G FAT

4 lean pork chops
2 garlic cloves, crushed
3 tablespoons tomato purée
1 teaspoon caraway seeds
1 tablespoon Dijon mustard
1 teaspoon cinnamon
1 teaspoon brown sugar
$\frac{1}{4}$ pint (150ml) cider
salt and freshly ground black
  pepper

You can leave out the caraway seeds in this recipe if you wish, but they do taste quite different when barbecued.

Remove any fat from the pork chops. Place the chops in an ovenproof dish.

Combine the remaining ingredients in a bowl and spread over both sides of the pork chops. Cover and leave to marinate for 1 hour.

When marinated, cook the chops on a barbecue or under a preheated hot grill for 6–8 minutes on each side.

Serve with a crisp salad, rice or potato salad.

Honey roast pork with prune and apple stuffing

Preheat the oven to 200°C, 400°F, Gas Mark 6.

Trim all the fat from the pork, then weigh the pork to calculate the cooking time and place on a chopping board. Season well with salt and pepper.

Dry-fry the onion in a non-stick pan until soft. Add the prunes, apple, sage and ¼ pint (150ml) of the stock. Cook briskly for 1–2 minutes then allow to cool.

Place three-quarters of the prune and apple mixture on the pork. Roll the pork up and tie with string. Place the pork in a roasting tin. Spoon the honey over the pork and pour ½ pint (300ml) of water around the meat. Cover with tin foil and cook in the oven. Allow 30 minutes per 1lb (450g), plus 30 minutes over.

Make the sauce by placing the remaining prune mixture in a saucepan. Add the wine and remaining stock and bring to the boil. Blend the cornflour with a little water and use to thicken the sauce. For a smooth sauce, place in a liquidiser and blend until smooth.

Serve the pork with the sauce and accompany with potatoes and fresh vegetables.

SERVES 6
PER SERVING:
441 KCAL/8.2G FAT

3lb (1.5kg) lean pork loin
1 medium onion, finely chopped
8oz (225g) 'no soak' prunes, pitted
1 cooking apple, peeled and grated
2 tablespoons chopped fresh sage
1 pint (600ml) vegetable stock
3 tablespoons clear honey
1 wineglass red wine
1 tablespoon cornflour
salt and freshly ground black pepper

Pork ragoût

Dry-fry the garlic and onions in a non-stick frying pan for 1 minute. Add the pork and continue cooking until the pork is slightly browned. Add the vegetables, beef stock and basil and season well with salt and pepper.

Bring to the boil, cover and simmer for 40–45 minutes or until the meat is cooked and the vegetables are tender. If necessary, remove the lid 5 minutes before the end of cooking to allow the sauce to reduce and thicken slightly.

Just before serving, garnish with the parsley.

SERVES 4
PER SERVING:
175 KCAL/4.5G FAT

1 garlic clove, crushed
8oz (225g) button onions, peeled
1lb (450g) lean pork fillet, trimmed and cubed
4oz (100g) button mushrooms
6oz (175g) courgettes, cut into julienne strips
1 medium green pepper, seeded and cut into strips
1 × 14oz (400g) can chopped tomatoes
$\frac{1}{4}$ pint (150ml) beef stock
1 tablespoon chopped fresh basil
salt and freshly ground black pepper to taste
chopped fresh parsley to garnish

Lemon pork

SERVES 4
PER SERVING:
198 KCAL/4.2G FAT

1lb (450g) lean pork tenderloin,
    cut into ½in (1cm) slices
12 spring onions, chopped
salt and freshly ground black
    pepper
2 tablespoons chopped fresh
    parsley to garnish

for the sauce
zest and juice of 2 small lemons
1 × 2in (5cm) piece root ginger,
    peeled and grated
4 tablespoons sherry
2 tablespoons light soy sauce
2 tablespoons clear honey
2 teaspoons cornflour

A quick and simple dish that also works well with chicken.

Heat a wok or large non-stick frying pan. Season the pork, place in the wok or pan and brown on both sides.

Combine all the sauce ingredients. Reduce the heat under the pan and pour the sauce over the pork, stirring continuously. Add the spring onions and simmer, uncovered, for 5 minutes, stirring occasionally.

Sprinkle with the parsley and serve with rice or noodles and salad.

Pork in spicy yogurt sauce

Remove any fat from the pork steaks. Place the steaks in a shallow heatproof dish.

Combine the remaining ingredients to make a sauce. Spread both sides of the pork steaks with the sauce. Place under a hot grill for 8–10 minutes each side.

Serve with boiled rice and vegetables.

SERVES 4
PER SERVING:
254 KCAL/5G FAT

4 lean pork steaks
8 tablespoons low-fat natural
   yogurt
1 tablespoon mild curry powder
2 tablespoons mango chutney
1 red chilli, finely chopped
1 tablespoon chopped fresh
   coriander
1 tablespoon chopped fresh
   mint
salt and freshly ground black
   pepper

Oriental pan-cooked pork

SERVES 4
PER SERVING:
135 KCAL/3.9G FAT

4 tablespoons Sharwoods plum
  sauce
1 teaspoon soy sauce
8oz (225g) lean pork tenderloin,
  thinly sliced
2 garlic cloves, crushed
1 red chilli, finely sliced
1 celery stick, cut into strips
4oz (100g) pak choi, shredded or
  quartered lengthways if
  small, or 4oz (100g) Chinese
  leaf, shredded
4 spring onions, sliced
salt and freshly ground black
  pepper

Mix together the plum and soy sauce in a bowl.

Dry-fry the pork, garlic and chilli in a large non-stick wok or saucepan for 3–4 minutes or until browned. Add the celery and cook for a further 1–2 minutes. Add the remaining ingredients and cook for 1–2 minutes.

Drizzle with the plum and soy sauce and serve immediately.

Pork saltimbocca with tomato and lemon sauce

Sage is most definitely the emphasis in this Italian dish. It combines with the tomatoes, lemon and onion to give an unusual flavour. The tomato sauce is very easy to prepare and can be used alongside many other dishes, particularly fish and chicken. The finished dish looks quite rustic, although, if you prefer, you could liquidise the sauce.

Choose lean pork steaks, free from bone, about $^1/_2$in (1cm) in depth (if they are too thick, a good thump with the rolling pin will do the trick). The thinner the slices, the quicker they will cook.

Preheat the oven to 150°C, 300°F, Gas Mark 2.

Remove any fat from the pork steaks and the Parma ham. Season the pork steaks well on both sides with salt and black pepper. Place a sage leaf on each side of the pork steaks and wrap around with a slice of Parma ham. Place in an ovenproof dish.

Combine the sauce ingredients and pour over the pork steaks. Place in the oven and bake for 30–35 minutes.

Serve with new potatoes and fresh vegetables of your choice.

SERVES 4
PER SERVING:
178 KCAL/5.7G FAT

4 lean pork steaks
4 thin slices lean Parma ham
8 large sage leaves
salt and freshly ground black
    pepper

for the sauce
1 × 14oz (400g) can chopped
    tomatoes
6 spring onions, finely chopped
zest and juice of 1 lemon
2 tablespoons chopped fresh
    parsley
1 garlic clove, crushed

Jamaican casserole

SERVES 4
PER SERVING:
275 KCAL/5G FAT

2 tablespoons plain flour
$\frac{3}{4}$ pint (450ml) stock
1lb (450g) lean pork steak,
    cubed
2 tablespoons mild curry powder
1lb (450g) sweet potatoes or
    ordinary potatoes, peeled and
    cut into $\frac{1}{2}$in (1cm) cubes
1 large or 2 small onions, sliced
1 lemon, sliced
1 yellow pepper, seeded and cut
    into chunks
salt and freshly ground black
    pepper

This recipe also works well with beef or lamb. The lemon slices will add lots of flavour during cooking. There is no need to remove them at the end of cooking, since they will become very soft and can be eaten.

Preheat the oven to 180°C, 350°F, Gas Mark 4.

Blend the flour with approximately 5 tablespoons of the stock to form a paste.

Place the meat, flour paste, remaining stock, curry powder, potatoes and onion in a large casserole dish. Season with salt and black pepper and stir well. Transfer to the oven and cook for $1\frac{1}{2}$–$1\frac{3}{4}$ hours until the meat is tender. Stir in the lemon slices and the peppers and cook for a further 15 minutes.

Serve with boiled rice, spinach and green beans or a selection of seasonal vegetables.

Sweet and sour pork

Dry-fry the pork fillet in a pre-heated wok or large non-stick frying pan for 5 minutes. Add the vegetables in the order listed in the ingredients, cooking each for 30 seconds before adding the next.

Drain the pineapple, reserving the juice, and stir into the pork mixture. Mix the pineapple juice with the vinegar, tomato purée, salt, honey and soy sauce and add to the pork mixture, continuing to stir for a few more minutes until the pork is well cooked.

Serve on a bed of boiled rice.

SERVES 4
PER SERVING:
168 KCAL/3.5G FAT

12oz (350g) lean pork fillet, thinly sliced into strips
1 small onion, finely chopped
1 carrot, sliced into julienne strips
½ green pepper, seeded and finely chopped
½ red pepper, seeded and finely chopped
8oz (225g) beansprouts
4oz (100g) mushrooms, sliced or chopped
1 small can pineapple chunks in natural juice
2 tablespoons malt vinegar
2 tablespoons tomato purée
pinch of salt
1 teaspoon honey
1 tablespoon soy sauce

Cantonese stir-fried pork

SERVES 4
PER SERVING:
258 KCAL / 7.1 G FAT

1lb (450g) lean pork tenderloin,
  thinly chopped
12 spring onions, sliced
8oz (225g) cucumber, cut into
  thin strips

for the marinade
1 red chilli, seeded and finely
  chopped
2 garlic cloves, crushed
6 tablespoons Hoisin sauce
4 tablespoons dark soy sauce
2 tablespoons sherry
2 tablespoons clear honey
zest and juice of 1 lemon

Mix together the marinade ingredients in a bowl. Add the pork slices and stir to ensure they are evenly coated. Cover and leave to marinate in the refrigerator for 10 minutes.

Heat a wok or large non-stick frying pan. Drain the pork, reserving the marinade, and stir-fry until browned. Add the reserved marinade and simmer for 2–3 minutes. Stir in spring onions and cucumber and heat through.

Serve immediately with rice or noodles and stir-fried vegetables or in Chinese pancakes.

Pork and sausage cassoulet

Cassoulet is generally a meal in itself, consisting of pieces of meat and sausage in a white bean stock thickened with breadcrumbs. Serve with green vegetables and crusty bread.

Preheat the oven to 180°C, 350°F, Gas Mark 4.

Grill the sausages and place in a casserole dish.

Mix together the pork, beans, onion, potatoes and tomatoes and add to the casserole dish. Season well with salt and black pepper.

Dissolve the mustard in the stock and pour over the casserole contents. Cover and cook in the oven for 1½ hours until the pork is tender.

When cooked, remove the lid and sprinkle the breadcrumbs on top of the casserole mixture. Return the casserole to the oven for a further 30 minutes until golden brown.

Just before serving, sprinkle with chopped parsley.

SERVES 6
PER SERVING:
440 KCAL/12.9G FAT

1lb (450g) low-fat sausages
1lb (450g) lean pork, cut into
    1in (2.5cm) cubes
1 × 14oz (400g) can white
    haricot beans, drained
1 large onion, roughly chopped
1lb (450g) potatoes, peeled and
    cut into even-sized pieces
1 × 14oz (400g) can chopped
    tomatoes
1 teaspoon mustard powder
¼ pint (150ml) beef stock
4oz (100g) fresh breadcrumbs
salt and freshly ground black
    pepper
chopped fresh parsley to garnish

Ranchero pie

SERVES 4
PER SERVING:
WITHOUT CHEESE:
479 KCAL/12.7G FAT
WITH CHEESE:
495 KCAL/13.6G FAT

1lb (450g) lean pork mince
1 onion, chopped
1 × 14oz (400g) can mixed
    beans in chilli sauce
4 tablespoons tomato passata
1 tablespoon mild chilli sauce or
    1 teaspoon chilli powder
1 tablespoon chopped fresh
    mixed herbs (e.g. chives,
    oregano, parsley)

for the topping
1½lb (675g) potatoes, peeled
    and chopped
1 × 7oz (200g) can sweetcorn,
    drained
2 tablespoons skimmed milk
1 tablespoon chopped fresh
    parsley
1oz (25g) grated low-fat cheese
    (optional)

Pork and beans – cowboy style! As a variation, you could make this recipe without the potato topping and serve the mince with rice, pasta or jacket potatoes. For a milder flavour, you could substitute kidney or baked beans for the chilli beans.

Preheat the oven to 190°C, 375°F, Gas Mark 5.

To make the topping, boil the potatoes until softened, then drain them. Mash the potatoes with the sweetcorn, milk and parsley.

Meanwhile, in a large non-stick saucepan, dry-fry the mince and onion for about 4–6 minutes, until they change colour. Add the beans, passata and chilli sauce or powder, bring to the boil and simmer for 3–5 minutes. Transfer the mixture to an ovenproof dish. Top with the mashed potato, and sprinkle with the cheese (if using). Bake in the oven for 20 minutes.

Serve with crusty bread and seasonal vegetables.

Gammon with pineapple rice

Cut the gammon steak into cubes and gently dry-fry with the onion in a non-stick pan. Add the pineapple and juice, the stock cube, rice and approximately $\frac{1}{2}$ pint (300ml) water and bring to the boil. Cover and cook for 10 minutes or until the rice is tender and most of the liquid is absorbed. Add more boiling water during cooking if necessary.

Stir in the peas, red pepper and soy sauce and season to taste. Finally, stir in the chives, heat through and serve immediately.

SERVES 1
PER SERVING:
431 KCAL/5.5G FAT

1 gammon steak
1 small onion, finely chopped
1 small can pineapple chunks in
    natural juice
$\frac{1}{2}$ vegetable stock cube
2oz (50g) [dry weight]
    brown rice
2oz (50g) canned or frozen peas
$\frac{1}{2}$ red pepper, sliced
dash of soy sauce
1 tablespoon chopped fresh
    chives
salt and freshly ground black
    pepper

Baked gammon with wholegrain mustard and apple sauce

If you wish, you can soak the gammon in a large bowl of cold water to remove some of the salt. Leave green (unsmoked) gammon for about 1 hour and smoked gammon for 3–4 hours.

SERVES 8
PER SERVING:
406 KCAL/19G FAT

1 × 3lb (1.5kg) lean gammon joint
wholegrain mustard
2–3 teaspoons demerara sugar
1 small Bramley apple (about 6–8oz/175–225g)
$3/4$–1 pint (450–600ml) dry cider or half cider and half chicken stock
$1^1/_2$–2 teaspoons arrowroot
2 tablespoons low-fat fromage frais
salt and freshly ground black pepper
1 bunch watercress to garnish (optional)

Preheat the oven to 180°C, 350°F, Gas Mark 4.

Place the gammon in a roasting tin, cover with foil and cook in the oven for about $1^1/_2$ hours (allow 30 minutes per 1lb/450g).

Half an hour before the gammon is cooked, remove the foil, peel off the rind and the fat. Spread a thin layer of wholegrain mustard over the joint and pat on the demerara sugar. Return to the oven and continue cooking until the coating is golden brown.

In the meantime, start to make the sauce. Peel and core the apple and slice or chop coarsely. Place in a small pan, cover with some of the cider and simmer gently until the apple is soft.

When the gammon is cooked, remove it from the roasting tin, place on a serving dish and keep hot. Pour away any juices in the tin and wipe the tin with kitchen paper to remove any fat, but leave any residual colouring from the sugar and mustard.

Pour the remaining cider and the apple sauce into the tin, place over a gentle heat and mix well with a wooden spoon, working the residual colouring into the cider and apple sauce. Flavour to taste with wholegrain mustard The sauce should be a light golden colour.

Bring gently to the boil and remove from the heat. Mix the arrowroot with a little water and pour into the tin. Return to the heat and bring to the boil again stirring all the time. Check the seasoning and the consistency of the sauce, adding salt and pepper and more arrowroot if required. Just before serving, stir in the fromage frais and recheck the seasoning.

Slice the gammon and arrange on a serving dish. Garnish with watercress if using. Serve with the sauce and accompany with potatoes and seasonal vegetables.

Pork and apple burgers

SERVES 4
PER SERVING:
296 KCAL/8.5G FAT

12oz (350g) lean pork mince
6 tablespoons unsweetened
    apple sauce
2oz (50g) fresh brown
    breadcrumbs
1 teaspoon dried sage
6oz (175g) mushrooms, sliced
a little vegetable stock
4 tomatoes, halved
4 small wholemeal pitta breads
salt and freshly ground black
    pepper

These burgers are delicious and nutritious, with minimum fat and maximum flavour. Ideal for all the family, they are also great for barbecues. Choose a chunky apple sauce for this recipe.

Place the pork, apple sauce, breadcrumbs and sage in a mixing bowl. Season with salt and pepper and mix until well combined. With well-floured hands, form the pork mixture into 4 burger shapes. Cover and chill until required.

Cook under a preheated grill for about 8–10 minutes each side, turning once.

Meanwhile, place the mushrooms in a small pan and add just enough stock to cover them. Bring to the boil then simmer gently for 2–3 minutes until the mushrooms are tender. Cook the tomatoes under the grill for about 5 minutes. Lightly toast the pitta breads if desired.

Serve the burgers with the pitta breads, tomatoes and mushrooms.

Poultry and Game

Poultry has come into its own in recent years as an extremely popular alternative to red meat. Most of the fat in poultry is in the skin, so once this is removed we are left with a very lean protein food which is extremely versatile. Minced, cubed, sectioned or kept whole, chicken and turkey can be used in everything from curries, casseroles and kebabs to fillings for jacket potatoes. I always buy chicken breasts 20 at a time and keep them in my freezer so that I am never short of a quick and easy meal. Be sure to thaw out frozen poultry thoroughly before cooking and never eat undercooked chicken or turkey.

Game offers a tasty alternative to chicken or turkey, and is now available, fresh or frozen, in many supermarkets. Buying ready-prepared joints takes away all the messy preparation often associated with game which has put many of us off cooking it for years.

In this section I have included some old favourites and some tasty new ideas for serving poultry and game. Enjoy them!

Devilled chicken

SERVES 4
PER SERVING:
177 KCAL/8.1G FAT

4 skinless chicken breasts
½ pint (300ml) tomato juice
2 tablespoons Dijon mustard
1 red chilli, seeded and finely
    chopped
1 tablespoon soy sauce
2 teaspoons paprika
2 teaspoons chopped fresh
    ginger
2 tablespoons chopped fresh
    parsley
salt and freshly ground black
    pepper

The term devilled refers to the 'heat' from the chilli and mustard. Although this dish is quite mild, you can make it hotter by adding more chilli if desired.

Preheat the oven to 190ºC, 375°F, Gas Mark 5.

Place the chicken breasts in an ovenproof dish or on a baking sheet. Season well on both sides.

Combine the remaining ingredients in a bowl and spoon over the chicken breasts.

Place the chicken in the oven and cook for 25–30 minutes until the juices run clear.

Skinless roast chicken with herby lemon sauce

Preheat the oven to 190°C, 375°F, Gas Mark 5.

Skin the chicken (chopping off the knuckles and wing tips makes this easier) and remove any visible fat.

Place the chicken on a large piece of aluminium foil in a roasting tin. Arrange the lemon slices over the breast and legs. Brush the chicken with the lemon juice and sprinkle the lemon zest, parsley and thyme over the chicken.

Wrap the chicken tightly in the foil, making sure that the wings and legs are tucked in. Place in the oven and cook for approximately 1½ hours.

Remove the chicken from the oven and unwrap the foil. Drain off the juices and place in a saucepan. Cover the chicken and return to the oven for a further 30 minutes.

Remove any fat from the reserved juices. Add enough water to the juices to make up the liquid to approximately 8fl oz (250ml). Stir in the cornflour and season to taste. Bring to the boil to thicken, stirring continuously.

Slice the chicken and arrange on a serving dish. Pour the herby lemon sauce over the chicken.

SERVES 6
PER SERVING:
190 KCAL/8.5G FAT

1 medium roasting chicken
    (approx. 3½–4lb/
    1.5–1.75kg)
1 lemon, cut into slices
zest and juice of 1 lemon
few sprigs of chopped fresh
    parsley and thyme
2 teaspoons cornflour
salt and freshly ground black
    pepper

Chicken and leek casserole

SERVES 4
PER SERVING:
286 KCAL/7.4G FAT

3–4 rashers lean back bacon

2 onions, sliced

1 garlic clove, crushed

1 × 14oz (400g) can chopped
   tomatoes

$\frac{1}{4}$ pint (150ml) cider or chicken
   stock

1 heaped teaspoon cornflour,
   mixed with a little water

4 chicken quarters or boned
   breasts, skinned

2 carrots, sliced

4 small leeks, trimmed

$\frac{1}{2}$ teaspoon dried basil

$\frac{1}{2}$ teaspoon mixed dried herbs
   or herbes de Provence

salt and freshly ground black
   pepper

Preheat the oven to 180°C, 350°F, Gas Mark 4.

Remove the rind and any fat from the bacon and cut the bacon into strips.

In a non-stick frying pan, dry-fry the bacon. Add the onions and garlic and cook for 1–2 minutes, stirring frequently. Stir in the tomatoes and the cider or chicken stock. Add the blended cornflour, stirring well.

Transfer the bacon mixture to an ovenproof casserole dish. Place the chicken pieces in the casserole dish. Add the remaining ingredients and season to taste with salt and black pepper. Cover and cook in the oven for 1–1$\frac{1}{2}$ hours until the chicken and vegetables are tender.

When the chicken is cooked, check the sauce. If it is too thin, transfer it to a pan and boil rapidly until reduced. Adjust the seasoning if necessary and pour the sauce over the chicken. Serve hot with new potatoes and green vegetables.

Stuffed chicken breasts

These mini chicken roulades make a good main course for a dinner party. You could use any seasonal vegetables of your choice to stuff the chicken breasts.

Preheat the oven to 180°C, 350°F, Gas Mark 4.

Remove the fillet from the back of each chicken breast and, using a sharp knife, scrape out the thick sinew and discard. Reserve the fillets. Place the chicken breasts on a board and cut through each breast from the thick side until you can open it out like an escalope.

Place a fillet in the centre of each breast, cover with a piece of cling film or greaseproof paper and hammer the breast out gently with a rolling pin.

Chop the vegetables finely and place half in a bowl. Add sufficient fromage frais to bind and half of the coriander or tarragon. Season with salt and pepper. Place a tablespoon of vegetables on each breast, roll up and secure each one with a small skewer or cocktail stick.

Place each chicken roll on a piece of aluminium foil. Season lightly and sprinkle with the lemon juice. Roll up each piece of chicken in the foil and seal tightly. Place in a baking tin and cook in the oven for 35–45 minutes or until tender.

In the meantime, cook the remainder of the vegetables, except the mushrooms, in the stock. When most of the liquid has evaporated, add the mushrooms and cook for a further 2–3 minutes.

When the chicken is cooked, make a white sauce: pour a little of the milk onto the cornflour and mix well. Heat the remainder of the milk in a saucepan until hot but not boiling. Slowly pour some of the hot milk onto the cornflour mixture, stirring continuously. Gradually stir in the rest of the milk. Mix the sauce well again and return to the pan with any residual stock from the vegetables.

SERVES 4
PER SERVING:
224 KCAL/6.2G FAT

4 × 4oz (4 × 100g) skinned
   chicken breasts
1/4 small red pepper
1/4 small green pepper
1/4 large carrot
1 medium onion
6 medium white mushrooms
1–2 tablespoons low-fat
   fromage frais
1 tablespoon chopped fresh
   coriander or tarragon
2–3 teaspoons lemon juice
1/2 pint (300ml) chicken stock
1/2 pint (300ml) skimmed milk
1/2oz (15g) cornflour
salt and freshly ground black
   pepper

Bring to the boil, stirring continuously, and cook for 2–3 minutes, still stirring. Add the vegetables and the remainder of the chopped herbs and season to taste with salt and pepper.

Remove the chicken breasts from the foil and remove the skewers or cocktail sticks. Arrange the breasts on a hot serving dish, pour a little of the sauce over and serve the rest separately.

Chicken korma

A korma is usually cooked in ghee or melted butter with a creamy sauce. In this recipe we use yogurt to achieve this creamy texture without the fat.

In a non-stick frying pan, dry-fry the onion until soft. Add the garlic and the chicken and cook for 2–3 minutes until the chicken changes colour.

Sprinkle the curry powder and flour over the chicken. Toss the chicken so that it is completely covered. Add the cinnamon and cook for 1 minute

Gradually add the stock, stirring well and season to taste with salt and black pepper. Simmer gently for 10 minutes until the sauce thickens.

Remove the pan from the heat, stir in the yogurt and coriander and serve immediately.

Serve with boiled rice and mango chutney.

SERVES 4
PER SERVING:
196 KCAL/5.9G FAT

1 medium onion, chopped
2 garlic cloves, crushed
1 lb (450g) diced lean chicken
2 tablespoons mild curry powder
1 tablespoon plain flour
1 teaspoon ground cinnamon
1/2 pint (300ml) chicken stock
1/2 pint (300ml) low-fat natural yogurt
2 tablespoons chopped fresh coriander
salt and freshly ground black pepper

Stoved garlic chicken

SERVES 4
PER SERVING:
449 KCAL/7.9G FAT

4 chicken portions
4oz (100g) lean back bacon
4 garlic cloves, chopped
2½lb (1.2kg) floury potatoes,
    cut into thin slices
2 large onions, sliced
2 teaspoons chopped fresh
    thyme or ½ teaspoon dried
    thyme
1 pint (600ml) chicken stock
salt and freshly ground black
    pepper
fresh chives to garnish

Garlic has a strong intense flavour when used in savoury dips and sauces. However, when cooked slowly over a long period it sweetens and has a totally different flavour.

Preheat the oven to 180°C, 350°F, Gas Mark 4.

Trim the chicken and remove any fat. Remove the rind and any fat from the bacon. Dry-fry the chicken, bacon and garlic in a wok or non-stick pan until the chicken is lightly browned.

Place a layer of potatoes and onion slices in a casserole dish and season well with salt, pepper and thyme. Arrange the chicken, bacon and garlic on top, then cover with the remaining potato and onion slices. Season again and add stock.

Cover and bake in the oven for approximately 1½–2 hours or until the chicken is tender and potatoes are cooked. Add more stock if needed.

Sprinkle with snipped chives and serve with a selection of fresh vegetables.

Thai chicken

Oil and coconut milk are common ingredients in Thai cookery. This fruity recipe gives the flavour of Thai cooking without the fat.

Preheat the oven to 190°C, 375°F, Gas Mark 5.

Place the chicken in an ovenproof dish and season well on both sides with salt and pepper.

Place the red pepper, onions and tomatoes in a bowl. Add the chilli, lime juice and zest, garlic, cumin and coriander and combine well.

Dissolve the cornflour with the pineapple juice and pour over the vegetables. Mix well and season with plenty of salt and pepper. Pour over the chicken and bake in the oven for 30–35 minutes.

Garnish with coriander and serve with jasmine rice.

SERVES 4
PER SERVING:
204 KCAL/7.4G FAT

4 skinned chicken breasts
1 red pepper, finely sliced
6 spring onions, finely chopped
6 plum tomatoes skinned, seeded and diced
1 green chilli, seeded and finely chopped
zest and juice of 2 limes
2 garlic cloves, crushed
1 teaspoon ground cumin
1 teaspoon ground coriander
1 tablespoon cornflour
$\frac{1}{2}$ pint (300ml) pineapple juice
salt and freshly ground black pepper
chopped fresh coriander to garnish

Honey chicken with spiced apricots

Spiced apricots complement sweet ginger-flavoured chicken in this easy-to-prepare recipe.

Cut 3 slashes in each chicken breast. Place in a shallow non-metallic dish and season with salt and pepper.

Drain the apricots, reserving the juice. Mix 2 tablespoons of the juice with the honey, soy sauce, garlic and root ginger and pour over the chicken. Cover and leave to marinate for at least 1 hour.

Remove the chicken from the marinade and cook under a preheated grill for 20 minutes, turning once or twice and basting with the marinade during cooking.

Place 2 tablespoons of apricot juice in a small pan. Add the apricots, spices and vinegar. Heat gently for 5 minutes until piping hot.

Serve the chicken with the spiced apricots, accompanied by potatoes and fresh vegetables of your choice.

SERVES 4
PER SERVING:
220 KCAL / 3.2G FAT

4 × 4oz (4 x 100g) skinned and boned chicken breasts
1 × 14oz (400g) can apricot halves in juice
3 tablespoons clear honey
1 tablespoon soy sauce
1 garlic clove, crushed
1 × 1in (2.5cm) piece root ginger, peeled and grated
$\frac{1}{4}$ teaspoon ground cloves
$\frac{1}{4}$ teaspoon ground ginger
1 tablespoon white wine vinegar
salt and freshly ground black pepper

Chicken and pineapple kebabs with chilli sauce

SERVES 4
PER SERVING:
329 KCAL/7.3G FAT

1 fresh pineapple
4 skinned and boned chicken
   breasts, cut into 1in (2.5cm)
   chunks
2 courgettes, thickly sliced
16 baby onions, skinned
16 button mushrooms

for the sauce
1 pint (600ml) tomato passata
   or thick tomato juice
2 fresh red chillies, seeded and
   finely chopped
2 tablespoons soy sauce
2 tablespoons chopped fresh
   coriander
1 teaspoon fennel seeds
salt and freshly ground black
   pepper

Fruity and spicy, with the bite of fennel seeds, these kebabs are cooked and served with a rich tomato sauce.

Slice off the top and bottom of the pineapple with a sharp knife. Remove the outside skin. Slice the pineapple in half lengthways and then half again lengthways. Cut away the centre core which may be tough and stringy. Cut each pineapple quarter into bite-sized chunks.

Thread alternate pieces of chicken, pineapple, courgettes, onions and mushrooms onto 4 large wooden skewers and place on a baking tray.

Mix all the sauce ingredients together in a bowl. Using a pastry brush, baste the kebabs with the sauce.

Cook the kebabs under a preheated hot grill, turning frequently, until the chicken is fully cooked through and the vegetables are slightly charred.

Serve with the remaining sauce and accompany with boiled rice and mixed salad.

Sticky ginger chicken

These drumsticks taste fantastic served hot or cold and are ideal for including in the school lunch box.

In a mixing bowl, mix together the lemon juice, sugar, ginger, soy sauce and pepper to form a glaze. Taste, and add a little salt if wished.

Remove the skin and any fat from the drumsticks or thighs. Slash the flesh on each one 2 or 3 times and toss the chicken in the glaze.

Cook the chicken under a moderately hot grill, turning them occasionally and brushing with the glaze. Cook until the juices run clear when the flesh is pierced with a skewer.

SERVES 4
PER SERVING:
154 KCAL/3.8G FAT

2 tablespoons lemon juice
2 tablespoons light Muscovado
   sugar
1 teaspoon grated fresh ginger
2 teaspoons soy sauce
8 chicken drumsticks or thighs
freshly ground black pepper
salt to taste (optional)

Coronation chicken

SERVES 4
PER SERVING:
287 KCAL/3.2G FAT

4 skinned and boned chicken
   breasts, cooked
8oz (225g) virtually fat free
   fromage frais
1 tablespoon curry powder
2 tablespoons mango chutney
8oz (225g) seedless grapes
2 tablespoons lemon juice
1 tablespoon chopped fresh
   parsley
salt and freshly ground black
   pepper
bunch of watercress to serve

This classic dish usually has lashings of high-fat mayonnaise. In this low-fat version, mixing the fromage frais with a few spices and additional flavours creates a delicious sauce.

Coarsely chop the cooked chicken and place in a mixing bowl.

Blend together the fromage frais, curry powder and mango chutney. Mix with the chicken, coating the chicken well.

Cut the grapes in half with a sharp knife, add to the chicken and combine all the ingredients well. At this point you can leave the dish to stand or store it in the refrigerator until ready to serve.

Just before serving, mix in the lemon juice and the parsley and season well with salt and pepper.

Serve with a watercress salad.

Mini chicken rissoles

These meaty nibbles are ideal party food. Children love them as well as grown-ups. You could substitute minced turkey or pork for the chicken.

Preheat the oven to 190°C, 375°F, Gas Mark 5.

Place all the ingredients in a large bowl and mix well. Mould the mixture into 16 small balls, each about the size of a golf ball. Place on a baking sheet.

Place in the oven and cook for 20–25 minutes.

Serve hot or cold with salad or a tomato sauce.

MAKES 16
PER RISSOLE:
86 KCAL/1.2G FAT

2lb (900g) lean minced chicken
1 small onion, finely chopped
1 garlic clove, crushed
2 teaspoons ground coriander
2 teaspoons ground cumin
1 tablespoon chopped fresh thyme
2 tablespoons chopped fresh parsley
1 teaspoon salt
1 tablespoon tomato purée

Roast turkey

SERVES 10
PER SERVING:
189 KCAL/3.2G FAT

1 × 12lb (5.4kg) fresh turkey
4oz (100g) herb stuffing mix
8oz (225g) canned chestnuts
   (drained weight)
1 pint (600ml) chicken stock
1 onion, chopped
2 tablespoons gravy powder

Preheat the oven to 180°C, 350°F, Gas Mark 4.

Wash the turkey in cold water and remove the giblets and any fat. Reserve the giblets.

Mix the stuffing mix with ½ pint (300ml) cold water and allow to stand for a few moments. Chop the chestnuts and add to the stuffing. Fill the neck end of the turkey with the prepared stuffing mixture.

Pour the chicken stock into a large roasting tin. Add the giblets and the onion. Place the turkey on a wire rack and place the rack in the roasting tin above the stock. Cover with aluminium foil and place in the oven. Allow a cooking time of 15 minutes per 1lb (450g) plus 20 minutes over. Allow for 30 minutes standing time after cooking. Turn the roasting tin round every hour to ensure even cooking.

One hour before serving, remove the turkey from the oven and remove the foil. Pour off most of the cooking liquid into a bowl or jug. Return the turkey (without the foil) to the oven for 30 minutes.

Meanwhile, place 4 large ice cubes in the turkey liquid. After 5 minutes, place the liquid in the refrigerator or freezer in order to cool it as fast as possible. The fat will then separate and thicken so that you can remove it before making the gravy.

To test if the turkey is completely cooked, pierce one of the legs with a skewer or sharp knife. If the juice runs out clear, the bird is cooked; if it is coloured with blood, return the turkey to the oven for a little longer. When cooked, leave the cooked turkey to stand in a warm place for 30 minutes, covered with the reserved foil to keep it moist and warm. This 'resting time' will make it easier to carve the turkey.

To make the gravy, heat the separated turkey liquid in a saucepan. Mix the gravy powder with a little cold water to form a paste and add to the turkey liquid, stirring well. You can thin the gravy using vegetable water from any vegetables you are cooking to accompany the turkey. Bring the gravy to the boil and then simmer gently until ready to serve.

Thai turkey stir-fry

For a less creamy sauce, you can prepare this dish without the fromage frais.

Heat a large wok or non-stick pan. Add the turkey and dry-fry for 5–6 minutes until it changes colour and the flesh starts to firm up. Add the garlic, ginger and chilli and cook for a further minute.

Grate a little zest from one of the limes, then squeeze out the juice from both limes. Add the lime zest and juice to the wok or pan, along with the wine and turmeric. Season well with salt and pepper. Add the green pepper and courgette. Cook for 2–3 minutes until very lightly cooked but remaining crisp.

Remove the wok or pan from heat and stir in the fromage frais and fresh coriander.

Serve with boiled rice and a crisp salad.

SERVES 2
PER SERVING:
238 KCAL / 2.2G FAT

2 turkey breast steaks, cut into strips
1 garlic clove, finely chopped
1 × 1 in (2.5cm) piece fresh ginger, peeled and finely chopped
1 fresh green chilli, seeded and chopped
2 limes
$1/2$ wineglass white wine
$1/2$ teaspoon turmeric
1 green pepper, cut into strips
1 courgette, cut into strips
3 tablespoons virtually fat free fromage frais
chopped fresh coriander
salt and freshly ground black pepper

Quick turkey bolognese

SERVES 2
PER SERVING:
172 KCAL/5.6G FAT

6oz (175g) turkey mince
1 chicken stock cube
1 × 7oz (200g) can chopped
   tomatoes
1/4 jar Bolognese sauce
1 teaspoon tomato purée
1/2 garlic clove, crushed, or 1
   teaspoon garlic purée
   (optional)

Place the turkey mince in a hot heavy-based pan and dry-fry until the mince changes colour.

Sprinkle the stock cube over the mince and add the remaining ingredients. Bring to the boil and simmer for 30 minutes.

Turkey burgers

MAKES 8
PER BURGER:
221 KCAL/4.8G FAT

1lb (450g) minced turkey breast
2oz (50g) fresh white
   breadcrumbs
1 medium onion, diced
1 tablespoon Worcestershire
   sauce
1 teaspoon French mustard
1 teaspoon dried herbs
1 egg or 2 egg whites
1 teaspoon salt
black pepper
8 small rolls or pitta breads to
   serve

You can spice up these simple turkey burgers by adding a little chilli powder, or try adding a little grated nutmeg and serve with a squeeze of fresh lemon.

Mix all the ingredients together in a large bowl until they bind. Form the mixture into 8 burger shapes. Place on silicone or waxed paper and refrigerate until required.

Cook under a preheated moderate grill or over a hot barbecue for 15–20 minutes, turning once during cooking, until the juices run clear when the burgers are pricked with a fork.

Serve the burgers hot in bread rolls or pitta bread and accompany with salad.

Herb-crusted duck with red wine sauce

There are many varieties and breeds of duck, varying in size and flavour. British Aylesbury and Gressingham have rich meat but unfortunately thick layers of fat. Barbary are less fatty with a large quantity of breast meat. When cooking a whole duck, it can be quite tricky getting the dark leg meat cooked through while keeping the moisture in the breast meat. I find the answer is to cook them separately. Duck breast may be slightly more expensive, but once the skin and fat are easily removed only lean meat remains, giving total portion control.

Remove the skin from the duck breasts and cut away any traces of fat. Place the duck in a large mixing bowl.

Place the salt, thyme, garlic, juniper, peppercorns and sugar in a food processor and blend until ground, or, alternatively, place all the ingredients in a thick plastic food bag and grind down with a rolling pin.

Rub the salt mixture over both sides of the duck. Pour the red wine over the duck. Cover and leave in the refrigerator to marinate for 1 hour.

Remove the duck from the marinade and pat dry with kitchen towel. Reserve the marinade. Place the duck on a baking sheet and grill under a hot preheated grill for 8–10 minutes, turning regularly.

Pour the marinade into a saucepan, and add the passata. Bring to the boil. Mix the cornflour with a little cold water and add to the pan, stirring continuously, to thicken the sauce. If you find the sauce too salty, add a little more cornflour.

To serve, slice each duck breast and arrange on a serving plate. Pour the sauce around the breasts.

SERVES 4
PER SERVING:
167 KCAL/5G FAT

- 4 × 4–6oz (4 × 100–175g) duck breasts
- 2 teaspoons coarse sea salt
- 1 tablespoon chopped fresh thyme
- 2 garlic cloves, crushed
- 6 juniper berries
- 4 whole black peppercorns
- 1 teaspoon sugar
- 1/2 pint (300ml) red wine
- 1/4 pint (150ml) tomato passata
- 1 tablespoon cornflour
- salt and freshly ground black pepper

Glazed duck breasts with cherry sauce

SERVES 4
PER SERVING:
299 KCAL/10.1G FAT

4 × 6–8oz (4 × 175–225g)
   duck breasts
2 tablespoons redcurrant jelly
$^1/_4$ teaspoon ground cinnamon
good pinch of freshly ground
   nutmeg
6oz (175g) canned or frozen
   dark sour cherries
$^1/_2$ teaspoon French mustard
2 tablespoons dark soy sauce
1 tablespoon red wine vinegar
$^1/_4$ pint (150ml) chicken stock
1 heaped teaspoon arrowroot
a few sprigs watercress to
   garnish

Duck is a delicious tender meat which continues to cook when left to stand. It is best cooked pink and allowed to rest for 5 minutes before slicing. If you find it is undercooked, place under a hot grill for a few seconds.

Preheat the oven to 220°C, 425°F, Gas Mark 7.

Remove the skin and fat from the duck breasts (you will find that it pulls off very easily). Using a sharp knife, remove any sinews from the underside.

Warm the redcurrant jelly in a pan and stir in the cinnamon and nutmeg. Taste, and add a little more cinnamon or nutmeg if you wish.

Place the duck breasts in a roasting tin and glaze with the redcurrant jelly, reserving the residue of the jelly in the pan. Cook in the oven for 18–20 minutes until the duck is tender but still slightly pink in the centre.

Meanwhile, stone the cherries, if necessary, and place them in the pan containing the residue of the redcurrant jelly. Add the French mustard, dark soy sauce, red wine vinegar and stock. Bring to the boil and cook gently for 6–8 minutes until the cherries are just tender. Mix the arrowroot with a little water, add to the pan and bring to the boil, stirring all the time. If using canned cherries, you only need to heat them through in the sauce but you may need a little more arrowroot to thicken the sauce.

When the duck breasts are cooked, cut each one into $^1/_2$in (1cm) slices along the length almost down to the base, and fan out. Arrange the 4 breasts in a semi-circle on a hot serving dish. Just before serving, use a slotted spoon to remove the cherries from the sauce and pile them at the bottom of the duck breasts. Pour a little sauce over each one and serve the rest of the sauce separately. Garnish the top edge of the dish with small sprigs of watercress.

Breast of pheasant
with wild mushrooms

Use fresh pheasant, if in season, or frozen pheasant. The latter can be bought throughout the year from most large supermarkets. Although only the breasts are used here, you can cut the legs in half and mix with 1–2 chopped chicken breasts to use in your favourite chicken casserole recipe, ideally one using red wine, and deep freeze for another occasion.

Many types of wild mushrooms are now cultivated and it is possible to buy some of them all year round. If you have difficulty in obtaining wild mushrooms, use open cup cultivated ones.

You could prepare the pheasant and stock a day in advance and refrigerate until required.

To remove the breast from the pheasants, first pull off the skin and use a small sharp knife to remove the wishbone. Use the knife to ease the breast away from the carcass, starting along one side of the breastbone. Cut off the legs and drumsticks and save for use in a casserole. Pull away the fillet (the long loose piece of meat at the back of the breast) and ease out the sinew in each one with the point of a small knife. Refrigerate the breast and fillets until later. Reserve the carcass.

Peel and trim the onions, carrots, leek and celery. Cut 1 onion and 1 carrot into slices and cut the remainder of the vegetables into medium dice.

To make the stock, wash the carcass well and place in a large pan. Add the sliced carrot and onion, cover with water and bring to the boil. Cover with a lid and simmer gently for 2 hours. Strain the stock into another saucepan. Discard the bones and vegetables and boil the stock rapidly until it has reduced to about 1/4 pint (150ml). Reserve.

Place the diced leek, celery and the remaining carrot and onion in a pan with a little water. Season lightly and simmer until the vegetables are tender. Drain and add the cooking liquor to the stock. Reserve the vegetables.

SERVES 4
PER SERVING:
405 KCAL/10.6G FAT

2 pheasants
2 medium onions
2 medium carrots
1 small leek
1 celery stick
12oz (350g) wild mushrooms
1/2 pint (300ml) white wine
1 large garlic clove
1 tablespoon fresh white
   breadcrumbs
1 tablespoon chopped fresh
   parsley
2 tablespoons brandy
salt and freshly ground black
   pepper
1 orange (optional)
small bunch of watercress to
   garnish

Preheat the oven to 200°C, 400°F, Gas Mark 6. Trim and clean the mushrooms. Season lightly and place in a pan. Add the wine and cook for 10–12 minutes or until tender. Drain, reserving the cooking liquor. Finely chop about 3oz (75g) of the mushrooms for use in the stuffing. With the remainder, leave chanterelles and trompettes whole, but cut shiitake or oyster mushrooms into thick slices. Reserve.

To make the stuffing, peel and crush the garlic. Place the small pieces of fillet in a food processor, together with the garlic, and work until finely chopped. Alternatively chop them finely by hand. Place in a bowl and mix the breadcrumbs, parsley, the 3oz (75g) chopped mushrooms and 1 tablespoon of brandy. Season lightly and mix well.

Place each breast on a board and cut a slit in the thin side to make a pocket. Place a quarter portion of stuffing in each pheasant breast. Press the edges of the slit together. Place the pheasant breasts in an ovenproof dish.

Make the sauce by placing the cooked diced vegetables with the reduced stock and cooking liquor from the vegetables and mushrooms in a liquidiser and blend until smooth. Transfer to a pan and heat, adding the remaining mushrooms and 1 tablespoon of brandy. Pour the sauce over the pheasant breasts and cook in the oven for 30–40 minutes depending on their size.

If you wish, you can use a canelle knife to decorate an orange and cut a few slices. Garnish the dish with the watercress and orange slices (if using) and serve with boiled potatoes and a selection of vegetables.

Pheasant casserole

SERVES 4
PER SERVING:
405 KCAL/13.8G FAT

1 large cock pheasant (or 2
　　medium hen)
2 medium onions, coarsely
　　chopped
$\frac{1}{2}$ pint (300ml) red wine
5 celery sticks, chopped into
　　1in (2.5cm) pieces
4 medium carrots, chopped into
　　1in (2.5cm) pieces
1 bay leaf
10oz (275g) mushrooms,
　　chopped
2 heaped tablespoons cornflour,
　　mixed with a little cold water
2 drops gravy browning
salt and freshly ground black
　　pepper

*This is a superb dish. It takes a long time to prepare, but for a
special dinner party it is well worth the effort.*

Preheat the oven to 200°C, 400°F, Gas Mark 6.

Place the pheasant (with the skin on) in a roasting tin. Roast
in the oven, allowing 15 minutes per 1lb (450g) plus 15 minutes
over.

When the pheasant is cooked, remove from roasting tin and
discard the fat. Allow to cool. Remove all the skin and cut the
meat into large chunks, removing all the bones. Place in a
casserole dish with the onions and wine. Season with salt and
black pepper, cover and leave to marinate overnight in the
refrigerator.

The next day, preheat the oven to 180°C, 350°F, Gas Mark 4.

Place the celery, carrots and bay leaf in the casserole dish.
Add $\frac{1}{4}$ pint (150ml) of water (or just enough water to cover the
ingredients). Bake in the oven for 1$\frac{1}{2}$ hours. Allow to cool again
and refrigerate overnight.

Three hours before serving, preheat the oven to 200°C,
400°F, Gas Mark 6. Remove the casserole from the refrigerator
and stir in the mushrooms and a little water if necessary. Cook for
1 hour, then reduce the oven temperature to 150°C, 300°F, Gas
Mark 2 and cook for a further 1$\frac{1}{2}$ hours.

Twenty minutes before serving, remove from the oven and
thicken the sauce with the blended cornflour and the gravy
browning. Season to taste. Return to the oven until ready to serve.

Serve with new potatoes and assorted vegetables.

Braised guinea fowl with celery

Guinea fowl is available from most supermarkets all year round. The texture of the meat is slightly firmer than that of chicken. It is a very lean bird and the flavour is midway between that of a chicken and pheasant. Either of these birds could also be used in this recipe, but if you haven't tasted guinea fowl before, do try it.

SERVES 4
PER SERVING:
206 KCAL/6.6G FAT

1 head celery
12 button onions
1 × 3lb (1.5kg) guinea fowl
$\frac{1}{2}$ teaspoon vegetable oil
7fl oz (200ml) white wine
7fl oz (200ml) chicken stock
1–2 teaspoons arrowroot
salt and white pepper

Preheat the oven to 180°C, 350°F, Gas Mark 4.

Trim the celery and cut the sticks into 3in (7.5cm) lengths. Pour boiling water over the onions, leave for a few minutes then drain and cool under the cold tap for a moment or two. You will then find that the onions are very easy to peel, but take care to remove as little of the root and stem ends as possible so that the centres do not 'pop' out during cooking.

Place the celery and onions in a pan and cover with boiling water. Season lightly with salt and simmer gently for 7–10 minutes. Drain well. If you are using a stock cube to make the stock, reserve the cooking liquor and use it instead of water to make the stock.

Remove any fat from inside the vent end of the bird. Brush the oil over the bottom of a heavy-based frying pan. Heat well and brown the guinea fowl on both sides.

Remove the guinea fowl from the pan and wipe the outside of the bird to remove any oil. Place the bird in an ovenproof casserole and add the celery, wine and stock. Cover with a tightly fitting lid and place in the oven. Cook for 40 minutes then add the button onions and continue cooking for another 30–45 minutes until the juices from the bird run clear and the vegetables are tender. Remove the bird and the celery and onions from the casserole, cover and keep hot.

Bring the cooking liquor to the boil and boil rapidly. Using a metal spoon, remove any froth which rises to the surface as this will be the fat which has seeped from the bird. When the stock is clear, mix a teaspoon of arrowroot with a little cold water and add to the pan. Bring to the boil, stirring all the time. If necessary, add more arrowroot mixed with water until the sauce is a pouring consistency. Check the seasoning and add pepper and, if necessary, more salt.

To serve the guinea fowl, place it on a serving dish, arrange the celery and onions around it, then carve it at the table. Serve the sauce separately.

Fish

White fish is high in protein and low in fat, easy to prepare and quick to cook, which makes it a great alternative to meat or poultry and invaluable in a low-fat diet. Make the most of fresh herbs, sauces and seasonings for maximum flavour.

Oily fish such as salmon and mackerel contain essential fatty acids that are important for good health, which is why they are included in this book, despite their higher fat content. You should aim to eat at least one portion a week, but remember if you need to lose weight, limit your intake to three portions a week maximum.

Some of the recipes in this section are incredibly easy to prepare, but I've also included a few more challenging ones and some seafood specialities that are suitable for dinner parties. If you've never tasted fish without lashings of oil, butter or batter before, start now!

Cod steak with herby stuffing crust

SERVES 4
PER SERVING:
143 KCAL/1.9G FAT

4 cod steaks
1 packet lemon and thyme
  stuffing
4 spring onions, very finely
  chopped
2 garlic cloves, very finely
  chopped
4oz (100g) finely chopped fresh
  parsley
2 beef tomatoes, thickly sliced

These crispy topped cod steaks benefit from being prepared the night before. Store in the refrigerator and, just before cooking, drizzle with lemon juice. If you wish, you could add 2oz (50g) grated low-fat Cheddar cheese to the stuffing mix.

Preheat the oven to 200°C, 400°F, Gas Mark 4.

Season the fish and place on a non-stick baking sheet.

Make up the stuffing as directed on the packet. Add the spring onion, garlic and chopped parsley and mix well together. Place a generous spoonful of the mixture onto the fish, spreading it evenly over the top of the fish. Arrange the tomato slices across the top.

Bake in the oven for approximately 10–15 minutes until the fish is cooked through and golden brown on top.

Serve with a low-fat parsley sauce.

Oriental cod with lime and wild rice

Cut the cod into 1 in (2.5cm) cubes and place in a dish. Mix together the lime zest and juice and the soy sauce and pour over the cod. Leave the cod to marinate until ready to cook.

Cook the rices together in boiling water. Drain and mix with the grated carrot, courgette and chopped mushrooms. Keep warm.

Pour the cod and the marinade into a saucepan and simmer for 6–8 minutes until the fish flakes.

Place the rice mixture in a serving dish and arrange the cod on top. Pour the marinade over and serve immediately.

SERVES 4
PER SERVING:
282 KCAL/2.3G FAT

2lb (1kg) cod fillet, skinned
zest and juice of 2 limes
4 tablespoons light soy sauce
12oz (350g) [dry weight] brown rice
2oz (50g) [dry weight] wild rice
2 carrots, grated
1 courgette, grated
2oz (50g) mushrooms, chopped

Gremolata fish cakes with sorrel sauce

SERVES 4
PER SERVING:
236 KCAL/1.8G FAT

1lb (450g) fresh cod
1lb (450g) mashed potato
2 baby leeks, finely chopped
2 tablespoons chopped fresh
    parsley
2 garlic cloves, crushed
zest and juice of 1 lemon
1 teaspoon salt
1 tablespoon chopped capers
4oz (100g) fresh sorrel
¼ pint (150ml) vegetable stock
1 tablespoon flour
1 pint (600ml) skimmed milk
salt and freshly ground black
    pepper

Gremolata is a mixture of parsley, lemon, garlic and sea salt and is usually used as a topping for meat or fish. Sorrel is a fresh herb with a limy flavour. You can use parsley instead of sorrel in this recipe if you prefer.

Grill the cod under a hot heat until lightly cooked. Flake the cod into a bowl, removing any skin and bones. Add the mashed potato.

In a non-stick frying pan, dry-fry the leeks and garlic until soft. Add to the potato mixture, then add the lemon juice and zest, parsley, salt and capers, mix well and season with salt and black pepper.

Shape the mixture into small balls, then using a palette knife, gently flatten them to form fish cakes. Dry-fry in a non-stick pan on both sides until golden brown and place in a low oven to keep warm.

Make the sauce by finely shredding the sorrel. Wilt it in a saucepan with the stock, sprinkle the flour over and cook for 1 minute to 'cook out' the flour. Gradually add the skimmed milk, stirring continuously to prevent lumps from forming. Season well and simmer until thick.

Serve the fish cakes hot with the sorrel sauce and seasonal vegetables.

Poached haddock florentine

Spinach and fish go so well together. You can use frozen spinach instead of fresh if you prefer – make sure you drain it well and then place it straight into the heatproof dish, as it needs no pre-cooking.

Prepare the fish by removing the skin and any obvious bones. Cut the fish into 4 pieces. Poach the fish in the skimmed milk for 8–10 minutes. Season well with salt and pepper.

Wash the spinach well and place in a large saucepan. Wilt the spinach over a low heat, then season with salt and pepper and fresh nutmeg.

Combine the yogurt with the mustard and parsley in a small bowl.

Place the spinach in the bottom of a heatproof dish. Place the haddock on top, spoon the yogurt sauce over, and place under a hot grill for 1–2 minutes until golden.

Serve hot with potatoes and fresh vegetables.

SERVES 4
PER SERVING:
307 KCAL/5.3G FAT

2lb (900g) haddock
½ pint (300ml) skimmed milk
4lb (2kg) fresh spinach
1 whole nutmeg, grated
4 tablespoons low-fat natural yogurt
2 teaspoons Dijon mustard
1 tablespoon chopped fresh parsley
salt and freshly ground black pepper

Fisherman's pie

SERVES 6
PER SERVING:
258 KCAL/2G FAT

1 ½ lb (675g) potatoes, peeled
2 tablespoons low-fat natural
    yogurt
12oz (350g) smoked haddock
12oz (350g) cod or white
    haddock
8oz (225g) peeled and cooked
    prawns
2 baby leeks, chopped
¼ pint (150ml) fish stock
1 tablespoon flour
½ wineglass white wine
1 tablespoon Dijon mustard
1 pint (600ml) skimmed milk
2 tablespoons capers
salt and freshly ground black
    pepper
chopped fresh parsley to
    garnish

A fish pie with lots of extras. Dijon mustard and white wine make a delicious creamy sauce, perfect to serve at any Captain's table.

Preheat the oven to 220°C, 425°F, Gas Mark 7.

Boil the potatoes in a saucepan of water until well done. Drain and mash until smooth. Mix in the yogurt and season well with salt and black pepper.

Remove the skin and bones from the fish and cut into bite-sized pieces, place in the bottom of an ovenproof dish. Add the prawns.

Place the leeks and the fish stock in a medium saucepan and cook for 1–2 minutes. Sprinkle the flour over and mix well. Cook for a further minute in order to 'cook out' the flour. Add the wine and mustard and beat well. Gradually add the skimmed milk, stirring continuously to prevent any lumps from forming. Bring to the boil, allowing the sauce to thicken. Pour over the fish and sprinkle the capers on top. Allow to cool for 20 minutes, then cover with the mashed potato, either using a fork or piping through a piping bag with a large star nozzle.

Place in the oven for 30–40 minutes until golden.

Just before serving, sprinkle with the chopped parsley. Serve with minted peas and other vegetables.

Smoked haddock boats

Pre-heat the oven to 180°C, 350°F, Gas Mark 4.

Wash and prick the potatoes and bake in the oven for 1½–2 hours. When soft, cut each potato in half lengthways. Scoop the insides of each potato half into a bowl, leaving the skins intact. Add the fromage frais to the bowl and season with salt and pepper. Stir in the smoked haddock and spoon the mixture back into the potato skins.

Turn the oven up to 200°C, 400°F, Gas Mark 6. Return the potatoes to the oven for a further 10–15 minutes.

Just before serving, sprinkle with chopped parsley.

SERVES 4
PER SERVING:
347 KCAL/2G FAT

4 large baking potatoes
2 tablespoons virtually fat-free
    fromage frais
4oz (100g) smoked haddock,
    cooked and flaked
salt and freshly ground black
    pepper
chopped fresh parsley to garnish

Baked plaice in mustard sauce

A golden rich sauce with a hidden kick transforms this dish into a bright colourful plate.

Preheat the oven to 180°C, 350°F, Gas Mark 4.

Make the sauce by softening the onion in the stock in a saucepan, sprinkle the flour over and cook for 1 minute to 'cook out' the flour. Add the mustard and turmeric. Gradually add the skimmed milk, stirring continuously to prevent any lumps from forming, and season well with salt and black pepper. Simmer until the sauce thickens.

Skin the plaice and arrange in an ovenproof dish, folding the tails under to form thick parcels. Pour the sauce over the fish and place in the oven for 15–20 minutes until cooked.

Serve hot with potatoes and plenty of vegetables.

SERVES 4
PER SERVING:
259 KCAL/3.9G FAT

1 medium onion, finely chopped
½ pint (150ml) vegetable stock
1 tablespoon flour
1 teaspoon mustard powder
1 pinch turmeric
1 pint (600ml) skimmed milk
4 large single fillets of plaice
salt and freshly ground black
    pepper
chopped fresh parsley to garnish

Grilled salmon with leek and tomato risotto

This dazzling dinner party recipe is full of interesting Continental flavours. Since salmon is an oily fish, this dish has a high fat content. However, since oily fish contains essential nutrients, it is acceptable within a low-fat diet, providing you eat no more than three servings a week.

SERVES 4
PER SERVING:
625 KCAL/25G FAT

1 medium onion, finely chopped
8oz (225g) [dry weight] risotto rice
1½ pints (900ml) fish stock
2 leeks, finely chopped
4 sun-dried tomatoes, chopped
4 salmon fillets
2 tablespoons lemon juice
20 cherry tomatoes
1 tablespoon chopped fresh chervil
salt and freshly ground black pepper
lemon slices and chopped fresh parsley to garnish

Dry-fry the onion in a non-stick pan until soft. Add the rice and fish stock and bring to the boil. Add the leeks and chopped tomatoes, cover with a lid and simmer over a low heat, stirring occasionally, for 20 minutes.

Prepare the salmon by removing skin and any bones. Season with salt and pepper. Place on a baking sheet, drizzle with lemon juice, and place under a hot grill for 8–10 minutes. One minute before the end of the cooking time, place the cherry tomatoes around the salmon and grill for 1 minute or until the skins pop.

To serve, stir the chopped chervil into the risotto. Place the risotto in the centre of a serving dish. Arrange the salmon on top of the risotto and place the tomatoes around the edges. Garnish with lemon slices and chopped parsley.

Monkfish and salmon kebabs

When cooked to perfection, monkfish is deliciously moist and full of flavour. These kebabs make fish cookery simple and fast.

Skin and bone the salmon, and remove any dark markings under the skin. Wash the monkfish well and cut away the fine membrane with a sharp knife. Cut both fish into 1 in (2.5cm) cubes.

Zest 2 of the limes into a shallow dish. Squeeze out the juice from both limes into the dish and add the lemon grass.

Take 8 small wooden or metal skewers. Cut the remaining lime into 4 thick slices, then cut each slice in half again and place a piece on each skewer. Thread alternate pieces of salmon and monkfish onto each skewer and then roll them in the lime and lemon grass mixture. Season well with salt and pepper and place on a baking sheet. Pour the remaining juice over.

Place the baking sheet under a hot grill or place the skewers over a hot barbecue for 3–4 minutes, turning the kebabs regularly. When cooked, sprinkle the kebabs with chopped parsley and crushed red peppercorns.

Serve hot with boiled rice and a mixed salad.

SERVES 4
PER SERVING:
203 KCAL / 10.3G FAT

1 lb (450g) salmon fillet
1 lb (450g) monkfish
3 limes
1 teaspoon finely chopped
  lemon grass
salt and freshly ground black
  pepper
chopped fresh parsley
pinch of crushed red
  peppercorns

Baked trout with rosemary and sea salt

This recipe can be prepared in advance. The rosemary really permeates into the fish to give an essence of the Mediterranean.

Rinse the trout well under cold running water. Scrape your finger along the inside of the backbone to remove any traces of blood. Use scissors to trim the tail and cut off all the fins. Place the fish on a baking sheet and slash the top with a sharp knife, making diagonal incisions.

Place a sprig of rosemary and a lemon slice in each incision. Sprinkle both the inside and outside of each fish with sea salt. Season well with salt and pepper and pour the apple juice over the fish.

Place under a hot grill and cook for 6–8 minutes on each side, or alternatively place in a moderate oven at 200°C, 400°F, Gas Mark 6 for 20–25 minutes.

Just before serving, drizzle with the hot juices and sprinkle with chopped parsley. Serve hot, with potatoes and plenty of seasonal vegetables.

SERVES 4
PER SERVING:
189 KCAL/5.9G FAT

4 large trout, gutted
4 large sprigs fresh rosemary
1 lemon, sliced
4 good pinches sea salt
1/4 pint (150ml) fresh apple juice
1 tablespoon chopped fresh
    parsley
salt and freshly ground black
    pepper

Turbot steaks *en papillote* with basil

SERVES 4
PER SERVING:
145 KCAL/3.7G FAT

4 × 4oz (4 × 100g) turbot steaks
1 baby leek, finely shredded
1 carrot, finely shredded
2oz (50g) button mushrooms,
    finely sliced
1 lemon, halved
1/2 wineglass dry white wine
4 basil leaves
salt and freshly ground black
    pepper

En papillote *is a French term for cooking inside a paper parcel. The parcel creates a vacuum which seals in all the flavours, allowing them to infuse during cooking. The same principle can be applied using foil and then cooking on a barbecue or chargrill.*

Preheat the oven to 220°C, 425°F, Gas Mark 7.

Cut out 4 large discs of greaseproof paper, using a dinner plate as a template. Place a turbot steak in the centre of each disc and season well with salt and black pepper. Scatter equal amounts of the vegetables over the 4 steaks. Squeeze the juice from the lemon halves and drizzle the lemon juice and the white wine over the top of the steaks. Season with salt and black pepper and place a basil leaf on each steak.

Bring the edges of the greaseproof paper together and twist over in small folds, starting at the bottom, folding over the top and down the other side so that the parcel looks the same shape as a Cornish pasty. The parcel should now be airtight. Place on a baking sheet and place in the oven for 10–12 minutes.

When cooked, place the parcels directly onto serving plates. Snip the top of the paper with scissors and fold back the paper. Serve with potatoes and seasonal vegetables.

Trout and spinach paupiettes with dill and cucumber sauce

These elegant paupiettes of trout are really quick and easy to prepare, especially if you ask the fishmonger to skin the fillets for you. To make sure that every bone is removed from the trout, slowly run a finger over each fillet to feel for any remaining bones, then as you find them, remove with a pair of clean tweezers, pulling them out towards the head end of each fillet.

Preheat the oven to 220°C, 425°F, Gas Mark 7.

Bring a large saucepan of water to the boil. Add the spinach and blanch it for 45–60 seconds, or until the spinach is wilted. Then immediately pour the spinach into a large colander and cool it quickly under a cold running tap. Allow to drain, then squeeze the spinach with your hands to remove all the excess water. Chop the blanched spinach and place in a bowl. Add 3 tablespoons of the yogurt (reserve the rest for the sauce), season to taste with salt and pepper and nutmeg and mix well.

Cut each fillet of trout in half lengthways to make 4 fillets. Place one of the trout fillets on a board, skin-side down ,with the tail end nearest to you, then make a small incision across the flesh at the tail end, stopping when the knife comes into contact with the skin. Then, holding the fillet firmly, slightly angle the knife between the skin and flesh and, using a gentle sawing action, carefully remove the skin. Repeat with the remaining fillets.

Place the trout fillets, skinned-side up, on a board, season with salt and pepper, and spread each one evenly with the spinach mixture. Roll each fillet up neatly from the head end to the tail and secure with a cocktail stick.

Place the paupiettes in a small ovenproof dish and sprinkle with the lemon juice. Add the lemon slices and sprigs of dill, cover the dish tightly with foil. Place in the centre of the oven and bake for 8–10 minutes, or until the trout turn opaque and the flesh flakes easily. Take care not to overcook or the trout will become dry.

SERVES 4
PER SERVING:
365 KCAL / 13.2G FAT

1 × 8oz (225g) packet baby spinach, washed and drained
3oz (75g) Total 0% Greek Yogurt
freshly grated nutmeg to taste
2 × 225g (2 × 8oz) filleted trout
2 tablespoons fresh lemon juice
2 slices lemon
2 sprigs fresh dill
salt and freshly ground black pepper
2 extra lemon slices to garnish (optional)

for the sauce
1/4 pint (150ml) well-flavoured fish or vegetable stock
2 tablespoons dry white wine (optional)
1 × 4oz (100g) piece cucumber, halved and thinly sliced
2 level teaspoons cornflour
2 tablespoons chopped fresh dill

Continued on page 230

Meanwhile, make the sauce. Pour the stock into a small saucepan, add the white wine, if using, and the cucumber. Bring to the boil then reduce the heat, partially cover the pan with a lid and simmer gently for 2–3 minutes until the cucumber is slightly softened.

Blend the cornflour with 2 teaspoons of water and stir it into the cucumber sauce. Add the chopped dill and bring to the boil, stirring continuously, until the sauce thickens slightly. Then reduce the heat and simmer for 1–2 minutes. Finally, stir in the remaining yogurt, season to taste with salt and pepper, and cook for a further minute.

Remove the cocktail sticks from the paupiettes, then carefully remove the paupiettes from the baking dish and arrange on warmed serving plates. Pour the cucumber and dill sauce over the paupiettes, garnish with lemon slices (if using) and serve immediately.

Cider and orange halibut steaks

SERVES 4
PER SERVING:
238 KCAL/3.3G FAT

4 halibut steaks
½ pint (300ml) sweet cider
¼ pint (150ml) orange juice
zest of 1 orange
1 garlic clove, crushed
4 spring onions, finely sliced
2 teaspoons chopped fresh dill
1 tablespoon arrowroot
4 orange wedges to garnish

An unusual combination of cider and orange makes this dish colourful and flavoursome.

Place the halibut steaks in a shallow ovenproof dish. Cover with the cider, orange juice and zest, garlic and spring onions. Place in the refrigerator and leave to marinate for 1 hour.

Preheat the oven to 200°C, 400°F, Gas Mark 6.

After marinating the steaks, pour off the juice into a bowl. Add the arrowroot and mix together, using a small whisk. Add the dill and pour the sauce over the fish. Bake in the oven for 20–25 minutes.

Garnish with orange wedges and serve with potatoes and a selection of vegetables.

Pan-fried tuna with pepper noodles

Fresh tuna tastes completely different from canned tuna. Its lean, meaty flesh holds together well, making it ideal to pan-fry or even barbecue. It benefits from being served slightly underdone, with a moist centre.

Trim the tuna steaks with a sharp knife, removing any unsightly dark fish. Season well with salt and black pepper.

Prepare the noodles by placing in boiling salted water for 2–3 minutes. Drain and refresh under cold running water.

Heat a griddle pan or non-stick frying pan, add the vegetable oil and then wipe out the pan with a piece of kitchen paper, taking care not to burn your fingers (use an oven glove if necessary).

Place the tuna, best side down, in the hot pan. As the tuna cooks it will change colour. Rather like a thermometer, the colour band will change and move up the fish. When it reaches halfway up the steaks, turn the steaks over and cook for a few minutes. Remove from the pan and place in a warm oven to keep hot.

Add the garlic and peppers to the pan and sauté quickly until they start to soften. Add the noodles, lime zest and juice and soy sauce. Cook for 1–2 minutes, turning regularly. Place the noodles on warmed serving plates and top with the tuna steak. Garnish each one with a slice of lime and red pepper.

SERVES 4
PER SERVING:
356 KCAL/8.6G FAT

4 fresh tuna steaks
8oz (225g) [dry weight] thread
    noodles
1 teaspoon vegetable oil
1 garlic clove, crushed
1 red pepper, seeded and finely
    sliced
1 yellow pepper, seeded and
    finely sliced
zest and juice of 1 lime
1 tablespoon light soy sauce
salt and freshly ground black
    pepper
4 lime slices and red pepper to
    garnish

Grilled lemon sole with dill sauce

Place the sole on a baking tray, season with salt and pepper and squeeze fresh lemon juice over. Grill under a hot heat for 5–7 minutes on each side. Keep warm in a hot oven while you make the sauce.

In a saucepan, heat the milk with the stock cube, mix the cornflour with a little water and add to the milk. Bring to the boil, stirring continuously. Add the chopped dill and simmer for 2–3 minutes.

Just before serving, stir in the fromage frais and adjust the seasoning.

Serve the sole hot with the sauce and seasonal vegetables.

SERVES 4
PER SERVING:
253 KCAL/3.7G FAT

4 lemon sole
1 lemon
1 pint (600ml) skimmed milk
1 fish stock cube
1 tablespoon cornflour
2 tablespoons chopped fresh dill
3 tablespoons low-fat fromage
    frais
salt and freshly ground black
    pepper

Steamed sea bass with chilli

Sea bass has an incredible flavour when gently cooked. It needs no sauce to mask the delicate flavour, just fresh vegetables or a salad.

Season the bass with salt and pepper and place in the top of a steamer. Scatter the spring onion slices, ginger and chilli over the fish. Sprinkle with the lime juice and steam the fish gently for about 5 minutes or until the fish turns pale pink and is just flaky.

Serve with salad or fresh vegetables.

SERVES 4
PER SERVING:
103 KCAL/2.6G FAT

4 sea bass steaks
4 spring onions, sliced
1 × 1 in (2.5cm) piece root
    ginger, finely chopped
1 garlic clove, crushed
2 red chillies, finely sliced
1 teaspoon lime juice
salt and freshly ground black
    pepper

Seared scallops with fresh vine tomatoes and basil

SERVES 4
PER SERVING:
129 KCAL / 2.4G FAT

1 shallot, finely chopped

$\frac{1}{2}$ teaspoon coriander seeds

1 garlic clove, crushed

$\frac{1}{2}$ wineglass rosé wine

2 teaspoons bouillon stock

8 vine tomatoes, skinned, seeded and finely diced

1 tablespoon finely shredded basil

1 teaspoon vegetable oil

20 queen scallops

salt and freshly ground black pepper

Scallops are a delicate seafood and are best bought in their large circular shells, but are mainly sold loose. Try to get fresh scallops, as frozen ones can be quite watery.

In a non-stick frying pan, dry-fry the shallot until soft. Add the coriander seeds and garlic and cook for 1 minute. Add the wine and the bouillon stock and cook until the liquid has reduced. Add the diced tomato and the basil, and season with salt and pepper.

Preheat a griddle pan or non-stick frying pan and add the oil. Wipe out the pan with kitchen paper, taking care not to burn your fingers (use an oven glove if necessary).

Add the scallops to the griddle pan or frying pan and cook for 2–3 minutes on each side. Do not overcook – they need to be just cooked in the centre. Add the tomato mixture and heat through. Season well.

Serve hot, with green beans and baby new potatoes.

Tuna chilli tortillas

Tortillas are fairly low in fat but can taste quite bland on their own. This spicy tuna filling transforms them into a Mexican treat.

Warm the tortillas in a low oven for a few minutes.

Combine the kidney beans and fromage frais with the chilli sauce. Fold in the tuna and mix well. Add the spring onions and mint and mix well

Shred the lettuce and cut the tomatoes in half.

Fill the tortilla shells with lettuce, then add the tuna mixture. Top with the tomatoes. Garnish with chopped parsley and lemon wedges.

SERVES 4
PER SERVING:
484 KCAL/2.5G FAT

8 large tortillas
1 × 14oz (400g) can red kidney
  beans, drained and rinsed
4 tablespoons low-fat fromage
  frais
2 teaspoons chilli sauce
2 spring onions, chopped
1 teaspoon chopped fresh mint
$\frac{1}{2}$ small crisp lettuce, shredded
1 × 14oz (400g) can tuna in
  brine, drained
8 cherry tomatoes
chopped fresh parsley and fresh
  lemon wedges to garnish

Spicy tomato king prawns

SERVES 4
PER SERVING:
58 KCAL/0.5G FAT

1 medium onion, finely diced

2 garlic cloves, crushed

1 red pepper, seeded and finely
diced

20 medium uncooked king
prawns, peeled

2 × 14oz (2 × 400g) cans
chopped tomatoes

2 teaspoons chilli sauce

1 teaspoon lemon grass

1 tablespoon bouillon stock
powder

2 tablespoons chopped fresh
parsley

salt and freshly ground black
pepper

*If you cannot find king prawns, this recipe works just as well with
small peeled prawns.*

Dry-fry the onion and garlic in a non-stick frying pan. Add the red
pepper and cook for a further minute. Add the prawns and quickly
seal (do not overcook). Cover with the tomatoes. Add the chilli
sauce, lemon grass and the bouillon stock powder. Bring the sauce
to the boil, and simmer for 1–2 minutes until the prawns are
cooked through. Season well with salt and black pepper.

Just before serving, sprinkle with the parsley. Serve with
boiled rice.

Vegetarian

There are about seven million vegetarians in the UK, and every week more and more people are choosing to adopt a vegetarian diet for all sorts of different reasons. Meat-eaters, too, are increasingly likely to enjoy the occasional vegetarian meal as an opportunity to add greater variety to their usual diet. Most vegetarians choose to exclude meat and fish from their diet; others avoid eggs and dairy products too, and true vegans avoid any food which has animal origins, including gelatine. Although it is perfectly possible for all these different types of vegetarians to maintain a healthy diet, it becomes progressively more important to ensure that the diet remains nutritionally balanced, because of the exclusion of certain groups of foods.

A healthy vegetarian diet

Vegetarians should try to follow the same healthy eating principles as meat-eaters, choosing foods from each of the major food groups – high protein sources, cereals and grains, dairy products (or non-dairy substitutes) and fruits and vegetables.

Protein

Protein is the nutrient which most people are concerned about in a vegetarian diet. Although it is true that meat is an excellent source of protein, most people in the UK eat far more protein than they actually need, and protein deficiencies very rarely occur. The quality of the protein is especially important for vegetarians

Proteins are made up of 20 different amino acids. Eight of these are considered to be essential – they cannot be produced in the body and must therefore be eaten. The other amino acids can all be made within the body from other amino acids, assuming sufficient protein is consumed. Meat is a high-quality protein because it provides all the essential amino acids, whereas most vegetable proteins lack one or more of the essential amino acids. However, by eating a variety of vegetable proteins, it is easy to ensure that all the essential amino acids are available to the body.

Foods such as beans, peas and lentils are all high in protein and are usually the main protein source in a vegetarian diet. Soya beans are one of the very few vegetable proteins which contain all the essential amino acids. Nuts are also an important protein source, although they are high in fat and should be eaten in moderation on a low-fat diet.

Textured vegetable protein (TVP) made from soya beans has been available for many years, but with the new vegetable proteins such as Quorn and tofu it is easier than ever to have a healthy, well-balanced diet which doesn't include animal products. Quorn is a protein based on mushrooms, and tofu is made from soya beans. Both are low in fat and can be used in many different recipes. They are good at absorbing the flavours and provide texture in dishes such as casseroles, curries or stir-fries.

Dairy products

Dairy products such as milk and cheese are important sources of calcium. Vegetarians who wish to avoid these foods should try to substitute them with non-dairy products such as soya milk and vegetarian cheese. Tofu is also rich in calcium.

Essential fatty acids (EFAs)

There are two families of essential fatty acids. First, there are the so-called omega-6 fatty acids, such as linoleic acid, which are found in some grains and seeds and commonly eaten in the form of corn oil or sunflower oil. The second family is the omega-3 fatty acids, such as linolenic acid, which are mostly eaten in oily fish but are also found in rape seed, walnut and soya oil. Some vegetarians worry that they many not be eating sufficient EFAs, especially if they are following a low-fat diet. However, in practice, this is unlikely to be a problem. The government recommends that EFAs should provide 1–2 per cent of our daily energy needs, approximately 5 grams a day. On average in the UK, we eat between 8 and 15 grams a day of EFAs and have a store of 500 grams in our body fat. However, if you are concerned, add just a drop of vegetable oil which is rich in essential fatty acids to your cooking or in salad dressings.

Vitamins and minerals

Vegetarians who eat a varied diet that includes plenty of cereals, fruit and vegetables should have no problem ensuring they meet all their nutritional needs for vitamins and minerals. However, it is important to take particular care with regard to certain vitamins and minerals for which is meat is a major source. The most important mineral is iron, since meat is a rich source of haem iron, which is particularly well absorbed by the body. Bread, fortified breakfast cereals, dark green leafy vegetables and dried fruit are all alternative sources of iron. Vitamin B12 is only found in animal products and therefore true vegetarians must take a B12 supplement.

Trio pepper pizza (see page 265)

Festive stuffed peppers

These tasty peppers add a colourful touch to any dinner party table. Serve with a mixed salad or plenty of seasonal vegetables.

Preheat the oven to 180°C, 350°F, Gas Mark 4.

Heat the oil in a pan and sauté the onion and celery until soft. Stir in the mushrooms and cook for 1 minute. Add the redcurrant jelly and stir until melted. Remove from the heat and cool the mixture slightly.

Chop the Quorn sausages in a food processor until well broken down. Stir in the cooling vegetables. Add the breadcrumbs, cranberries, stuffing mix, parsley, brandy and 1/4 pint (150ml) of water and mix well.

Fill the pepper halves generously with the sausage mixture, taking care not to compact the filling too tightly. Place on a baking sheet and bake in the centre of the oven for about 25 minutes until the peppers are soft and the Quorn stuffing is golden brown.

SERVES 4
PER SERVING:
335 KCAL/7.4G FAT

1 tablespoon sunflower oil
1 onion, finely chopped
1 celery stick, finely chopped
2oz (50g) button mushrooms, thinly sliced
1 tablespoon redcurrant jelly
11oz (300g) packet Quorn frozen sausages
4oz (100g) fresh breadcrumbs
4oz (100g) water chestnuts
4oz (100g) fresh or defrosted cranberries
2oz (50g) sage and onion stuffing mix
2 tablespoons chopped fresh parsley
4 tablespoons brandy
2 large red peppers, halved lengthways and seeded
2 large green peppers, halved lengthways and seeded
salt and freshly ground black pepper

Garlic, pasta and lentil bake

SERVES 4
PER SERVING:
426 KCAL/3.3G FAT

6oz (175g) [dry weight] red
    lentils
6oz (175g) [dry weight] pasta
    bows
1 large onion, chopped
2 garlic cloves, crushed
1 large carrot, diced
2 celery sticks, chopped
2 green or red peppers, seeded
    and chopped
1 × 7oz (200g) can plum
    tomatoes
2 tablespoons tomato purée
1 vegetable stock cube
salt and freshly ground black
    pepper
1 × 3$\frac{1}{2}$oz (90g) packet garlic
    and herb stuffing mix

Rinse the lentils. Place in a pan and cover with water. Cook for about 20 minutes until tender. Drain. Meanwhile cook the pasta according to the instructions (but without oil). Drain well. Place the onion, garlic and carrot in a pan with a little water, cover and simmer until the carrot is almost cooked. Add the celery and peppers to the pan and cook for a couple of minutes.

Preheat the oven to 200°C, 400°F, Gas Mark 6.

Combine the vegetables with the lentils, tomatoes, tomato purée, stock cube and seasoning in a large pan and heat through gently.

Make up the stuffing mix, adding half as much water again as indicated on the packet (the stuffing needs to be fairly sloppy).

Place a layer of cooked pasta in the base of a large ovenproof dish. Follow with a layer of lentil mixture then a thin layer of stuffing. Continue like this and finish with a layer of stuffing. Fork the top and bake in the oven for 20 minutes until brown and crisp.

Stuffed aubergine

This recipe can be used as a main course and served with unlimited salad or vegetables. Choose smooth-skinned fresh aubergines, since wrinkled or bruised ones may be old and leathery.

Cut the aubergine in half lengthways and scoop out the flesh. Sprinkle the insides of the aubergine and the flesh with salt and leave for 20 minutes. Rinse well and chop the flesh.

Meanwhile, cook the lentils in boiling water for 25–30 minutes until tender. Drain.

Preheat the oven to 180°C, 350°F, Gas Mark 4.

Place the oil in a saucepan and sauté the onion for 5 minutes until it begins to soften. Add the chopped aubergine, pepper and mushrooms and sauté for 5 minutes. Stir in the mustard and herbs and season well.

Drain the tomatoes, reserving the juice. Chop the tomato flesh and add to the pan with the cooked lentils. Spoon into the aubergine shells. Bake in the oven for 45 minutes until the aubergine is tender.

Just before the end of cooking time, stir a little tomato juice into the cornflour to form a smooth paste. Add the remaining stock and juice. Heat gently, stirring continuously, until thickened. Season to taste and pour the sauce over the aubergine.

SERVES 4
PER SERVING:
162 KCAL/1.0G FAT

2 large aubergines
4oz (100g) [dry weight] Puy lentils, soaked
1 teaspoon olive oil
1 onion, finely chopped
1 red pepper, seeded and finely chopped
4oz (100g) mushrooms, chopped
1 teaspoon wholegrain mustard
1 teaspoon chopped mixed herbs
1 × 14oz (400g) can tomatoes
2 teaspoons cornflour
1/4 pint (150ml) vegetable stock
salt and freshly ground black pepper

Spinach, lentil and mushroom strudel

An excellent dinner party dish that can be made in advance. Serve with a spicy red pepper sauce and a selection of seasonal vegetables.

This recipe makes two strudels. Filo pastry comes in many different sizes, so you can make larger or smaller strudels to suit. The strudels can be placed in a plastic box and deep frozen.

Preheat the oven to 200°C, 400°F, Gas Mark 6.

Place half the onions and half the garlic in a pan. Wash the lentils and add to the pan, cover with water and boil for 20–30 minutes until the lentils are almost tender. If there is too much liquid in the pan, strain most of it off. Add the garam masala and the chopped tomatoes and cook until the mixture is quite dry, stirring frequently to prevent the mixture from sticking to the base of the pan. Season to taste with salt and black pepper. Place in a bowl and leave until cold.

Heat 1 teaspoon of oil in a small pan, add the remaining chopped onion and crushed garlic and cook over a gentle heat until soft. Add the mushrooms and 3–4 tablespoons of water to the pan. Season lightly and cook until the mushrooms are soft and all the liquid has evaporated. Check the seasoning, stir in the grated cheese and leave until required.

If using fresh spinach, remove the stalks and wash well in several changes of water. Place the fresh or frozen spinach in a pan and add a little water. Season lightly with salt, cover with a lid, bring to the boil and cook for 3–4 minutes. Drain well and press out as much water as possible with a potato masher. Turn out on to a board and chop well. Place in a bowl and check the seasoning.

For each strudel lay 3 or 4 sheets of filo pastry out on a lightly greased baking sheet. Brush each filo sheet with the egg mixture. Cover with another sheet and repeat. Distribute the lentil mixture over half the width of each pastry layer (i.e. along the length of

SERVES 6
PER SERVING:
290 KCAL/11.1G FAT

2 medium onions, finely chopped
2 garlic cloves, crushed
6oz (175g) [dry weight] orange lentils
1 teaspoon garam masala
1 × 7oz (200g) can chopped tomatoes
1 teaspoon oil
8oz (225g) mushrooms, finely chopped
2oz (50g) low-fat vegetarian Cheddar cheese, grated
1lb (450g) fresh spinach or 8oz (225g) frozen chopped spinach
6–8 sheets filo pastry (approx. 12 × 9in (30 × 23cm)
1 egg, beaten with 2 tablespoons skimmed milk
1 bunch watercress
1–2 tomatoes, cut into quarters
salt and freshly ground black pepper

one side) leaving a 1 in (2.5cm) border all the way round. Cover with the spinach, spreading it out as evenly as possible, and then cover with mushrooms.

Fold the other half of each pastry layer over and seal the edges with water. Brush a little egg over the surface and bake in the oven for 25–30 minutes until crisp and golden brown.

Lift the strudels onto a hot serving dish. Just before serving, garnish with watercress and quarters of tomatoes. Cut the strudels into quarters at the table. Serve with hot chilli sauce (see page 399).

Grilled polenta with fresh wild mushrooms

Polenta is coarsely ground maize. Bramata is the best quality and is rather like a coarse flour. Like pasta, it is a good base to incorporate many flavours. Since it is fat free it forms an ideal alternative to rice or potatoes and can be purchased in a readymade state or part-cooked as an instant polenta. However, to get the authentic flavour, it is best made from scratch, using bramata flour. A large batch can be frozen in pieces and then cooked from frozen as required.

Weigh the polenta flour into a large jug so that it can be poured easily.

Place the stock in a large saucepan. Add the sage and half the garlic and bring to the boil. Slowly add the polenta in a continuous stream, stirring with a whisk to prevent lumps forming then, using a wooden spoon, beat well until combined.

Reduce the heat and simmer for 40–45 minutes until the polenta starts to leave the sides of the pan. Pour into a shallow dish or baking tray and allow to cool and set.

In a non-stick frying pan dry-fry the shallot with the remaining garlic until soft. Add the mushrooms and cook for 2–3 minutes, seasoning well with salt and plenty of black pepper. Add the lemon juice, soy sauce and most of the parsley (reserve a little for the garnish) and simmer for 1–2 minutes.

Cut the set polenta into squares and place face-down onto a baking tray. Grill under a high heat for 1–2 minutes until golden brown. Spoon the mushroom mixture onto the polenta and sprinkle with the remaining chopped parsley.

SERVES 4
PER SERVING:
231 KCAL / 2.4G FAT

8oz (225g) bramata polenta flour
2 pints (1.2 litres) vegetable stock
1 tablespoon chopped fresh sage
2 garlic cloves, crushed
1 medium shallot, finely diced
1lb (450g) fresh mixed wild mushrooms (e.g. oyster, shiitake, ceps)
juice of 1 lemon
1 tablespoon light soy sauce
1 tablespoon chopped fresh parsley
salt and freshly ground black pepper

Lentil roast

This creamy tomato lentil roast with a crunchy topping can be eaten cold with salad.

Wash the lentils well, drain and place in a large pan. Cover with water. Tie the bay leaf, parsley stalks and thyme together with string and add to the pan. Bring to the boil. Add the chopped onions, crushed garlic, cumin and sliced celery to the lentils. Add the stock cube and simmer until the lentils and vegetables are tender and the liquid has almost evaporated.

Preheat the oven to 180°C, 350°F, Gas Mark 4.

Meanwhile, peel the apple, cut into quarters and remove the core. Cut the quarters into small dice. When the lentils are tender, remove the bunch of herbs and continue cooking, stirring continuously, until the mixture is quite dry. Stir the diced apple, peppers, tomatoes, and quark or yogurt into the lentil mixture. Mix well and season to taste with salt and black pepper.

Pile the mixture into an ovenproof dish and bake in the oven for about 1 hour until the top is springy like a sponge.

Serve with seasonal vegetables.

SERVES 4
PER SERVING:
376 KCAL/2G FAT

12oz (350g) [dry weight] orange lentils

1 bay leaf

2–3 parsley stalks

1 sprig fresh thyme

2 large onions, chopped

1–2 garlic cloves, crushed

1 teaspoon ground cumin

2–3 celery sticks, sliced

1 vegetable stock cube

1 dessert apple

$\frac{1}{2}$ green pepper, seeded and diced

$\frac{1}{2}$ red pepper, seeded and diced

1 × 14oz (400g) can chopped tomatoes

3oz (75g) quark or low-fat natural yogurt

salt and freshly ground black pepper

Spicy chickpea casserole

SERVES 4
PER SERVING:
426 KCAL/5.7G FAT

8oz (225g) [dry weight]
    chickpeas, soaked overnight
1 medium onion, chopped
1 × 14oz (400g) can chopped
    tomatoes
2 vegetable stock cubes
$\frac{1}{2}$ teaspoon ground coriander
2 heaped teaspoons cumin
    seeds
$\frac{1}{2}$ teaspoon chilli powder
8oz (225g) [dry weight] brown
    rice
8oz (225g) mushrooms, sliced
1 tablespoon chopped fresh
    coriander
salt and freshly ground black
    pepper

*This recipe tastes better if you make it up in advance to allow all
the flavours to combine and then simply reheat it before serving.*

Fast-boil the chickpeas for 10 minutes, then simmer for a further
20–25 minutes until fairly soft. Meanwhile, place the onion and
tomatoes into a medium saucepan with one of the stock cubes.
Add the coriander, cumin, chilli and season with salt and black
pepper. Bring to the boil and simmer gently for 10 minutes.

Cook the rice according to the packet instructions, adding the
remaining vegetable stock cube to the cooking water. Drain well
and keep hot.

When the chickpeas are almost cooked, drain them, then rinse
with boiling water. Stir the chickpeas into the tomato and spice
mixture. Add the mushrooms and simmer for a further 5 minutes.
Season well with salt and black pepper. Add the fresh coriander.

Serve the chickpeas with the rice and fresh vegetables of your
choice.

Chickpea and fennel casserole

This wholesome and flavoursome dish takes just 25 minutes to prepare. Fennel has a distinctive aniseed flavour and can be quite strong, so adjust the quantity according to your personal taste.

Gently cook the chickpeas, bulgar wheat, celery, fennel and garlic in a little stock for about 5 minutes. Add the remaining ingredients, except the mint, and simmer for 20 minutes.

Garnish with the fresh mint and serve with fresh vegetables of your choice.

SERVES 2
PER SERVING:
316 KCAL/7.3G FAT

1 × 14oz (400g) can chickpeas, drained
1oz (25g) [dry weight] bulgar wheat
2 teaspoons fennel seeds, crushed
1 garlic clove, crushed
6oz (175g) celery, diced
6oz (175g) whole green beans, chopped
½ pint (300ml) vegetable stock
1 tablespoon soy sauce or to taste
salt and freshly ground black pepper
2 tablespoons chopped fresh mint to garnish

Chickpea and mixed vegetable stew

SERVES 4
PER SERVING:
244 KCAL/8.7G FAT

1 tablespoon sunflower oil
2 medium carrots, halved
    lengthways and sliced across
1 medium to large potato,
    peeled and chopped
$^1/_2$ cauliflower, cut into florets
8oz (225g) courgettes, chunkily
    chopped
2–3oz (50–75g) green beans,
    cut in half across
1 teaspoon ground coriander
2 vegetable stock cubes
$^3/_4$ pint (450ml) water or light
    stock
$^1/_4$ pint (150ml) tomato passata
1 medium red pepper, seeded
    and diced
4oz (100g) okra, topped and
    tailed and cut in half across
2 green chillies, seeded and
    chopped
1 tablespoon tikka paste or
    other marinating paste
1 × 14oz (400g) can chickpeas,
    drained and rinsed
salt and freshly ground black
    pepper

This stew is packed with unusual and common varieties of vegetables. Serve on a bed of couscous with a crisp green salad.

Heat the oil gently in a medium saucepan and gently fry the carrots, potato and cauliflower. Stir the mixture from time to time to prevent it from sticking to the bottom of the pan.

Add the courgettes, green beans and coriander and cook slowly for another 5 minutes. Add the stock cubes, water or stock, tomato passata, red pepper, okra, chillies, tikka paste and chickpeas and cook for 20–30 minutes.

Serve immediately.

Blackeye bean casserole

Fresh ginger and soy adds a slightly oriental theme to this dish. As a variation, try serving it with stir-fried rice mixed with fresh beansprouts.

Place the blackeye beans in plenty of water in a saucepan. Cover and bring to the boil and simmer for 30–35 minutes. Drain well.

Cook the rice according to the packet instructions, adding the vegetable stock cube to the cooking water. When cooked, drain well and keep hot.

In a separate pan, gently heat the vegetables, chestnuts, chilli, ginger and garlic in a little of the vegetable stock.

Mix the soy sauce and cornflour with a little vegetable stock, add the remainder of the stock and stir into the vegetables, stirring continuously. Add the drained beans and simmer for a further 8–10 minutes. Season to taste and serve with the rice.

SERVES 2
PER SERVING:
373 KCAL/3.8G FAT

2oz (50g) blackeye beans
4oz (100g) [dry weight] brown rice
1 vegetable stock cube
2oz (50g) onion, diced
6oz (175g) mushrooms, sliced
4oz (100g) celery, cut into thin strips
3oz (75g) carrots, cut into thin strips
2oz (50g) water chestnuts, thinly sliced
$\frac{1}{2}$ teaspoon chilli powder
$\frac{1}{2}$ teaspoon grated fresh ginger or ground ginger
1 garlic clove, crushed
$\frac{1}{4}$ pint (150ml) vegetable stock
1 tablespoon soy sauce
$\frac{1}{2}$oz (15g) cornflour
freshly ground black pepper

Bean and burgundy casserole

SERVES 6
PER SERVING:
326 KCAL / 4G FAT

6oz (175g) [dry weight] green
   lentils
1 tablespoon vegetable oil
2 medium onions, finely
   chopped
2 garlic cloves, crushed
2 teaspoons cumin seeds
1 teaspoon dried oregano
1/2 pint (300ml) red wine
1 × 14oz (400g) can chopped
   tomatoes
3/4–1 pint (450–600ml)
   vegetable stock
1 bay leaf
1lb (450g) firm old or new
   potatoes, peeled and cut into
   large dice
1–2 large carrots, sliced
8oz (225g) leeks, cut into 1in
   (2.5cm) lengths
1 × 14oz (400g) can red kidney
   beans, drained and rinsed
6–8oz (175–225g) small
   button mushrooms
1 small cauliflower, broken into
   florets (optional)
salt and freshly ground black
   pepper
1 tablespoon chopped fresh
   parsley to garnish

*You could halve the quantities in this recipe to serve just 3 people.
This dish can also be frozen. Allow the casserole to defrost at room
temperature or in a microwave before reheating it. If you reheat it
on top of the stove, you may need to add some more stock or a little
water to keep the dish moist.*

Soak the lentils in cold water for at least an hour. Drain.

Heat the oil in a large pan and cook the onions gently until
soft. Add the garlic, cumin seeds and oregano and cook for a
further 2–3 minutes. Add the drained lentils, wine, tomatoes, 3/4
pint (450ml) of the vegetable stock and the bay leaf. Bring to the
boil, cover the pan and simmer for 10–15 minutes.

Add the potatoes, carrots, leeks and kidney beans to the pan.
Bring back to the boil again, adding more stock if necessary, and
simmer for a further 10 minutes.

Add the mushrooms and cauliflower (if using) to the pan and
continue cooking for a further 7–10 minutes or until the lentils
are tender.

When the lentils are tender, remove the bay leaf from the pan
and season the vegetables to taste with salt and pepper. Just
before serving, pour the casserole into a hot serving dish and
sprinkle the chopped parsley over the top.

Stir-fry Quorn

Heat the oil in a wok or non-stick pan. Add the Quorn, ground coriander and spring onions and cook for a few minutes.

Add the remaining vegetables and the grated ginger. Continue to cook until the Quorn and vegetables are cooked but the vegetables are still crunchy. Add the soy sauce and lemon juice. Season to taste and serve immediately.

SERVES 4
PER SERVING:
130 KCAL/1.8G FAT

1 teaspoon sunflower oil
16oz (450g) Quorn chunks
2 teaspoons ground coriander
8 spring onions, chopped
4oz (100g) pak choi or spring
    greens
4oz (100g) mange tout
2 medium carrots, cut into
    julienne strips
grated root ginger to taste
1–2 teaspoons soy sauce
juice of 1 lemon
salt and freshly ground black
    pepper

Tofu Indonesian-style

SERVES 4
PER SERVING:
145 KCAL/6.4G FAT

10oz (275g) regular tofu
1 tablespoon sunflower oil
4oz (100g) baby carrots, thinly
   sliced
6oz (175g) baby sweetcorn, cut
   in half at a slant
6oz (175g) mange tout, topped
   and tailed
4oz (100g) turnip or white
   radish, peeled and thinly
   sliced

for the sauce
2 teaspoons arrowroot
1 tablespoon tamari or other soy
   sauce
1 lime leaf or bay leaf
2 small red and green chillies,
   sliced and seeded
1×2in (5cm) piece lemon grass
2 teaspoons fresh ginger juice
approx. $\frac{1}{4}$ pint (150ml)
   vegetable stock

Tamari is a good quality soy sauce from Japan and is available in many healthfood stores. If you can't find it, you can substitute any soy sauce.

Ginger juice is easily made by using unpeeled root ginger. Grate the ginger and squeeze out as much of the juice as possible.

Cut the tofu into 20 pieces and leave to drain on kitchen paper.

Heat the oil and sweat the vegetables in a semi-covered pan for 5 minutes, stirring continuously.

Mix all the sauce ingredients together, adding only sufficient vegetable stock to form a smooth sauce. Add the tofu and pour the sauce and tofu over the vegetables. Cover, and cook for 8 minutes.

Season and serve on a bed of boiled brown rice.

Tofu kebabs

These kebabs can be made up in advance and stored, covered, in the marinade until ready for use. They are ideal for barbecues.

Place all the ingredients for the marinade in a shallow dish and mix until well combined.

Cut the tofu into chunks and pat dry. Add to the marinade and toss until well coated. Cover and allow to marinate in the refrigerator for at least 3 hours.

Thread alternate pieces of tofu, pepper, onion and courgette onto 8 small skewers and brush with the remaining marinade.

Cook under a preheated grill or over a barbecue for 10 minutes, turning frequently, until the tofu is golden. Serve with the pitta breads.

SERVES 4
PER SERVING:
203 KCAL/4.2G FAT

2 × 10½oz (2 × 285g) packets fresh tofu, drained
2 red peppers, seeded and diced into 1in (2.5cm) pieces
16 baby onions, peeled
2 small courgettes, cut into thick slices
4 small pitta breads

for the marinade
4 garlic cloves, crushed
½ teaspoon chilli powder
½ teaspoon ground cumin
½ teaspoon ground coriander
½ teaspoon ground ginger
1 teaspoon garam masala
5oz (150g) low-fat natural yogurt

Sweet potato and fruit curry

SERVES 4
PER SERVING:
236 KCAL/2.6G FAT

1 medium onion, chopped
1 garlic clove, crushed
2 green chillies finely chopped
1 × 1in (2.5cm) piece green
    ginger, finely chopped
½ pint (300ml) vegetable stock
2 teaspoons garam masala
1 teaspoon ground coriander
1 teaspoon ground cumin
1lb (450g) sweet potato, cut
    into 1in (2.5cm) chunks
8oz (225g) green beans,
    trimmed and cut into 1in
    (2.5cm) lengths
1lb (450g) cauliflower, broken
    into small florets
1 red pepper, seeded and cut
    into small pieces
½ pint (300ml) tomato passata
salt to taste
2 bananas

Place the onion, garlic, chillies and ginger in a non-stick pan, cover with a lid and dry-fry for 5 minutes on a gentle heat. Add a little vegetable stock if the pan becomes too dry.

When the onion is soft add 2fl oz (50ml) of the stock, sprinkle the spices into the pan and cook for a further minute, stirring continuously. Add the sweet potato, beans, cauliflower and pepper to the pan and cook over a moderate heat for 2–3 minutes, stirring continuously. Pour in the remaining vegetable stock and the passata, season with salt. Cover the pan and cook gently for 10 minutes.

Slice the bananas and add to the pan. Cook for a further 10 minutes or until the vegetables are tender.

Serve with boiled brown rice and low-fat natural yogurt mixed with chopped cucumber and a little fresh mint.

Leek and courgette dhansak

A dhansak is an Indian curry traditionally made with meat and thickened with lentils. The dish is usually started by frying the onion in ghee or butter. Here, we replace the meat and the fat with a selection of fresh vegetables which, when combined with spices, gives a really tasty vegetarian dish. You could substitute any seasonal vegetables – cauliflower works particularly well.

Prepare the potatoes, leeks and courgettes by chopping into bite-size pieces.

Dry-fry the onions and garlic in a non-stick pan until soft. Add the potatoes, leeks, courgettes and red pepper and cook over a medium heat for 2–3 minutes.

Add the spices and the chillies, stirring well to coat the vegetables, and cook for a further minute in order to 'cook out' the spices.

Add the lentils and stir the stock and tomato purée into the mixture. Season well with salt and freshly ground black pepper. Cover and simmer for 35–40 minutes.

Serve with boiled rice spiced with a little lemon zest, and a simple cucumber yogurt salad.

SERVES 4
PER SERVING:
302 KCAL/3G FAT

1lb (450g) small waxy potatoes
8oz (225g) young leeks, washed
8oz (225g) small courgettes
2 medium onions, chopped
2 garlic cloves, crushed
1 red pepper, seeded and diced
1 tablespoon ground coriander
1 tablespoon ground cinnamon
1 tablespoon ground cumin
1 tablespoon fennel seeds
2 fresh green chillies, seeded
   and chopped
4oz (100g) [dry weight] red
   lentils
1 pint (600ml) vegetable stock
3 tablespoons tomato purée
salt and freshly ground black
   pepper

Dahl

Dahl is an Indian accompaniment to spicy curries and hot flavoured dishes. Served with a jacket potato or even topped with mashed potato, it makes a good lunch.

In a non-stick saucepan, fry the onion in the oil until soft. Add the garlic, lentils and spices and cook for 1 minute to allow the spices to 'cook out'. Add the tomatoes and stock, and cover and simmer for 20–25 minutes until the liquid has been absorbed by the lentils.

   Taste, and season with salt and black pepper. Pour into a serving dish and sprinkle with the parsley.

SERVES 4
PER SERVING:
227 KCAL/2G FAT

2 medium onions, finely
   chopped
1 teaspoon oil
1 garlic clove, crushed
8oz (225g) [dry weight] orange
   lentils
½ teaspoon turmeric
½ teaspoon garam masala
1 × 7oz (200g) can tomatoes
½ pint (300ml) vegetable stock
salt and freshly ground black
   pepper
1 tablespoon chopped flat leaf
   parsley

Vegetable chilli

SERVES 4
PER SERVING:
187 KCAL/1.4G FAT

1 × 14oz (400g) can tomatoes

8oz (225g) can red kidney
    beans, washed and drained

1 teaspoon tomato purée

2 teaspoons oil-free sweet pickle
    or Branston

1 garlic clove, crushed

1 eating apple, peeled and
    chopped

1 onion, chopped

4oz (100g) broad beans

4oz (100g) peas

4oz (100g) carrots, chopped

4oz (100g) potatoes, peeled and
    chopped

1 teaspoon chilli powder

3 chillies, seeded and finely
    chopped

4fl oz (120ml) vegetable stock

1 bay leaf

The simplest of recipes, this is ideal for entertaining, or you could make a large batch and freeze in single portions.

Place all the ingredients in a saucepan and cover with a lid. Simmer for 1 hour over a low heat, stirring occasionally. Remove the lid and continue to cook until the liquid is reduced and the mixture is of a thick consistency.

Serve on a bed of boiled rice.

Stir-fried vegetables with ginger and sesame marinade

To make the ginger juice, use unpeeled root ginger. Grate the ginger and squeeze out as much of the juice as possible.

Heat the oil in a wok and quickly fry the onion until soft. Add the mange tout and cook for about 1 minute, stirring continuously to stop them from going brown. Add the red pepper and cook for another 3 minutes. Add the beansprouts and Chinese cabbage and cook until both look tender, stirring from time to time.

Meanwhile, make the marinade by mixing all the ingredients together thoroughly. Pour over the vegetables and bring the mixture back to the boil. Cover with a lid, turn the heat down and cook for a further 3–4 minutes to finish cooking the vegetables.

Serve straight away on a bed of boiled rice.

SERVES 4
PER SERVING:
140 KCAL/5.5G FAT

- 1 1/2 tablespoons sunflower oil
- 1 onion, cut in half and shredded
- 12oz (350g) mange tout, topped and tailed
- 1 large red pepper, seeded and cut into strips
- 10oz (275g) mung beansprouts
- 1 medium Chinese cabbage, shredded

for the marinade
- 3 tablespoons fresh ginger juice
- 3 teaspoons arrowroot
- 3 tablespoons tamari
- 1 teaspoon toasted sesame oil
- 3fl oz (75ml) light stock or water

Trio pepper pizza

SERVES 6
PER SERVING:
216 KCAL/1.1G FAT

8oz (225g) white bread flour
1 teaspoon salt
2 teaspoons dried yeast
$\frac{1}{4}$ pint (150ml) warm water
4 tablespoons tomato passata
1 red onion, finely chopped
$\frac{1}{2}$ each red, yellow and green
    pepper, finely sliced
1 tablespoon chopped fresh
    mixed herbs
1 teaspoon sea salt
8 cherry tomatoes, halved

A colourful family dish that is quick and easy to prepare. You can vary the toppings – try mushrooms, diced courgette and aubergine.

Most pizza bases contain fat, but this recipe shows you how to make a successful base without using any fat.

Sift the flour and salt into a large mixing bowl.

Blend the yeast with the water until the yeast has dissolved. Make a well in the centre of the flour and add the liquid. Stir with a knife to bring the dough together. Turn out on to a floured surface and knead until smooth. Cover with a damp cloth and leave for 10 minutes.

Preheat the oven to 200°C, 400°F, Gas Mark 6.

Knead the dough again. Roll it out into a large circle and place on a baking sheet.

Spoon the tomato passata over the base, leaving a border around the edge. Arrange the onions, peppers and herbs on top and sprinkle with the salt.

Bake in the oven for 20 minutes.

Sweetcorn and potato cakes with spicy tomato sauce

In a large bowl mix together the potato, vegetable stock and sweetcorn. Add the onions, parsley and season with nutmeg and salt and black pepper. Shape the potato mixture into 8 round patties.

Place the flour, egg white and breadcrumbs in individual shallow dishes. Dip the potato cakes into the flour, then into the beaten egg and finally the breadcrumbs until well coated. Chill for at least 30 minutes.

To make the sauce, place the vegetable stock, onion and garlic in a small pan, cover and cook over a low heat for about 5 minutes until the onion is soft. Add the remaining ingredients and simmer for 10 minutes.

To cook the potato cakes, line the grill tray with foil and very lightly grease (using no more than $1/4$ teaspoon of oil). Cook the potato cakes under a preheated grill for about 3 minutes on each side, turning once.

Serve the potato cakes with the tomato sauce.

SERVES 4
PER SERVING:
244 KCAL/1.6G FAT

1lb (450g) potatoes, cooked and mashed
1 tablespoon vegetable stock
16oz (400g) frozen sweetcorn
4 spring onions, chopped
2 tablespoons chopped fresh parsley
a little nutmeg
2 tablespoons seasoned flour
1 egg white, lightly beaten
4 tablespoons dried wholemeal breadcrumbs
salt and freshly ground black pepper

for the sauce
2 tablespoons vegetable stock
1 small onion, chopped
1 garlic clove, crushed
1 × 14oz (400g) can chopped tomatoes
1 teaspoon wholegrain mustard
1 teaspoon chilli sauce

Mushroom filo triangles

MAKES 8 TRIANGLES
PER TRIANGLE:
154 KCAL / 6.4G FAT

1lb (450g) mushrooms, finely
    chopped
1 onion, chopped
1–2 garlic cloves, crushed
¼ pint (150ml) vegetable stock
2 tablespoons fresh
    breadcrumbs
1 tablespoon chopped fresh
    tarragon or parsley
pinch of nutmeg
8 sheets filo pastry approx.
    7–8in (18–20cm) wide
    × 14in (36cm) long
1 egg
1 tablespoon milk
2 tablespoons sesame seeds
salt and freshly ground black
    pepper
salad to garnish

Raw filo pastry contains very little fat. It is only when it is brushed with butter or oil that it becomes a high-fat option. When using filo pastry, take care to cover any sheets you are not using with a damp cloth, since this pastry becomes dry if left uncovered.

The quantities in this recipe can be halved, if you wish, or any extra triangles can be stored in an airtight plastic box, frozen and reheated when required. If you freeze them, try to avoid knocking the box too much while it is in the freezer, as the triangles are fragile and break easily when frozen.

Serve 1 triangle per person for a starter or 2 per person for lunch.

Preheat the oven to 200°C, 400°F, Gas Mark 6.

Place the mushrooms, onion, garlic and stock in a pan and cook gently until the vegetables are tender, then raise the heat, stirring frequently, until all the liquid has evaporated and mixture is dry.

Stir in sufficient breadcrumbs to make the mixture firm, add the chopped tarragon or parsley and season with a pinch of nutmeg and salt and black pepper to taste. Allow to cool.

Cut the sheets of filo pastry in half lengthways. Take 2 pieces of the pastry and cover the remainder with a damp cloth. Lay the 2 pieces on top of each other to form a strip, and brush very lightly with water all around the edges. Divide the mushroom mixture into 8 portions and place a portion on one end of the strip. Fold one corner of the pastry over to the long side to form a triangle. Press the sides down to seal them, then fold the triangle over again. Repeat with the remaining filo sheets.

Beat the egg with the milk. Brush the triangles with the egg and milk and sprinkle with sesame seeds. Bake in the oven for 20–25 minutes or until golden brown. Garnish with salad and serve warm.

The easiest vegetable pie ever

As the name suggests, this vegetable pie is foolproof. It can be made in individual pie dishes or served as a hearty centrepiece.

Preheat the oven to 200°C, 400°F, Gas Mark 6.

Bring a large pan of water to the boil, add the frozen vegetables and return to the boil. Cook for 3–4 minutes. Drain, reserving $1/2$ pint (300ml) of the cooking liquid. Place the vegetables in an ovenproof pie dish.

Mix the cornflour with a little of the milk to form a paste, then stir in the remaining milk and the reserved vegetable water. Crumble the stock cube into the liquid. Cook gently in a saucepan, stirring continuously, until the sauce has thickened. Alternatively, cook in a microwave on High for 3–4 minutes, whisking once or twice during the cooking time. Stir in the cheese and season well.

Pour the sauce over the vegetables. Brush each sheet of filo with a little oil, scrunch up slightly and place on top of the vegetables. Repeat until all the vegetables are covered. Bake in the oven for 20 minutes or until the pastry is golden.

Serve with new potatoes and salad.

SERVES 4
PER SERVING:
260 KCAL/5.7G FAT

1 × 1lb 11oz (750g) bag frozen casserole mixed vegetables
6oz (175g) frozen cauliflower
4oz (100g) frozen peas
3 tablespoons cornflour
$1/2$ pint (300ml) skimmed milk
$1/2$ vegetable stock cube
2 $1/2$oz (65g) half-fat vegetarian Cheddar cheese
4–5 sheets filo pastry
2 teaspoons sunflower oil
salt and freshly ground black pepper

Sweet pepper and mushroom frittata

A frittata is like a large omelette filled with cooked vegetables, started on the top of the stove and then finished under a hot grill.

Beat the eggs with salt and black pepper and add 3 tablespoons of water.

Dry-fry the peppers, onion, garlic and mushrooms in a non-stick pan for about 5 minutes until softened. Remove from the pan with a slotted spoon and leave the pan to reheat for a few moments.

Pour the egg mixture into the pan, let the base cook slightly, then spoon the vegetables and cheese over the egg base. Cover with a lid, turn the heat down and leave to cook for about 7 minutes until the mixture has risen and set. Place under a preheated hot grill until golden brown.

Loosen the edges with a spatula and turn out. Serve hot or cold with broad beans and new potatoes.

SERVES 4
PER SERVING:
179 KCAL/11.6G FAT

6 eggs
1 small green and 1 small red pepper, seeded and sliced
1 onion, sliced
2 garlic cloves, crushed
8oz (225g) closed cup mushrooms
3 tablespoons grated Parmesan cheese
salt and freshly ground black pepper

Butterbean and pumpkin fricasée with asparagus

SERVES 4
PER SERVING:
176 KCAL/1.4G FAT

1 × 14oz (400g) can butter
  beans
2 garlic cloves, finely chopped
2 onions, finely chopped
1 tablespoon vegetable bouillon
  powder
1 teaspoon ground coriander
1 wineglass white wine
2 teaspoons chopped fresh
  rosemary
12oz (350g) pumpkin, peeled
  and diced into 1in (2.5cm)
  pieces
8oz (225g) baby leeks, cut into
  1in (2.5cm) pieces
4oz (100g) asparagus tips
3 tablespoons low-fat fromage
  frais
salt and freshly ground black
  pepper

This rich supper dish is an ideal standby dish for that unexpected instant meal. If fresh pumpkin is unavailable, use butternut squash or even sweet potatoes.

In a non-stick wok, dry fry the onion and garlic for 2–3 minutes until soft. Add the bouillon powder, coriander and white wine and stir well. Bring to the boil and add the rosemary, pumpkin and leeks. Lay the asparagus on top. Cover with a lid and simmer for 10 minutes.

Test the pumpkin, it should be tender when cooked. If the pumpkin is cooked, remove the pan from the heat and stir in the fromage frais. Season with salt and pepper.

Serve with boiled rice or potatoes.

Rice

There are many varieties of rice, mainly Asian in origin, which forms the second most important food to wheat.

After harvesting, the whole kernels are processed through a cleaning schedule which, as well as removing the outer husk, removes the inedible surface starch. We are then left with brown rice which still contains its outer bran layer. If the rice is polished and cleaned again, the bran layer is removed along with the germ to leave white grain rice. Both brown and white rice can then be steam treated or par-cooked and then dried to form what is known as easy cook rice.

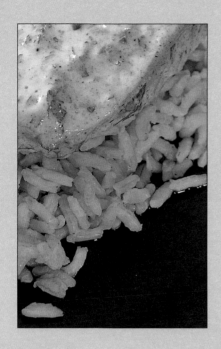

Common varieties

American long-grain rice Available white or brown. Each grain has a long narrow kernel, 4–5 times longer than its width. It is a good flavoursome grain. The grains cook very loosely and remain separated after cooking.

Basmati Available white or brown. Grown in the foothills of the Himalayas, this thin grain has a light aromatic flavour. Shorter than American long-grain rice, it becomes fluffy during cooking. It can be soaked in advance to withstand long cooking.

Easy cook Available white or brown. This is par-cooked by a steam process and then dried. It cooks much more quickly than other forms of rice and produces loose, separate grains.

Thai fragrant rice Available white. A sweet, fragrant rice that becomes slightly sticky during cooking, with the grains tending to clump together. It produces a light, fluffy texture.

Arborio and carnoroli Available white. These Italian short, broad grains are used in risotto dishes because of their ability to absorb liquid, which plumps up the grain. The grains become creamy and slightly sticky during cooking and give a nutty flavour.

Calasparra Spanish in origin, this is a hardy grain suitable for paellas. The grains remain firm during cooking and produce a slightly sticky texture.

Wild Not a grain as such but a grass harvested from the lakeland shores of Minnesota in the United States. It requires cooking for up to 50 minutes and has a nutty, earthy flavour and a chewy texture.

Red Camareine This is a reddish-brown grain which comes from the wetlands of Camareine in France. It takes on a similar appearance to wild rice during cooking and has a woody, nutty flavour and slightly sticky texture.

Pudding rice These short, fat, smooth grains are used in puddings as a thickening agent and produce a creamy, smooth texture.

Flaked rice These are shavings of rice and are used in puddings. This rice cooks quickly and produces a smooth, light texture.

Other rice products

Sake A Japanese rice wine similar to a very dry sherry. It is used in savoury dishes.

Mirin This is similar to Sake but slightly sweeter and is used in marinades and dressings.

Rice vinegar Available clear, red, yellow or black, this has a slightly sharp flavour and is used in stir-fries, dressings and marinades.

Rice noodles These white dry threads vary in thickness. They only need to be soaked in boiling water to reconstitute and are used in stir-fries or steamed dishes.

Ground rice This is used as a thickening agent in puddings and desserts and is gluten free.

Rice flour A very fine flour used for Chinese dim sum (dumplings). It is gluten free and can be used as a substitute for wheat flour.

Rice paper Edible baking parchment used for individual cakes and nougart.

Fat-free fluffy rice

SERVES 8
PER SERVING:
201 KCAL/0.3G FAT

1 lb (450g) [dry weight] long-
    grain or basmati rice
1 heaped teaspoon salt
4–5 cardamom seeds (optional)
$\frac{1}{2}$ teaspoon turmeric (optional)

Rinse the rice and place in a large non-stick pan. Fill the pan with cold water. Add the salt, cardamom seeds and turmeric (if using). Bring to the boil, stirring occasionally to prevent the rice from clumping, and simmer rapidly for 10–12 minutes.

Place the rice in a colander and rinse well under the cold tap until the residue salt has been washed away.

Return the rice to the pan, cover with a lid and leave on a very low heat for at least half an hour, turning the rice occasionally with a non-scratch spoon to aid cooking. The rice will be ready when it is fluffy and soft to bite. If it is not quite cooked, add a tablespoon of water, stir, then replace the lid and cook for a little longer. Remove the cardamom seeds (if using) before serving.

Savoury rice

This basic savoury rice can be served hot or cold with a light citrus dressing.

Heat the base of a saucepan and add the onion. Lower the heat, cover the pan and cook for a few minutes, stirring occasionally, until the onion is lightly coloured. Stir in the rice, add the chicken stock and bring to the boil. Season lightly with salt and pepper then cover the pan and simmer over a moderate heat for about 10 minutes until almost tender.

When the rice is almost tender, add the tomatoes, peas, sweetcorn, tarragon and half the parsley. Mix well and continue cooking for a further 3–5 minutes. If necessary, add a little more stock while the rice is cooking to prevent it from drying out, or, if too much stock is left when the rice is cooked, raise the heat and boil the stock away, stirring frequently to prevent the rice from sticking to the pan.

When the rice and vegetables are cooked, pile into a hot dish. Just before serving, sprinkle the remainder of the parsley over the top.

SERVES 4
PER SERVING:
228 KCAL/2.5G FAT

1 large onion, finely chopped
2 garlic cloves, crushed
6oz (175g) [dry weight] easy cook rice
3/4 pint (450ml) chicken stock
2 tomatoes, skinned, seeded and coarsely chopped
4oz (100g) frozen peas
4oz (100g) frozen sweetcorn or canned sweetcorn, drained
2 teaspoons chopped fresh tarragon
1 tablespoon chopped fresh parsley
salt and freshly ground black pepper

Wild mushroom risotto

SERVES 4
PER SERVING:
236 KCAL / 2.3G FAT

1 medium onion, finely chopped
2 garlic cloves, crushed
good pinch of saffron
8oz (225g) [dry weight] arborio
   or risotto rice
1 pint (2.2 litres) vegetable
   stock
½ glass white wine
1 lb (450g) fresh mixed wild
   mushrooms
2 tablespoons virtually fat free
   fromage frais
1 tablespoon chopped fresh
   chives
salt and freshly ground black
   pepper

Delicate wild mushrooms in a golden saffron risotto, flavoured with white wine – a delight!

In a non-stick pan, dry-fry the onion and garlic until soft. Add the saffron and the rice and gradually stir in the stock and wine. Each time the stock is absorbed, stir in a little more. Repeat until all the stock is absorbed. Add the mushrooms and cover with a lid for 2 minutes in order to lightly steam the mushrooms. Fold in the fromage frais and remove from heat. Season with salt and pepper, add a drop more wine if the rice needs to loosen slightly.

     Just before serving, sprinkle with the chopped chives, and garnish with green salad.

Thai pilaff

This fragrant rice, spiked with lime and sweetened with pineapple, goes well with chicken or fish. If you wish, you could add some dry-fried meat or prawns to the rice before you place it in the oven.

Preheat the oven to 190°C, 375°F, Gas Mark 5.

In a non-stick pan dry-fry the onion and garlic until soft. Add the rice and stock, stir in the remaining ingredients. Transfer to an ovenproof dish or casserole. Cover and place in the oven for 30 minutes.

Remove from the oven and serve immediately with grilled chicken or steamed fish.

SERVES 4
PER SERVING:
302 KCAL/1.3G FAT

1 medium onion, finely diced
1 garlic clove, crushed
10oz (275g) [dry weight] Thai fragrant rice
1¼ pints (750ml) chicken stock
1 red chilli, seeded and finely chopped
zest and juice of 2 limes
1 × 14oz (400g) can pineapple chunks in juice, drained
1 teaspoon cumin ground
6 plum tomatoes, skinned, seeded and chopped
2 tablespoons chopped fresh parsley
salt and freshly ground black pepper

Red beans and rice

SERVES 4
PER SERVING:
254 KCAL/2.2G FAT

2 medium onions, chopped
2 garlic cloves, crushed
4oz (100g) [dry weight] long-
    grain rice
4 celery sticks, chopped
1/2 bulb fennel, chopped
1/2 pint (300ml) vegetable stock
2 × 14oz (2 × 400g) can kidney
    beans, drained and rinsed
2 × 14oz (2 × 400g) can
    chopped tomatoes
2 tablespoons tomato purée
1/2 teaspoon cayenne pepper
2 teaspoons chopped fresh
    thyme
salt and freshly ground black
    pepper
a little low-fat natural yogurt

An American cowboy treat. The rice thickens this rich tomato casserole.

In a non-stick pan, dry-fry the onion and garlic until soft. Add the rice, celery and fennel. Stir in the stock. Add the drained kidney beans, tomatoes, tomato purée, cayenne pepper and thyme. Season with salt and black pepper. Cover and simmer gently for 20 minutes.

Remove the lid and stir well. Continue cooking until all the liquid is absorbed.

Place in individual bowls, drizzle with yogurt and serve hot with crusty bread.

Smoked ham and prawn jambalaya

Jambalaya arrived in New Orleans from Spain in the late 1700s. The name probably comes from the Spanish word for ham.

Dry-fry the onion and garlic in a non-stick pan until soft. Add the celery, tomatoes, tomato purée and chilli and simmer for 10 minutes. Add the rice, smoked ham, prawns, grated nutmeg and herbs and simmer for a further 2–3 minutes, making sure the ham and prawns are heated through. Season to taste.

Serve with a side salad.

SERVES 4
PER SERVING:
225 KCAL/3.1G FAT

2 medium onions, chopped
2 garlic cloves, crushed
2 celery sticks, diced
1 × 14oz (400g) can chopped tomatoes
2 tablespoons tomato purée
1 red chilli, seeded and finely chopped
8oz (225g) cooked long grain rice
8oz (225g) smoked ham, cut into bite-sized pieces
8oz (225g) peeled and cooked prawns
1 tablespoon chopped fresh mixed herbs (e.g. chives, parsley and tarragon)
freshly grated nutmeg
salt and freshly ground black pepper

Leek and sun-dried tomato risotto cakes

SERVES 4
PER SERVING:
262 KCAL/3.6G FAT

1 large onion, finely chopped

2 garlic cloves, crushed

8oz (225g) [dry weight] risotto
rice

1 pints (1.2 litres) vegetable
stock

2 leeks, finely chopped

4 sun-dried tomatoes, finely
chopped

1 tablespoon chopped fresh
chervil

2 tablespoons plain flour

salt and freshly ground black
pepper

These risotto cakes can be made in advance and refrigerated or frozen. Defrost at room temperature before reheating.

In a non-stick pan dry-fry the onion and garlic until soft. Add the rice, and gradually stir in the stock a little at a time until most of the stock has been absorbed. Stir in the chopped leeks, tomatoes, chervil and remaining stock. Season with salt and pepper and allow to cool.

Mould the risotto mixture into fish cake shapes, allowing 1 large or 2 small cakes per person. Use the flour to prevent them from sticking to your hands. Shape with a palette knife.

Preheat a non-stick frying pan. Dry-fry the risotto cakes for 2–3 minutes on each side until lightly golden.

Serve hot with a mixed salad.

Dolmades
(stuffed vine leaves)

This can be served as a main course for 6 people or as a starter for 12 people. You can freeze the stuffing and any leftover vine leaves.

Prepare the vine leaves according to the packet instructions. In a non-stick frying pan, dry-fry the onion until soft. Add the cooked rice, paprika and cayenne pepper and stir well.

Remove the pan from the heat. Stir in the sultanas, mint and tomatoes. Season well.

Place a spoonful of the mixture in the centre of a vine leaf, fold the side in and roll into a cigar shape. Repeat with the remaining leaves and mixture, allowing 2–4 dolmades per person.

Place the dolmades in a steamer and steam for 8–10 minutes. Serve with salad and chopped cucumber mixed with low-fat natural yogurt, or with a hot tomato sauce.

MAKES 16 DOLMADES
PER DOLMADE:
34 KCAL/0.3G FAT

1 × 12oz (350g) packet vine
    leaves
1 medium onion, finely chopped
8oz (225g) cooked rice
1 teaspoon paprika
$\frac{1}{4}$ teaspoon cayenne pepper
2oz (50g) sultanas
1 teaspoon chopped fresh mint
3 tomatoes, seeded, skinned and
    chopped
salt and freshly ground black
    pepper

Vegetable rice bake

SERVES 4
PER SERVING:
367 KCAL/8.4G FAT

1 teaspoon olive oil
1 small onion, sliced
1 red pepper, sliced
2 courgettes, sliced
1 small aubergine, cubed
225g (8oz) mushrooms, sliced
1 × 400g (14oz) can chopped
     tomatoes with herbs
2 tablespoons tomato purée
1lb (450g) cooked brown rice
2 small eggs, beaten
1 tablespoon sunflower seeds
salt and freshly ground black
     pepper

Pre-heat the oven to 180°C, 350°F, Gas Mark 4.

Heat the oil in a large pan and fry the onions for 3–4 minutes until softened. Add the red pepper, courgettes, aubergine and mushrooms to the pan and add 3 tablespoons water. Cover and cook gently until the vegetables begin to soften. Stir in the tomatoes and tomato purée, bring to the boil and simmer for 10 minutes. Season to taste with salt and pepper. Pour into a shallow ovenproof dish.

Place the cooked rice in a mixing bowl, add the eggs and sunflower seeds. Season well and mix until combined. Spread over the tomato mixture and level the top. Bake in the oven for 30 minutes until the top is golden brown.

Paella

Traditionally, paella is cooked in a large shallow pan that has handles on both sides. This recipe will fill a 12–14in (30–35cm) pan. However, you can easily use a large shallow casserole or dish, or perhaps you might find it easier to cook in two smaller dishes.

The correct rice to use for paella is Valencia or Calasparra rice, but as this is not always easy to find, I use an Italian arborio or risotto rice.

Most supermarkets and many fishmongers now sell squid ready prepared. However, if you are unable to find them, I have given instructions on how to prepare them at the end of this recipe. Squid and mussels are a characteristic feature of a paella, so if you haven't eaten them before, do try them.

Preheat the oven (if using) to 170°C, 325°F, Gas Mark 3.

Place the saffron in a small bowl and cover with 2–3 tablespoons of boiling water. Leave until required.

Cut the prepared squid into rings and any tentacles in half. Remove the membrane from the outside of the monkfish (if using). Cut through the fish from the thin side and cut away from the bone. Cut each piece into two lengthways then cut into medallions about ½in (1cm) thick.

Wash the mussels in several changes of water. Discard any which are damaged or which stay open when immersed in cold water. Scrub them well. Scrape off any small barnacles and pull off the 'beard' (the long strand which attaches the mussels to the rocks). Wash well again.

If you wish, you can remove the heads from the prawns but it does add to the traditional look of the dish if you leave them on.

Dry-fry the chicken in a preheated pan until coloured. Remove from the pan. Add the onion, leek, garlic and the stock to the pan and simmer gently for 5–6 minutes until the onion starts to soften.

SERVES 6
PER SERVING:
417 KCAL/8.8G FAT

2 good pinches saffron strands or 1 small sachet powdered saffron

10oz (275g) prepared squid tails or 1lb (450g) monkfish or 10oz (275g) fillet of other firm fish such as cod or halibut

1lb (450g) mussels

6–8 large prawns in shells

4 skinned chicken breasts

1 medium onion, finely chopped

1 medium leek, finely sliced

4 garlic gloves, crushed

1½ pints (900ml) fish or chicken stock

12oz (350g) [dry weight] arborio rice

1 medium red pepper, finely diced

4 medium tomatoes, diced

4oz (100g) frozen peas

1½–2 level teaspoons salt

freshly ground black pepper

chopped fresh parsley

2 lemons

Continued on page 286

Wash the rice and stir into the stock. Add the red pepper, chopped tomatoes, peas and the saffron-coloured liquid. Mix well and season to taste with salt and black pepper. Stir in the squid and fish and arrange the chicken, mussels and prawns evenly on top. Cover with foil or a tight-fitting lid. If you wish, you can carry on cooking the paella over a gentle heat or on top of the barbecue, but you must watch it carefully to see if it needs more stock or water to prevent it from boiling dry. I prefer to put it in the oven to ensure that the chicken is well cooked. If choosing the latter method, place in a preheated oven at 170°C, 325°F, Gas Mark 3 and cook for 30–35 minutes until the rice and chicken are tender and liquid has been absorbed. It is important NOT to stir the rice while it is in the oven or it will cook unevenly. To test if it is cooked, take a grain or two carefully from the centre of the pan.

When the paella is cooked, remove it from the oven or the heat. Cover it with damp greaseproof paper and leave for 4–5 minutes.

Cut the lemons into wedges. Just before serving, sprinkle the chopped parsley over the dish and garnish with the lemon wedges. If you are using a pan with handles, wrap a napkin around each one before taking the pan to the table.

Preparing squid

Pull the head and tentacles away from the tail section. Cut the tentacles just above the eyes and discard the rest of the body. Cut out or squeeze out the small round cartilage from the base of the tentacles and discard. Cut each piece in two. Remove any reddish-brown membrane from the outside of the tail and discard. Cut about 1/2in (1cm) piece off the end of each tail. Run cold water through the tube to clean the inside thoroughly and wash the end piece of each tail. Cut the tails into rings. The squid is now ready to use.

Veggie biriani

SERVES 4
PER SERVING:
306 KCAL/3.6G FAT

1 teaspoon sunflower oil

$^1/_2$ teaspoon cumin seeds

$^1/_4$ teaspoon crushed coriander
  seeds

1 small onion, chopped

1 garlic clove, crushed

$^1/_2$ teaspoon turmeric

8oz (225g) potatoes, diced

8oz (225g) carrots, diced

1 pint (600ml) vegetable stock

8oz (225g) cauliflower florets

4oz (100g) green beans topped
  and tailed and cut into 2in
  (5cm) lengths

8oz (225g) [dry weight] brown
  basmati rice

Heat the oil in a large pan, add the cumin and coriander seeds and cook for a few seconds until the seeds start to crackle. Add the onion and garlic and cook for about 5 minutes until they begin to soften. Add the turmeric, potatoes, carrots and about 6 tablespoons of the stock, cover and cook for about 5 minutes.

Add the cauliflower, green beans, rice and the remainder of the stock. Bring to the boil, stir, then reduce the heat. Cover and simmer for 30 minutes until the rice is tender and the stock has been absorbed. If the rice is not tender but the stock has been absorbed, add a little more water and cook for a few more minutes. If the rice is too wet, increase the heat and boil off the excess stock.

Pasta

All pasta is cut from the same wheat, but there is a vast selection of shapes. Generally, the shape of pasta should correspond with the style of the sauce it is served with. However, this is no longer a hard and fast rule, and if you cannot find the type of pasta called for, then use something similar. Ring the changes and experiment with different shapes. Some recipes, though, are traditional combinations such as spaghetti bolognese or lasagne.

Here are some common types of pasta. *Bucatini:* long thick spaghetti with a thin hollow centre; *Conchiglie:* shells; *Fettucine:* long flat noodles; *Fusilli:* corkscrews; *Lasagne:* wide flat sheets; *Linguine:* flat spaghetti; *Penne:* quills (thin tubes); *Ravioli:* stuffed squares or circles; *Rigatoni:* ridged tubes; *Spaghetti:* long thin strands; *Spaghettini:* long thin spaghetti; *Zite:* medium tubes.

As a guideline, use 1oz (25g) dry weight pasta per person when serving as a starter and 2oz (50g) dry weight pasta per person for a main course, although non-dieters may have more.

It is a tradition in Italy to serve ample Parmesan cheese with many pasta dishes. Parmesan cheese should be used with moderation, as 4oz (100g) provides 452 kcal and 32.7g fat. A $\frac{1}{4}$oz (4 teaspoons/10g) portion, grated, provides 45 kcal and 3.3g fat.

Chicken or turkey tagliatelle with ginger

SERVES 4
PER SERVING:
447 KCAL/6.2G FAT

4 rashers lean smoked bacon,
 trimmed
4 chicken or turkey breasts,
 skinned and cubed
1 onion, chopped
8oz (225g) mushrooms
1 piece root ginger (approx.
 1–2in/2–5cm square),
 peeled and grated
1 medium-sized jar traditional
 Ragù
8oz (225g) [dry weight]
 tagliatelle
2 tablespoons low-fat natural
 yogurt

Chop the bacon into small squares and dry-fry in a large non-stick saucepan. Add the chicken or turkey and dry-fry for 5 minutes. Add the onion and mushrooms to the pan and dry-fry. Add the root ginger and cook for 2 minutes, then add the Ragù. Stir and heat through.

Place a lid on the saucepan to keep the sauce warm while you prepare the tagliatelle.

Cook the tagliatelle in a large pan of boiling salted water until tender. Drain. Just before serving mix in the yogurt to either the sauce or the drained tagliatelle for a creamy effect.

Serve the chicken or turkey and sauce on the bed of tagliatelle.

Turkey chilli pasta

This recipe is similar to a turkey bolognese, with the pasta shells incorporated in the sauce. However, if you wish, you could cook and serve the pasta separately.

In a large non-stick saucepan, dry-fry the turkey mince with the onion and until the mince changes colour and forms a firm consistency. Add the remaining ingredients and simmer for 20–25 minutes until the pasta is cooked.

Serve hot with a side salad or crusty bread.

SERVES 4
PER SERVING:
247 KCAL/1.8G FAT

12oz (350g) turkey mince
1 medium onion, chopped
2 garlic cloves, crushed
1 red chilli, seeded and finely chopped
1 × 14oz (400g) can chopped tomatoes
2 teaspoons freeze-dried fines herbes
2 tablespoons tomato purée
$\frac{1}{2}$ pint (300ml) chicken stock
6oz (175g) [dry weight] pasta shells
salt and freshly ground black pepper
1 tablespoon chopped fresh parsley

Crunchy bacon and spaghetti

SERVES 4
PER SERVING:
261 KCAL/2.6G FAT

8 thin rashers lean smoked
   bacon
8oz (225g) [dry weight]
   wholemeal spaghetti
1 × 14oz (400g) can chopped
   tomatoes
8oz (225g) mushrooms, thinly
   sliced
8oz (225g) frozen sweetcorn
2 tablespoons Branston pickle
salt and freshly ground black
   pepper
1 tablespoon chopped fresh
   basil to garnish

In this recipe you can cook the bacon in advance and then leave it to cool on kitchen paper to allow the fat to be absorbed.

Trim any fat from the bacon. Grill the bacon on both sides.

Cook the spaghetti in boiling salted water in a saucepan for 10 minutes. While the spaghetti is cooking, place the tomatoes in a saucepan and add the mushrooms, sweetcorn and pickle. Cook on a moderate heat then allow to simmer for 10 minutes.

Wipe off any traces of fat from the bacon with kitchen paper, then snip the bacon into bite-sized pieces (using scissors) and add to the tomato mixture. Season to taste.

By the time the spaghetti is cooked, the bacon and tomato mixture will be ready to serve. Drain the spaghetti, place on a serving plate and top with the bacon and tomato mixture. Just before serving, sprinkle with the basil.

Rich spaghetti bolognese

This classic Italian dish consists of lean minced beef in a rich herby sauce. Traditionally, the beef and onions are fried in olive oil. In this low-fat version, we dry-fry the minced beef to release the fat. Adding the sundried tomatoes gives a strong, robust flavour, but make sure you use the dried ones in packets, since the ones in jars contain oil.

Dry-fry the minced beef in a non-stick pan until it starts to change colour. Remove the mince from the pan and wipe out the pan with kitchen paper. Return the meat to the pan, add the garlic and onion and continue cooking for a further 2–3 minutes, stirring the ingredients well. Add the carrots and crumble the stock cubes over the top. Add the tomatoes, tomato purée, herbs and sundried tomatoes and mix well to allow the stock cubes to dissolve. Reduce the heat to a gentle simmer, season, cover with a lid, and continue to cook for 30 minutes until the sauce thickens.

Meanwhile, bring a large pan of salted water to the boil. Add the spaghetti and cook for 20–25 minutes until the spaghetti is soft but slightly firm in the centre. Drain through a colander.

Arrange the spaghetti on warmed serving plates and pour the sauce on top. Garnish with fresh herbs.

SERVES 4
PER SERVING:
521 KCAL/12.8G

1lb (450g) lean minced beef
2 garlic cloves, crushed
1 large onion, finely diced
2 medium carrots, finely diced
2 beef stock cubes
2 × 14oz (2 × 400g) cans
    chopped tomatoes
2 tablespoons tomato purée
1 tablespoon chopped fresh
    mixed herbs (oregano,
    marjoram, basil, parsley)
8 sundried tomatoes, finely
    chopped
8 oz (225g) [dry weight]
    spaghetti
salt and freshly ground black
    pepper
chopped fresh herbs to garnish

Fusilli with smoked duck and green pepper

A quick and rather special pasta dish. Duck benefits from being cooked slightly pink so that it retains its moisture and flavour.

Cook the fusilli in salted boiling water until al dente, then drain.

Meanwhile, prepare the duck breasts by cutting into fine slices. Preheat a non-stick frying pan. Add the duck, pepper and garlic. Cook quickly, turning with a wooden spatula, for 2–3 minutes until the duck is sealed. Add the ginger, soy sauce and lemon juice. Season with salt and pepper.

Add the cooked pasta to the pan and combine with the duck. Serve immediately.

SERVES 4
PER SERVING:
253 KCAL/4.4G FAT

8oz (225g) [dry weight] fusilli pasta
2 × 4oz (2 × 100g) skinned duck breasts
2 green peppers, seeded and finely sliced
2 garlic cloves, crushed
1 tablespoon chopped fresh ginger
2 tablespoons light soy sauce
juice of 1 lemon
salt and freshly ground black pepper

Pasta with prawns

SERVES 4
PER SERVING:
225 KCAL/1.6G FAT

4 spring onions, finely chopped

1 green pepper, seeded and
diced

2 small courgettes, sliced

2 fresh tomatoes, finely chopped

1 small green chilli, finely
chopped (optional)

2 garlic cloves, finely chopped

1 × 11oz (295g) can Campbell's
condensed half-fat mushroom
soup

4oz (100g) peeled prawns

2 tablespoons chopped fresh
coriander

8oz (225g) [dry weight] penne
or rigatoni pasta tubes

In a wok or non-stick frying pan, dry-fry the onions, green pepper, courgettes, tomato, chilli and garlic until soft. Pour the mushroom soup into the pan (do not dilute), and add the prawns and half the chopped coriander. Cook on a low heat until heated through.

Meanwhile, cook the pasta in salted boiling water until tender. Drain and add to the sauce mixture. Mix well to combine all the ingredients.

Transfer the mixture onto warmed plates, and sprinkle with the rest of the chopped coriander. Serve with a green salad.

Pasta twirls with scallops and bacon

Trim all the fat from the bacon and discard. Cut the bacon into strips. Dry-fry the bacon in a non-stick pan until almost tender but without colour. Drain off any fat.

Add the garlic and cook for a moment or two. Add the tomatoes, white wine and mushrooms. Season to taste. Bring to the boil and simmer for about 8 minutes.

Add the scallops and continue cooking for a further 1–2 minutes until the mushrooms are tender and the sauce has reduced. Scallops need only a little cooking, just until they become opaque (they are better undercooked than overcooked or they will become tough). In the meantime, cook the pasta according to the instructions. Drain well and stir into the sauce. Pile into a hot serving dish and serve.

SERVES 4
PER SERVING:
205 KCAL/2G FAT

4 lean rashers smoked back
  bacon
1 garlic clove, crushed
2 leeks, thinly sliced
1 × 7oz (200g) can tomatoes
¼ pint (150ml) white wine
6 large mushrooms, diced
6oz (175g) scallops
4oz (100g) [dry weight] pasta
  twirls
salt and freshly ground black
  pepper

Creamy leek and tuna pasta

SERVES 4
PER SERVING:
337 KCAL/2.6G FAT

8oz (225g) [dry weight] pasta
  shapes
1 medium onion, chopped
2 medium leeks, washed and
  finely chopped
1 garlic clove, crushed
2 tablespoons plain flour
$\frac{1}{4}$ pint (150ml) vegetable stock
$\frac{1}{2}$ pint (300ml) skimmed milk
2 teaspoons Dijon mustard
1 × 7oz (200g) can tuna in
  brine, drained
1 tablespoon chopped fresh
  chervil
salt and freshly ground black
  pepper
4 lemon slices or wedges to
  garnish

This pasta dish with a creamy fish sauce is ideal when you have guests round for supper. Try adding a dash of white wine or a few chopped capers to the sauce.

Cook the pasta in boiling salted water until al dente.

Meanwhile, dry-fry the onion and leeks in a non-stick frying pan until soft. Add the garlic, sprinkle the flour over then gradually stir in the stock, making a roux. Cook for 1 minute, stirring well.

Gradually mix in the milk. Add the Dijon mustard and tuna. Simmer for 2–3 minutes on a low heat. Finally, add the chervil and season to taste.

Serve the sauce on a bed of pasta. Garnish with the lemon slices or wedges.

Golden cauliflower pasta

If you adore cauliflower cheese, you'll love this pasta dish which gives a good balance of pasta and cauliflower with a crispy topping.

Cook the pasta shells in boiling salt water until tender. Drain well.

Preheat a non-stick frying pan and dry-fry the onion until soft. Add the garlic, cauliflower and spices and cook for 1 minute, stirring continuously.

Pour the soup into the pan. Rinse out the soup can with the skimmed milk and add to the pan. Simmer gently for 10–15 minutes until the cauliflower is just cooked. Season to taste and sprinkle with parsley.

Add the drained pasta shells and heat through. Pour into a casserole dish and grate the cheese over the top. Place under a hot preheated grill until brown and golden. Serve with a mixed salad.

SERVES 4
PER SERVING:
270 KCAL/3.5G FAT

8oz (225g) [dry weight] pasta shells
1 large onion, finely chopped
2 garlic cloves, crushed
1 small cauliflower, broken into florets
1 teaspoon ground turmeric
1 teaspoon ground cumin
1 × 11oz (295g) can Campbell's condensed half-fat mushroom soup
¼ pint (150ml) skimmed milk
2 tablespoons chopped fresh parsley
2oz (50g) low-fat Cheddar cheese
salt and freshly ground black pepper

Tagliatelle with wild mushrooms

SERVES 4
PER SERVING:
217 KCAL/1.7G FAT

2oz (50g) dried wild mushrooms
1 shallot, finely chopped
1/2 pint (300ml) vegetable stock
1 tablespoon chopped fresh
    thyme
8oz (225g) [dry weight]
    tagliatelle
2 teaspoons Dijon mustard
2–3 tablespoons low-fat natural
    yogurt
1 tablespoon chopped fresh dill
salt and freshly ground black
    pepper

Wash the mushrooms well and place in a saucepan with the shallot, stock and thyme. Bring to the boil. Reduce the heat, cover, and simmer for 20 minutes.

Meanwhile, cook the tagliatelle in boiling salted water until tender. Drain.

Add the mustard to the mushroom mixture, remove from the heat, then stir in the yogurt and dill. Season well and serve with the cooked pasta.

Mushroom pesto

Pesto is a basil paste or sauce made from olive oil, basil garlic and pine nuts. Once the paste is made, simply add to the cooked drained pasta and return the pan to the stove. Heat gently with a little of the cooking liquor from the pasta pan.

Place all the ingredients except the tagliatelle into a food processor and blend until smooth. You may find you need to add the mushrooms in batches, adding more as the mixture blends down. Check the seasoning.

Cook the pasta in boiling salted water until tender. Drain.

Heat the mushroom sauce in a saucepan for 2–3 minutes. Add the cooked pasta, reheat and serve.

SERVES 4
PER SERVING:
104 KCAL/4.1G FAT

1 1/2 lb (675g) chestnut
    mushrooms
3 garlic cloves, crushed
juice of 2 lemons
2 tablespoons light soy sauce
2 teaspoons pesto sauce
1 teaspoon sea salt
freshly ground black pepper
8oz (225g) [dry weight]
    tagliatelle

Lasagne

SERVES 4
PER SERVING:
517 KCAL/21G FAT

1 lb (450g) lean minced beef
2 medium onions, finely
    chopped
2 garlic cloves, crushed
1 medium red pepper, seeded
    and diced
1 tablespoon chopped fresh
    oregano
2 beef stock cubes, made up
    with $\frac{1}{2}$ pint (300ml) water
1 × 14oz (400g) can chopped
    tomatoes
2 tablespoons tomato purée
8oz (225g) 'no pre-cook' lasagne
8–10 large fresh basil leaves

for the topping
$\frac{1}{2}$ pint (300ml) low-fat natural
    yogurt
1 egg, beaten
1 teaspoon English mustard
    powder
1 tablespoon grated Parmesan
    cheese
salt and freshly ground black
    pepper

Preheat the oven to 190°C, 375°F, Gas Mark 5.

Dry-fry the minced beef in a preheated non-stick pan until it starts to change colour. Remove the meat from the pan. Wipe out the pan with kitchen paper and return the meat to the pan. Add the onions and garlic and cook for a further 2–3 minutes until soft, stirring the mixture well. Add the red pepper, oregano, stock, tomatoes and tomato purée and mix well. Reduce the heat to a gentle simmer, season, cover with a lid, and cook for 30 minutes.

Place a thin layer of the sauce in an ovenproof dish. Cover with sheets of lasagne but do not overlap them since they will expand with cooking. Continue layering with the remaining sauce and lasagne sheets, adding a few basil leaves between each layer.

Combine all the topping ingredients and pour over the lasagne mixture.

Place in the oven and cook for 40–45 minutes.

Serve with a crisp mixed salad.

Quick and low-fat courgette lasagne

Preheat the oven to 190°C, 375°F, Gas Mark 5.

Heat the oil in a frying pan and fry the onion until tender. Add the courgettes and green pepper and fry gently for a few more minutes. Add the tomatoes, tomato purée, bouillon powder or vegetable stock cube and dried basil, and bring the mixture to the boil. Break up the tomatoes and simmer for 10 minutes. Season well.

Place a layer of the tomato mixture on the base of a lasagne dish, top with 4 sheets of lasagne, then repeat the tomato layer and the lasagne sheets. Finish with a layer of the tomato mixture.

Whisk the topping ingredients together and pour over the tomato and lasagne mixture. Bake in a preheated oven for 25–30 minutes.

Serve hot or cold with a crisp salad.

SERVES 4
PER SERVING:
161 KCAL/6.1G FAT

1 teaspoon olive oil
1 onion, chopped
8oz (225g) courgettes, diced
1 green pepper, seeded and
   diced finely
1 × 14oz (400g) can tomatoes
2 tablespoons tomato purée
2 teaspoons bouillon powder or
   1 vegetable stock cube
2 teaspoons dried basil
8 'no pre-cook' wholemeal
   lasagne sheets
salt and freshly ground black
   pepper

for the topping
10oz (275g) low-fat natural
   yogurt or fromage frais
1 egg, beaten
1 teaspoon ground cumin

Rigatoni with herb sauce

SERVES 4
PER SERVING:
324 KCAL/4.7G FAT

8oz (225g) [dry weight] rigatoni
pasta
2 garlic cloves, crushed
1 medium onion, finely chopped
½ wineglass white wine
1 teaspoon chopped fresh
thyme
1 teaspoon chopped fresh
rosemary
1 teaspoon chopped fresh
oregano
1 tablespoon chopped fresh
basil
1 tablespoon chopped fresh
parsley
1 tablespoon chopped fresh
chives
½ pint (300ml) skimmed milk
1 vegetable stock cube
1 tablespoon cornflour, blended
with water
2 tablespoons low-fat fromage
frais
4 tablespoons grated Parmesan
salt and freshly ground black
pepper

This wine and fresh herb sauce with rigatoni makes a light and tasty pasta dish. If you wish, you can omit the Parmesan and substitute 4 tablespoons of finely chopped lean cooked ham.

Cook the pasta in boiling salted water, then drain.

Meanwhile, make the sauce by dry-frying the onion and garlic in a non-stick frying pan until soft. Add the wine, herbs, and milk. Bring to the boil, then thicken with the blended cornflour. Beat well to form a smooth sauce.

Remove the pan from the heat and stir in the fromage frais. Season well. Add the cooked pasta. Pour the sauce over and mix well.

Just before serving, sprinkle with the Parmesan.

Chilli pasta bake

This rich tomato bake has a hint of chilli. If you prefer, you can omit the chilli and substitute 1 chopped red pepper.

Preheat the oven to 190°C, 375°F, Gas Mark 5.

Cook the pasta in boiling salted water until tender, then drain.

In a large non-stick saucepan dry-fry the courgette, leeks and garlic for 2–3 minutes. Add the chilli, herbs and passata. Stir in the cooked pasta and season to taste.

Transfer the mixture to an ovenproof dish and sprinkle with Parmesan. Bake in the oven for 30–35 minutes or until golden brown.

Just before serving, drizzle with the yogurt. Serve with a crisp salad or crusty bread.

SERVES 4
PER SERVING:
250 KCAL/3.3G FAT

8oz (225g) [dry weight] pasta shapes
2 courgettes, diced
2 medium leeks, washed and diced
2 garlic cloves, crushed
1 red chilli, seeded and finely chopped
1 tablespoon chopped fresh oregano
1 tablespoon chopped fresh parsley
1 pint (600ml) tomato passata
2 tablespoons grated Parmesan
3 tablespoons low-fat natural yogurt
salt and freshly ground black pepper

Salads

Never before has there been such a variety of salad leaves in the supermarkets, from Iceberg, Lollo Rosso to sweet Romaine and Little Gem. We have become a nation of green leaf experts! Lettuce leaves need no longer mean limp, wilted leaves. We have exciting peppery rocket from Italy, baby spinach and corn salad 'mash' from France, and bunches of fresh herbs that blend and partner many salad leaves.

You can purchase prepacked salad leaves which provide an instant selection of tasty leafy flavours, from green salad to herb salad and now gourmet selection and continental leaves, as well as bunches of fresh watercress. Recently, vegetable tops have been added to salads for colour, and stronger-flavoured leaves such as beetroot tops and turnip tops are full of vitamins and nutrients.

It is very important to serve salad clean and fresh. Wash very carefully in plenty of cold water, then dry with a salad spinner or kitchen paper. Leaves can easily bruise, so handle them with care.

The beauty of salads is the dressing. This can transform a plain vegetable into something quite delicious.

Herby fish salad

SERVES 4
PER SERVING:
184 KCAL / 1.3G FAT

14oz (400g) white fish, skinned
10oz (275g) new potatoes,
   sliced, cooked and cooled
1 × 7oz (200g) can red kidney
   beans, drained and rinsed
1 × 7oz (200g) can sweetcorn,
   drained
1 medium green pepper, seeded
   and diced
freshly ground black pepper

for the dressing
1 tablespoon lemon juice
2 teaspoons dried tarragon or
   dill
1 tablespoon wine vinegar
chopped fresh parsley to garnish

Poach the fish in a covered pan with a little water for
approximately 8 minutes. Remove any bones and flake roughly.
Leave to cool.

Place the sliced potatoes, kidney beans, sweetcorn and diced
pepper in a bowl. Add the fish and season well.

Place the dressing ingredients in a jar and shake vigorously.
Pour over the salad and toss gently until well coated.

Prawn and pasta salad

Combine the cooked pasta shells and prawns in a serving bowl.

In a small bowl stir together the yogurt, tomato purée and Tabasco sauce. Pour onto the pasta mixture and toss well.

Just before serving, sprinkle with the spring onions.

Serve either at room temperature or slightly chilled.

SERVES 4
PER SERVING:
255 KCAL/2.2G FAT

1 lb (450g) [cooked weight] pasta shells

1 lb (450g) peeled and cooked prawns

5 oz (150g) low-fat natural yogurt

1 tablespoon tomato purée

a few drops Tabasco sauce to taste

3 spring onions, chopped

Sardine, beetroot and red apple salad

SERVES 2
PER SERVING:
158 KCAL / 6.1G FAT

1 × 120g (4.2oz) can sardines in
    brine
2oz (50g) low-fat natural yogurt
3oz (75g) cooked and grated
    beetroot
1 red apple, grated (leave the
    skin on)
black pepper to taste
1 small lettuce

Drain and mash the sardines. Mix in the yogurt, stir in the beetroot and apple, and season well. Chill until ready to serve, and serve on a bed of lettuce.

Couscous salad

Couscous is fine grains of semolina rolled in flour. Most prepacked couscous has been pre-cooked and just requires soaking in order to reconstitute it.

In a saucepan, bring the stock to the boil, add the spices then the couscous and stir well. Remove from the heat and cover with a lid for 1 minute.

Pour the couscous into a large bowl. Add the vegetables and herbs, mixing well, and season to taste.

Just before serving, drizzle with the lemon juice. Serve hot or cold.

SERVES 4
PER SERVING:
114 KCAL/1.3G FAT

14fl oz (400ml) vegetable stock
$1/4$ teaspoon ground turmeric
$1/4$ teaspoon paprika
$1/4$ teaspoon ground coriander
6oz (175g) couscous
2 salad tomatoes, diced
1×3in (7.5cm) piece cucumber, peeled and diced
1 red pepper, seeded and finely diced
2 spring onions, finely chopped
2 tablespoons chopped fresh mint
2 tablespoons chopped fresh parsley
juice of $1/2$ lemon
salt and freshly ground black pepper

Potato and watercress salad

SERVES 6
PER SERVING:
129 KCAL / 2.4G FAT

1–1½lb (450–675g) new
   potatoes
4oz (100g) lean back bacon
4 spring onions *or* 2 tablespoons
   chopped fresh chives
1 bunch fresh watercress
1 tablespoon chopped fresh
   parsley

for the dressing
5oz (150g) low-fat natural
   yogurt
2–3 teaspoons French mustard
1 teaspoon caster sugar or
   artificial sweetener to taste
1 tablespoon wine vinegar
salt and freshly ground black
   pepper

Scrub baby potatoes and cook whole, or scrape large ones and cut into pieces. Cook in boiling salted water until just tender. Drain well and place under cold running water until completely cold. Drain well. If using large potatoes cut them into dice.

In the meantime, remove any fat from the bacon and grill the rashers until they are crisp. Drain on kitchen paper.

Trim and slice the spring onions. Coarsely chop the watercress. Place the potatoes in a bowl with the spring onions or chives and the watercress. Crush the bacon into small pieces and sprinkle into the mixture.

Mix all the ingredients for the dressing together and taste to check the seasoning. Pour over the potatoes and mix well. Sprinkle with the chopped parsley, cover and refrigerate until required.

Thai noodle salad

Thai salad dressings often include flavoured oils. In this recipe the combination of apple and lime juice is a more than adequate substitution.

Cook the noodles according to the packet instructions. Drain and rinse well.

Place the onion, tomatoes and cucumber in a large mixing bowl. Add the noodles, lime zest and juice, chilli and coriander and mix well. Divide the mixture equally between 4 serving bowls.

Combine the dressing ingredients in a bowl and pour over the salad.

SERVES 4
PER SERVING:
106 KCAL/0.2G FAT

4oz (100g) [dry weight]
    vermicelli rice noodles
1 small red onion, finely diced
4 ripe tomatoes, skinned, seeded
    and finely diced
$\frac{1}{2}$ cucumber, peeled and cut
    into julienne strips
zest and juice of 1 lime
1 red chilli, seeded and finely
    chopped
2 tablespoons chopped fresh
    coriander

for the dressing
2 tablespoons fresh apple juice
2 tablespoons fresh lime juice
1 teaspoon sugar
2 teaspoons Thai fish sauce or
    oyster sauce
salt and freshly ground black
    pepper

Lentil salad

SERVES 4
PER SERVING:
130 KCAL / 4.1G FAT

1 teaspoon sunflower oil

1 onion, sliced

2 celery sticks, sliced

2 garlic cloves, crushed

6oz (175g) brown or green
   lentils soaked for at least 1½
   hours

1 × 14oz (400g) can blackeyed
   beans, drained and rinsed

½ each red, green and yellow
   peppers, seeded and diced

4oz (100g) cucumber, diced

6 tablespoons reduced-fat salad
   dressing

1oz (25g) Parmesan

Heat the oil in a saucepan and fry the onion, celery and garlic for 5 minutes until softened.

Add the lentils and ½ pint (300ml) boiling water. Cover and simmer gently for 30–45 minutes until the lentils are tender (the cooking time will vary according to how long the lentils have been soaked). Drain, if necessary, and allow to cool.

When the lentil mixture is cold, stir in the beans, peppers and cucumber. Add the dressing and toss well. For an attractive effect, use a potato peeler to produce thin shavings of the Parmesan cheese (or use grated Parmesan). Sprinkle the Parmesan over the salad.

Duo of courgettes and flageolets en salade

Steam the courgette slices for 6 minutes. In the meantime, prepare the dressing by mixing all the dressing ingredients together.

When the courgettes are ready, place them in a mixing bowl and pour the dressing on top. Leave to cool and marinate for 10–15 minutes.

Add the onion, flageolet beans and seasoning, and mix well but gently. Leave to stand until completely cold.

Garnish with a pinch of sesame seeds.

SERVES 4
PER SERVING:
76 KCAL / 4 G FAT

12oz (350g) courgettes, sliced at a slant
½ red onion, sliced
1 × 14oz (400g) can flageolet beans, drained and rinsed
salt and freshly ground black pepper
pinch of sesame seeds to garnish

for the dressing
1 tablespoon pesto sauce
2 tablespoons chopped fresh basil
2 tablespoons lemon juice

Broad bean and mint salad

SERVES 2
PER SERVING:
116 KCAL / 1.7G FAT

8oz (225g) shelled broad beans
5oz (150g) low-fat natural
   yogurt
fresh mint
1 teaspoon sugar
salt and freshly ground pepper
   to taste
shredded lettuce

Cook the broad beans in a pan of boiling salted water for 10–15 minutes. Drain the beans and allow to cool.

Mix the yogurt in a bowl with 1–2 tablespoons of cold water, adding sufficient water to obtain the consistency of your preference.

Place the mint on a chopping board. Sprinkle the sugar on top, then chop the mint with a sharp knife or chopper. Stir the mint into the yogurt and season with salt and pepper. Add the broad beans and stir well.

Arrange the shredded lettuce in a serving bowl and pour the broad bean mixture over the top. Serve well chilled.

Italian salad

SERVES 6
PER SERVING:
40 KCAL / 0.3G FAT

1 medium head radicchio
1/2 head chicory frisée (curly
   endive)
1 Little Gem lettuce
1 × 3–4oz (75–100g) packet
   Rocket or lamb's lettuce
1 × 15oz (425g) can artichoke
   hearts (optional)
4oz (100g) French beans
oil-free vinaigrette

Wash the radicchio, chicory frisée, Little Gem lettuce and Rocket or lamb's lettuce and drain well. Shred the lettuce into large pieces.

Drain the artichoke hearts (if using) and cut each one into quarters.

Top and tail the French beans and cut each one into 3–4 pieces. Cook in boiling salted water until tender. Drain and place under cold running water until really cold. Drain well again.

Mix the lettuce and vegetables together in a large bowl. Just before serving pour over a little oil-free vinaigrette and toss well.

Greek salad

Instead of the traditional high-fat feta cheese and olives, I have used low-fat quark and black seedless grapes in this Greek-style salad. This makes it look similar to the real thing, and taste delicious while keeping the calories and fat to a minimum.

Combine all the salad ingredients in a large bowl. Using 2 dessertspoons, shape the quark into small balls. Place on a plate and season with salt and pepper. Drizzle over the lemon juice and sprinkle with parsley. Arrange the salad on 4 individual plates. Place some quark on top of each salad, and scatter with the grapes.

Combine all the dressing ingredients in a small bowl. Just before serving, pour the dressing over the salad.

Serve with a jacket potato and natural yogurt mixed with chives.

SERVES 4
PER SERVING:
101 KCAL / 1.1G FAT

1 crisp Romaine lettuce
1 cucumber, diced
6 ripe tomatoes, quartered
1 red onion, diced
1 green pepper, seeded and
    diced
8oz (225g) quark
juice of 1 lemon
2 tablespoons chopped fresh
    parsley
salt and freshly ground black
    pepper
12 black seedless grapes, halved

for the dressing
$1/4$ pint (150ml) apple juice
2 tablespoons white wine
    vinegar
1 tablespoon Dijon mustard
pinch of sugar
salt and freshly ground black
    pepper

Waldorf salad

Traditionally, Waldorf salad includes apple, celery and high-fat walnuts and mayonnaise. here is a tasty low-fat alternative which looks deliciously creamy.

Quarter and core the apples and cut into dice. Place in a bowl, and add the lemon juice. Add the celery and spring onions . Mix in the butter beans and parsley, season well.

Mix all the dressing ingredients together in a small bowl and pour over the salad. Mix well, and serve with cooked cold meat or smoked fish.

SERVES 4
PER SERVING:
137 KCAL/0.8G FAT

2 sweet dessert apples
2 tablespoons lemon juice
4 celery sticks, diced
6 spring onions, finely sliced
1 × 14oz (400g) can butter
    beans, drained and rinsed
1 tablespoon chopped fresh
    parsley
salt and freshly ground black
    pepper

for the dressing
6oz (175g) virtually fat-free
    fromage frais
2 tablespoons cider vinegar
1 tablespoon lemon juice
$\frac{1}{4}$ teaspoon ground turmeric
2 teaspoons sugar
salt and freshly ground black
    pepper

Cucumber salad

SERVES 8
PER SERVING:
17 KCAL/0.1G FAT

1 cucumber
salt
1–2 teaspoons caster sugar
white wine vinegar to taste

Peel the cucumber, if you wish, and slice very finely. If you have a slicing attachment on your food processor or if you have a mandolin, use either of these for the best results.

Place the cucumber in a sieve and sprinkle lightly with salt. Leave for 20–30 minutes, then rinse under the cold tap and pat dry with kitchen paper.

Place the cucumber in a dish. Add the sugar and white wine vinegar to taste to give a sweet and sour taste.

Cover and refrigerate until required. Serve chilled.

Cucumber raita

SERVES 6
PER SERVING:
28 KCAL/0.4G FAT

1 small cucumber
salt
10oz (275g) low-fat natural
    yogurt
$1/2$ teaspoon ground cumin
1 teaspoon caster sugar
$1/4$ teaspoon chilli powder
    (optional)
1–2 teaspoons lemon juice or to
    taste
1–2 tablespoons chopped fresh
    mint

If you wish you can peel the cucumber, but it looks more cheerful if the skin is left on. Cut the cucumber into short lengths and cut each piece into half down the centre. Scoop out the seeds with a teaspoon and chop the flesh into small dice or grate coarsely. Place in a sieve and sprinkle with a little salt and leave for 20–30 minutes.

Rinse the salt from the cucumber and drain well. Place the yogurt in a bowl and beat in the ground cumin, sugar and chilli powder (if using). Add the lemon juice and chopped mint..

Cover and refrigerate for at least 1 hour before serving.

Tomato and orange salad

Slice the tomatoes from the core end. Cut the peel from the oranges and, using a sharp knife, cut out the segments of orange. Arrange the tomato slices in concentric rings on a round plate and place a circle of orange segments between each ring.

Mix the orange juice with balsamic vinegar and season with salt and pepper. Pour over the tomatoes and sprinkle with the basil.

Cover and refrigerate until required.

SERVES 8
PER SERVING:
32 KCAL / 0.2G FAT

1 lb (450g) firm ripe tomatoes
3–4 oranges
3–4 tablespoons orange juice
balsamic vinegar to taste
salt and freshly ground black
    pepper
chopped fresh basil to garnish

Coleslaw

Make the dressing by mixing the flour, sugar (if using), salt and mustard together in a small pan, then blend in the vinegar and $^1/_4$ pint (150ml) water. Stir or whisk until smooth then bring slowly to the boil. Allow to boil for 5 minutes, stirring all the time.

Whisk the egg (if using) in a bowl and pour the boiling dressing over the egg. Mix well, then stir in the yogurt. Check the seasoning and add the artificial sweetener (if using). Allow to stand until cold, then cover and refrigerate until required.

Shred the cabbage very finely, and grate the carrots. Trim the leek or spring onions and slice thinly. Place in a bowl and stir in as much of the dressing as is necessary to coat the vegetables. The vegetables can be prepared well in advance, but it is best to mix them with the dressing no more than 1–2 hours before serving.

Cover and refrigerate until required.

SERVES 6
PER SERVING:
65 KCAL / 1.9G FAT

8oz (225g) white cabbage
2 medium carrots
1 small leek *or* 3–4 spring onions

for the dressing
1 tablespoon flour
2 tablespoons sugar or artificial
    sweetener to taste
2 teaspoons salt
1 tablespoon made-up English
    mustard
$^1/_4$ pint (150ml) malt vinegar
1 egg (optional)
5oz (150g) low-fat natural
    yogurt

Facing page: (top) coleslaw; (middle) potato and watercress salad; (bottom) tomato and orange salad.

Vegetables

play a crucial role in any diet. They are particularly valuable in a low-fat diet because they offer bulk and many nutrients yet relatively few calories. If we can find new ways of making them look more appealing and taste even more interesting they can be a great help in a weight-loss or weight-maintenance campaign. Some of these recipes use vegetables that may be new to you. Try them and see how you like them and so broaden your repertoire.

Globe artichokes with vinaigrette

SERVES 4
PER SERVING:
51 KCAL/0.6G FAT

4 large globe artichokes
1 lemon, halved
¼ pint (150ml) fresh apple juice
3 tablespoons lemon juice
1 teaspoon sugar
2 teaspoons Dijon mustard
salt and freshly ground black
    pepper

Prepare the artichoke by breaking off the stalk and pulling away any fibres from the base. Even out the base by cutting off a slice with a sharp knife. Rub immediately with lemon to prevent discoloration.

Cut the top off the artichoke, about a third of the way down the vegetable, and trim the outer leaves with scissors, removing the ends of the leaves.

Plunge the artichokes into a pan of boiling salted water and simmer for 35–45 minutes until a central leaf pulls away easily. Drain and place the artichokes, upside-down, on a cake rack to remove the excess water. Grasp the centre leaves with your fingers, twist and pull them out to reveal the central choke. Carefully spoon out the choke with a teaspoon.

Combine the apple juice, lemon juice, sugar and mustard and season to taste. Spoon the vinaigrette into the centre of the artichokes and serve immediately.

Asparagus with chive sauce

Trim the asparagus and tie into 4 equal bunches with string. Place in a pan of salted boiling water and cook until tender. Drain and arrange on a serving plate.

Combine the yogurt, turmeric, lemon juice and chives and season to taste. Spoon the sauce over the asparagus. Place under a preheated hot grill until the sauce bubbles and gently browns.

SERVES 4
PER SERVING:
59 KCAL/1.2G FAT

1½lb (675g) fresh asparagus
6oz (175g) Total 0% Greek Yogurt
¼ teaspoon ground turmeric
1 tablespoon lemon juice
1 tablespoon chopped fresh chives
salt and freshly ground black pepper

Country style broad beans

If fresh broad beans are unavailable you can use frozen ones. If you are using a stock cube to make your stock, only make it half strength or you will find the sauce is too salty.

Pod the broad beans. Trim the spring onions and cut the stems into short lengths, leaving the bulbs whole. Remove any fat from the bacon and cut the meat into strips.

Place the beans, onions and bacon in a saucepan and pour the stock over. Bring to the boil and simmer gently for 10–15 minutes until the beans are tender.

Remove the beans and onions from the stock with a slotted spoon. Mix the cornflour with a little water to a smooth paste. Stir it into the stock and bring to the boil, stirring continuously. Continue boiling rapidly until it has the consistency of a thin sauce.

Return the vegetables to the pan. Boil for a minute or two to reheat them. Check the seasoning and pour into a hot serving dish. Cover and keep hot.

Just before serving, sprinkle the chopped parsley or chervil over the vegetables.

SERVES 4
PER SERVING:
128 KCAL/2.7G FAT

2lb (1kg) broad beans
10–12 spring onions
3oz (75g) lean bacon
3/4 pint (450ml) chicken or
    vegetable stock
1 tablespoon cornflour
salt and freshly ground black
    pepper
1 tablespoon chopped fresh
    parsley or chervil to garnish

Petits pois à la Français

SERVES 4
PER SERVING:
54 KCAL/1G FAT

1lb (450g) frozen petits pois
8 spring onions, finely sliced
1 Little Gem lettuce
2–3 sprigs fresh mint, finely
    chopped
salt and freshly ground black
    pepper

Frozen peas are a great standby for an instant vegetable. Try this French recipe to ring the changes and add some texture and a different flavour. You can use the same principle with baby broad beans or fine green beans.

Place the frozen peas and spring onions in a saucepan. Cover with water and bring to the boil. Simmer for 5–6 minutes until cooked.

Drain the vegetables into a colander and return to the saucepan.

Finely shred the lettuce and fold into the pea and onion mixture. Fold in the chopped mint. Season well with salt and pepper. Pile into a warmed serving dish and serve immediately.

Broccoli with orange

SERVES 4
PER SERVING:
120 KCAL/1.3G FAT

1 orange
1 large onion
1–1½lb (450–675g) broccoli
¼ pint (150ml) orange juice
salt

This is a simple but delicious way of serving broccoli. It goes particularly well with fish.

Thinly pare the peel from the orange and cut into very fine julienne strips. Blanch the strips in boiling water until just tender, drain and place under cold running water until cold. Drain again and reserve until later. Cut all the pith from the orange and cut out the segments.

Cut the broccoli into small even-sized florets and cook in boiling salted water for 7–8 minutes or steam for about 20 minutes. Drain boiled ones well and add salt to steamed ones.

Heat the orange juice in a pan and boil for a few minutes until it thickens slightly. Add the broccoli and orange segments. Stir carefully so that the broccoli is coated with the orange juice. Pile into a hot serving dish and sprinkle the reserved julienne strips over the top. Serve hot.

Brussels sprouts with chestnuts

Make a small nick in each chestnut with a sharp knife and then blanch them quickly in boiling water for 2 minutes. Peel off the skins while hot. Keep the chestnuts whole.

Trim and wash the sprouts and cook in boiling salted water until just tender. Meanwhile, place the chestnuts in a small saucepan with the stock. Cover and cook gently. Drain the sprouts and mix with the chestnuts, pour into a warmed serving dish and season with freshly ground black pepper.

SERVES 8
PER SERVING:
131 KCAL/2.8G FAT

1lb (450g) chestnuts
1–2lb (450–900g) brussels
  sprouts
375ml (13fl oz) chicken stock
freshly ground black pepper

Braised cabbage with cider

Preheat the oven to 150°C, 300°F, Gas Mark 2.

Cut the stalks out of the cabbage quarters. Blanch the cabbage in boiling salted water for 5 minutes. Drain well and arrange in a casserole dish.

Sauté the onion in a hot wok or pan until soft. Add the flour and cook for 1 minute. Gradually stir in the cider and stock and bring to the boil, stirring continuously. Season with salt and pepper. Add the chopped apples, then pour the mixture over the cabbage. Cover and bake in the oven for 1–1½ hours.

SERVES 8
PER SERVING:
49 KCAL/0.5G FAT

1 green cabbage, trimmed and
  quartered
1 onion, finely chopped
2 level tablespoons plain flour
½ pint (300ml) chicken stock
salt and freshly ground black
  pepper
8oz (225g) cooking apples,
  peeled and chopped

Spinach timbales

SERVES 4
PER SERVING:
42 KCAL / 1.5G FAT

1 ½lb (675g) fresh spinach
1 vegetable stock cube
pinch of grated nutmeg

Preheat the oven to 200°C, 400°F, Gas Mark 6.

Wash the spinach and remove the stalks. Choose 12 large leaves. Blanch the large leaves quickly in boiling water for 5 seconds then plunge into ice cold water. Dry off on kitchen paper.

Line 4 ramekin dishes with the spinach leaves, allowing them to cover the inside of the dish with a slight overhang.

Dissolve the stock cube in 1 pint (600ml) of boiling water. Add the spinach and cook for a minute or two. Drain well and chop finely. Return the chopped spinach to the saucepan and heat gently to remove the excess moisture. Season with nutmeg.

Spoon the chopped spinach into the ramekins and fold over the overhanging leaves. Place the ramekins in a roasting tin. Pour sufficient water into the tin so that it comes halfway up the sides of the ramekins. Cover completely with foil and bake in the oven for 10–15 minutes.

To serve, turn out onto a serving plate.

Hot beetroot with balsamic vinegar

Wash the beetroot well and place in a large pan. Cover the beetroot with water and bring to the boil. Simmer for 35–40 minutes until tender. Drain the beetroot and rinse with cold water, rubbing the skins away. Cut the top and bottom off and slice into baton pieces.

In a non-stick frying pan dry-fry the spring onions for 2–3 minutes. Add the beetroot. Mix well, season and flavour with the balsamic vinegar.

Serve hot.

SERVES 4
PER SERVING:
58 KCAL/0.2G FAT

1½lb (675g) fresh beetroot
6 spring onions, finely sliced
2–3 teaspoons balsamic vinegar or to taste
salt and freshly ground black pepper

Carrots with ginger and orange

Cook the carrots in lightly salted water until almost tender but still crisp. Drain and return to the saucepan.

Meanwhile in a small bowl, mix the cornflour, sugar, salt, ginger and orange juice. Pour the mixture over carrots and cook over a low heat for 2–3 minutes.

Remove from the heat and place in a serving dish.

SERVES 4
PER SERVING:
78 KCAL/0.4G FAT

1lb (450g) carrots, sliced
2 teaspoons cornflour
1 teaspoon sugar
¼ teaspoon salt
1 teaspoon chopped fresh ginger
¼ pint (150ml) orange juice

Spicy mushrooms

SERVES 4
PER SERVING:
28 KCAL/1.1G FAT

1lb (450g) mushrooms
1 tablespoon lemon juice
1 teaspoon chopped fresh
  parsley
1 teaspoon chopped fresh
  chives
2 garlic cloves, crushed
1 small onion, chopped
2 chicken stock cubes
6fl oz (175ml) hot water
salt and freshly ground black
  pepper

Preheat the oven to 180°C, 350°F, Gas Mark 4.

Wash and trim the mushrooms, leaving the stalks in place to prevent shrinkage. Place the mushrooms in an ovenproof dish with the stalks upwards. Sprinkle with the lemon juice, parsley, chives, garlic and onion. Season well with salt and pepper.

Dissolve the stock cubes in the hot water and pour around the mushrooms. Bake in the oven for about 20 minutes.

Serve immediately in preheated small dishes.

Dry-fried garlic mushrooms

SERVES 4
PER SERVING:
14 KCAL/0.5G FAT

1lb (450g) mushrooms
1 onion, finely diced
2 garlic cloves, crushed
salt and freshly ground black
  pepper

Preheat the oven to 180°C, 350°F, Gas Mark 4.

Cut the mushrooms in half and place the mushrooms and onions in a non-stick pan. Add the garlic and season with salt and pepper. Slowly dry-fry the onions and mushrooms for about 5 minutes, stirring occasionally. Transfer to an ovenproof dish. Cover and bake in the oven for 10 minutes.

Parsnip gratin

Spicy creamed parsnips with a crispy topping are a delicious accompaniment to any meat or vegetarian main dish. Choose small firm parsnips, as these have a much sweeter flavour than large ones. Large parsnips are often tough and woody and become stringy when mashed.

Peel the parsnips and cut into chunks. Boil in salted water until tender. Drain well and mash with a fork or potato masher. Fold in the garlic, cumin, parsley and fromage frais. Season well with salt and pepper.

Pile into an ovenproof dish and place under a preheated grill until golden brown.

SERVES 4
PER SERVING:
159 KCAL/2.5G FAT

2lb (900g) parsnips
1 garlic clove, crushed
2 teaspoons ground cumin
1 tablespoon chopped fresh
   parsley
2 tablespoons low-fat fromage
   frais
salt and freshly ground black
   pepper

Ratatouille

SERVES 4
PER SERVING:
65 KCAL/0.7G FAT

2 medium onions, sliced

8oz (225g) courgettes, sliced

2 small aubergines, sliced

1 large green pepper, seeded
    and finely sliced

1 × 14oz (400g) can tomatoes

2 garlic cloves, crushed

2 bay leaves

2 teaspoons chopped fresh
    thyme

salt and freshly ground black
    pepper

a little chopped fresh basil to
    garnish

Preheat a non-stick frying pan. Dry-fry the onion in the pan until soft. Add the courgettes, season and cook for a further 2–3 minutes. Pour the onion and courgettes into a large saucepan.

Return the frying pan to the stove, add the aubergine and green pepper, season and dry-fry for 4–5 minutes, then transfer to the large pan.

Pour the tomatoes into the frying pan. Add the garlic, bay leaves and thyme, bring to the boil then pour over the vegetables. Simmer the vegetables for 10 minutes to combine the flavours.

Just before serving, sprinkle with fresh basil.

Lemon-glazed vegetables

Scrape the potatoes and carrots. Top and tail the French beans, courgettes and mange tout. Cut each bean into 2–3 pieces. If the courgettes are very small, just cut into 4 down the length, otherwise cut in half and then quarter them lengthways.

Cook the potatoes in a pan of boiling salted water until tender.

In another pan of boiling salted water, cook the carrots for about 4 minutes. Add the French beans and cook for a further 4–5 minutes. Finally, add the courgettes, mange-tout and baby sweetcorn for a few minutes. Try to keep the vegetables slightly crisp.

Drain the vegetables, reserving about $1/4$ pint (150ml) of the mixed vegetable water. Keep the vegetables hot.

Add the sugar, mustard and lemon juice to the reserved vegetable water and boil until syrupy. Return the vegetables to the pan and turn carefully to coat them with the glaze. Pile into a hot serving dish.

Just before serving, sprinkle with the lemon zest and chopped coriander.

SERVES 4
PER SERVING:
178 KCAL/1.3G FAT

1lb (450g) small new potatoes
6oz (175g) small new carrots
6oz (175g) French beans
6oz (175g) baby courgettes
4oz (100g) mange tout
4oz (100g) baby sweetcorn
$2^{1}/_{2}$oz (65g) sugar
2 teaspoons French mustard
4–5 tablespoons lemon juice
zest of 1 lemon
1 tablespoon chopped fresh
  coriander

Roasted Mediterranean vegetables

SERVES 4–6
PER SERVING:
73 KCAL/1.7G FAT

2 red peppers
1 green pepper
1 yellow pepper
1 lb (450g) medium courgettes
6–8 garlic cloves
1 teaspoon olive or vegetable
 oil
salt and freshly ground black
 pepper
fresh chopped herbs to garnish

Grilling and peeling the peppers gives them an extra flavour and makes them sweeter. Do not be alarmed by the amount of garlic in this recipe. It really is quite mild to taste after roasting.

Preheat the oven to 200°C, 400°F, Gas Mark 6.

Cut out the stalk and inner core from the peppers and discard. Cut the peppers into quarters. Remove any seeds and pith from the inside. Place them, skin-side up, on a working surface and press lightly with one hand to flatten them out. Place the peppers, still skin side up, under a hot grill, moving them around if necessary until the skins are charred all over. Place in a bowl, cover with clingfilm and allow to cool for 15 minutes. This enables the skin to be peeled off easily. Discard the skin, then cut each piece of pepper into 3–4 strips.

Trim the courgettes and cut into 2in (5cm) lengths. Cut in half lengthways, then cut each piece into 3–4 wedges according to the thickness of the courgette, but keep them as thick as possible (thin slices will shrivel in the oven).

Peel the garlic cloves and keep whole. Place the courgettes and garlic in a pan of boiling salted water and blanch for about 3 minutes. Drain well.

Heat the oil in a non-stick ovenproof pan. Add the peppers, courgettes and garlic, and sprinkle lightly with salt and black pepper. Toss them in the oil and cook in the oven for 30–35 minutes. Stir them around once or twice during the cooking time so that they cook evenly. Do not overcook the vegetables, as the courgettes taste much better when they have a 'bite'.

Using a slotted spoon, remove the peppers, courgettes and garlic from the pan and place onto kitchen paper. Carefully blot them to remove all the excess oil, then arrange the vegetables in a hot serving dish.

Just before serving, sprinkle a few fresh herbs of your choice over the top. Serve hot.

Potatoes with spinach

Tiny new potatoes are best for this dish, but you could also use larger ones or firm old potatoes and cut into 1in (2.5cm) dice.

Preheat a non-stick sauce pan. Add the mustard seeds. Cook over a gentle heat for a few seconds until the seeds begin to 'pop'. Remove from the heat and add the coriander and chilli powder and mix well. Add the onions and garlic. Cook together for 3–5 minutes. Add the potatoes and dry-fry for 2–3 minutes. Add the spinach, tomatoes and the stock.

Cover and cook gently for 20–30 minutes until the potatoes are tender and only a little liquid remains in the pan. Check the pan occasionally to make sure the mixture doesn't burn on the bottom and add a little more liquid if necessary.

Transfer the mixture to a hot serving dish. Just before serving, sprinkle the chopped fresh coriander, over the top.

SERVES 4
PER SERVING:
159 KCAL / 1.6G FAT

2 teaspoons black mustard
   seeds
$1\frac{1}{2}$ teaspoons ground coriander
$\frac{1}{4}$ teaspoon chilli powder
2 large onions, sliced
2 garlic cloves, crushed
1lb (450g) potatoes, peeled and
   cut into dice
12oz (350g) frozen leaf spinach
2 tomatoes, chopped
$\frac{1}{4}$ pint (150ml) vegetable stock
chopped fresh coriander to
   garnish

Honeyed minty potatoes

New potatoes are delicious when they first come into season, but as the season progresses some of them lose their flavour. Serving them this way makes them more interesting.

Scrape the potatoes and cook in boiling salted water until tender. Drain well and keep hot.

Just before serving, heat the honey in a pan and add the balsamic vinegar. Mix well together. Add the cooked potatoes to the pan and stir well until they are coated with the honey and vinegar mixture. Add the mint, mix well and place on a hot serving dish.

SERVES 4
PER SERVING:
129 KCAL/0.3G FAT

1–1½lb (450–675g) small new potatoes
salt
2–3 tablespoons clear honey
1–1½ tablespoons balsamic vinegar
1 tablespoon chopped fresh mint

Marquise potatoes

SERVES 4
PER SERVING:
142 KCAL/0.7G FAT

1 ½lb (675g) old potatoes
1 egg white
1–2 tablespoons tomato purée
salt and white pepper
pinch of nutmeg (optional)
a few drops oil
2 medium tomatoes
parsley sprigs to garnish

The potato shapes in this recipe can be prepared in advance and refrigerated or frozen until required. To freeze, leave the potato shapes on the baking sheet and place in the freezer. When the shapes are frozen, remove them from the sheet and place in a single layer in a plastic box, then seal the box. When required for use, place the shapes on a lightly oiled baking sheet while still frozen and allow to defrost at room temperature before baking.

Preheat the oven to 220°C, 425°F, Gas Mark 7.

Peel the potatoes and boil in salted water until tender. Drain well and mash.

Whisk the egg white until frothy and stir into the potatoes. Stir in sufficient tomato purée to give an attractive pink colour. Season to taste with salt, white pepper and a pinch of nutmeg if desired. Lightly brush a non-stick baking sheet with oil.

Place the potato mixture in a piping bag with a ½in (1cm) rosette nozzle and pipe out 8 beehive shapes (about the size of a whipped cream walnut) onto the baking sheet.

Peel the tomatoes and remove the seeds. Chop the flesh finely and season well with salt and pepper. Make a small hole in the top of each potato shape (the end of a wooden spoon is ideal for this) and fill one with a little of the chopped tomato.

To bake, place in the oven for 15–20 minutes or until the outsides are crisp and the ridged edges of the piped potato are browned.

Remove each one carefully from the baking sheet, using a metal spatula, and place on a hot serving dish. Just before serving, garnish the potatoes with a few small sprigs of parsley.

Kinga's Hungarian potatoes

In a non-stick saucepan, dry-fry the onion until soft. Remove from the heat and add the potatoes, paprika, bouillon powder, bay leaf and 3/4 pint (450ml) of water.

Return the pan to the stove and bring to the boil, seasoning with black pepper. Reduce the heat, cover and simmer for 10 minutes. Stir in the cornflour and milk mixture and simmer until the sauce thickens. Pour into a serving dish and sprinkle with fresh parsley.

SERVES 4
PER SERVING:
199 KCAL/0.6G FAT

1 medium onion, finely chopped
2lb (900g) potatoes, peeled and diced
1 tablespoon mild/sweet paprika
1 tablespoon vegetable bouillon powder
3/4 pint (450ml) water
3 bay leaves
freshly ground black pepper
1 tablespoon cornflour, mixed with 3 tablespoons skimmed milk
chopped fresh parsley

Rosemary boulangère potatoes

SERVES 6
PER SERVING:
103 KCAL/0.3G FAT

1–1½lb (450–675g) old
   potatoes
6–8oz (175–225g) onions
½ pint (300ml) vegetable or
   chicken stock
1 teaspoon dried rosemary
salt and freshly ground black
   pepper

The attachment on a food processor or mixer is ideal for slicing the potatoes and onions because the vegetables will cook more quickly if they are thinly and evenly sliced.

Preheat the oven to 200°C, 400°F, Gas Mark 6.

Peel and thinly slice the potatoes and onions.

Pour the stock into a saucepan, bring to the boil and cook the onions in it for 3–4 minutes.

Place a layer of potatoes in the base of an ovenproof dish. Sprinkle half the rosemary over and season lightly with salt and pepper. Using a slotted spoon, remove the onions from the stock and place them on top of the potatoes. Add a little more salt and pepper. Cover with the remainder of the potatoes, sprinkle with the remaining rosemary, and season with salt and pepper.

Pour the remaining stock over the potatoes, cover with a lid or aluminium foil and bake in the oven for 1–1¼ hours until the vegetables are tender. Check them once or twice during cooking and press them down so that the top layer is kept moist. Remove the lid or foil for the last 20 minutes of the cooking time so that the potatoes turn golden brown on top.

Duchesse potatoes

Beat the yogurt, nutmeg and salt and pepper into the potatoes. Place the mixture in a saucepan, add the egg yolk and mix well over a low heat until the mixture leaves the base of the pan clean.

Place the mixture in a piping bag fitted with a vegetable star nozzle. Pipe into rosettes onto a well-greased baking sheet. Brown under a grill or in the top of a hot oven.

Just before serving, garnish with watercress.

SERVES 4
PER SERVING:
97 KCAL/1.7G FAT

2oz (50g) low-fat natural yogurt
pinch of nutmeg
1lb (450g) potatoes, peeled,
    cooked and sieved
1 egg yolk
salt and freshly ground black
    pepper
watercress to garnish

Lyonnaise potatoes

Preheat the oven to 200°C, 400°F, Gas Mark 6.

Cut the potatoes and onions into thin slices. Place alternate layers of potato and onion slices in a casserole dish, sprinkling a little garlic between each layer.

Heat the milk in a saucepan and dissolve the stock cube in the milk. Pour sufficient milk mixture over the vegetables so that it almost reaches the top layer. Cover and cook in the oven for 45–60 minutes or until tender.

Just before serving, garnish with chopped parsley.

SERVES 4
PER SERVING:
148 KCAL/0.8G FAT

1lb (450g) potatoes, scrubbed
    but not peeled
2 large Spanish onions
1 garlic clove, crushed
1/2 pint (300ml) skimmed milk
1 vegetable stock cube
chopped fresh parsley

Coronation potatoes

SERVES 4
PER SERVING:
164 KCAL/0.6G FAT

1½lb (675g) potatoes, peeled and cut into large chunks

1 garlic clove, crushed

1 small onion, finely chopped

1 tablespoon curry powder

1 tablespoon tomato purée

1 tablespoon mango chutney

4oz (100g) canned apricots in juice, drained and chopped

5oz (150g) low-fat natural yogurt

salt and freshly ground black pepper

1 tablespoon chopped fresh coriander

Place the potatoes in a saucepan and just cover with cold water. Bring to the boil and simmer for 15–20 minutes until just cooked. Drain and keep hot.

Dry-fry the garlic and onion in a non-stick pan for 3–4 minutes until the onion is transparent. Add the curry powder and the tomato purée and sauté for a further minute. Mix in the mango chutney and apricots and cook gently for a further 2–3 minutes. Remove from the heat, place in a food processor and liquidise until smooth. Stir in the yogurt and season to taste with salt and pepper.

Place the potatoes in a serving dish and pour the curry sauce over them. Just before serving, sprinkle with chopped coriander.

Puddings

are a great way to round off any meal, and this section contains a wide choice of hot and cold ones. All are low in fat, but the calorie content may vary. In my low-fat diets I generally allow 100 calories per portion. If you are trying to lose weight and there's a pudding recipe you fancy with more calories, then go ahead, but make sure you precede it with a lighter main course to balance out the calories. If you are giving a dinner party, simply choose whichever one you fancy and if the calorie content is higher than my recommended amount, perhaps give yourself a smaller serving if you are feeling strong-willed. Otherwise, indulge yourself and resolve to do some extra exercise the next day!

Summer fruit salad

SERVES 4
PER SERVING:
130 KCAL/0.4G FAT

4oz (100g) black grapes

4oz (100g) seedless green
    grapes

4oz (100g) strawberries

2–3 small tangerines

$^1/_2$ honeydew melon

1 large crisp eating apple

2–3 tablespoons lemon juice

$^1/_2$ pint (300ml) orange or apple
    juice

artificial sweetener to taste

Cut the black grapes in half and remove the seeds. Leave the green grapes whole. Hull and slice the strawberries. Peel the tangerines and break into segments. Remove the seeds from the melon and slice the flesh, discarding the skin. Peel, core and slice the apple.

Mix all the fruit together and stir in the lemon juice, making sure that the apple is well coated. Pour the orange or apple juice over the fruit and mix well. Sweeten to taste with artificial sweetener.

Place in a bowl, cover with a lid or cling film, and chill in the refrigerator for at least an hour before serving.

Spiced tropical fruit salad

To make the syrup, remove the seeds from the chillies and discard. Chop the chillies finely. Dissolve the sugar or Canderel in 12fl oz (350ml) water and boil for 5 minutes. Add the chopped chillies. Taste frequently and remove the chillies when the syrup seems hot enough.

Using a potato peeler, thinly pare off the zest of 1 lime, cut into fine shreds and blanch for 5–10 minutes in boiling water. Drain and refresh under cold water. Squeeze out the juice from both limes and reserve.

Place the remaining fruit in a bowl. Add the lime shreds and the lime juice. Pour the chilli syrup over the fruit. Refrigerate for 30–60 minutes before serving.

SERVES 4
PER SERVING:
208 KCAL/0.8G FAT

2 limes
$^1/_2$ medium melon, chopped
2 kiwi fruit, sliced
$^1/_2$ small ripe pineapple, cut into chunks
1 orange, broken into segments
2 bananas, sliced
1 star fruit, sliced

for the syrup
1–2 small chillies
2oz (50g) sugar or Canderel to taste

Mixed berry brûlée

SERVES 4
PER SERVING:
204 KCAL/0.2G FAT

6oz (175g) blueberries
2 tablespoons caster sugar
6oz (175g) raspberries
6oz (175g) strawberries, hulled
   and sliced
16oz (450g) Total 0% Greek
   Yogurt
4 tablespoons demerara sugar

Place the blueberries in a small saucepan. Add a little water and the caster sugar. Cook gently over a low heat until the fruit starts to pop. Turn off the heat, add the raspberries and strawberries and mix well. Spoon into 4 ramekin dishes and chill.

When the fruit is chilled, preheat the grill until it is very hot. Just before you are ready to serve, spread the yogurt over the fruit, covering the fruit completely. Sprinkle with sugar and immediately place under grill until the sugar caramelises.

Serve immediately.

Fruit brûlée

You can use any assortment of fruit for this sweet. Oranges, grapes and apples form a good base; pears, plums, raspberries, strawberries and redcurrants all provide a contrast in flavour and texture. Even in winter, a few frozen raspberries can be used, but frozen strawberries are not recommended as they are too moist.

Using a small serrated knife, peel the oranges and cut out the segments. Wash the grapes, cut them in half and remove the pips. Peel and dice the apples and pears. Remove the stones from the plums and cut into pieces. Wash the raspberries, strawberries and redcurrants. Toss the apples and pears in the lemon juice. Drain all the fruit well so that it is quite dry. Place the fruit in a heatproof dish and chill.

Preheat the grill until it is very hot. Just before you place the dish under the grill, spread the yogurt over the fruit and sprinkle the sugar on top. (It is important that this is done immediately before grilling, otherwise the sugar melts and does not caramelise.) Place the dish as high under the grill as possible and watch it all the time to see that it caramelises evenly. Turn the dish, if necessary, and take care that the sugar doesn't burn.

Allow to cool, then chill before serving.

SERVES 4
PER SERVING:
176 KCAL/0.3G FAT

1lb (450g) fresh fruit (e.g. oranges, grapes, apples, pears, plums, raspberries, strawberries, redcurrants)
1–2 tablespoons lemon juice
16oz (450g) Total % Greek Yogurt
4–5 tablespoons demerara or palm sugar

Mango and yogurt mousse

You can use fresh mangoes in this recipe instead of canned ones. You will need two, weighing about 8oz (225g) each. Alternatively, you can substitute any canned fruit for the mangoes, but make sure it is canned in juice.

Place 2 tablespoons of water in a small microwave or heatproof bowl and sprinkle the gelatine over. Dissolve the gelatine either by placing the bowl over a small pan of boiling water or placing it in the microwave on High for about 30 seconds or until dissolved.

Drain the mangoes and discard any syrup. Purée the mango flesh and lemon juice in a liquidiser, food processor or through a fine vegetable mill. Stir in the dissolved gelatine and leave until the mixture is just starting to set.

Fold in the yogurt or fromage frais. Taste and add a little sugar or artificial sweetener if desired.

Whisk the egg whites until they form stiff peaks and fold them carefully into the mixture. Pour the mixture into a wetted 1 pint (600ml) mould or pour into individual moulds. Chill overnight. Turn out and serve.

SERVES 4
PER SERVING:
129 KCAL/0.5G FAT

$\frac{1}{2}$oz (15g) packet powdered gelatine
1 × 10oz (275g) can mangoes
1 tablespoon lemon juice
10oz (275g) low-fat natural yogurt or fromage frais
a little caster sugar or Canderel to taste (optional)
2 egg whites

Raspberry yogurt ice

SERVES 4
PER SERVING:
69 KCAL/0.6G FAT

8oz (225g) raspberries
caster sugar or Canderel to taste
    (optional)
2 egg whites
8oz (225g) low-fat raspberry
    yogurt
3–4 oz (75–100g) extra
    raspberries (optional)
small piece of angelica

Chill a 1 pint (600ml) china bowl in a freezer or in the freezer compartment of a refrigerator.

Wash the raspberries. Drain them and press them through a nylon sieve until only the seeds remain. Add caster sugar or sweetener if you wish.

Whisk the egg whites in a clean dry bowl until they form stiff peaks. Place the yogurt in a separate bowl and, using a metal spoon or spatula, carefully fold in the egg whites.

Spoon one-third of the yogurt and egg mixture into the base of the chilled bowl. Cover with half the raspberry purée. Continue like this and finish with a layer of yogurt mixture. Cover well and freeze overnight until solid.

To serve, lightly moisten a plate. Dip a knife in hot water and run it round the inside of the bowl to free the yogurt ice. Turn out onto the centre of the plate. Decorate the base with the whole raspberries and small leaves of angelica. For the best results, place the yogurt ice in the refrigerator for about 15 minutes to allow it to soften slightly.

Fresh mango and lime sorbet

Sorbet, while always low in fat, can be high in calories, as glucose syrup is often used to give it a smooth and creamy taste. Here, I have kept the calorie content to a minimum, resulting in a fresh, light dessert which resembles granita.

In a saucepan dissolve the sugar in ½ pint (300ml) water and bring to the boil. Remove from the heat and allow to cool.

Peel the mangoes and remove the flesh from the stone. Place in a food processor with the lime zest (reserve a little zest) and juice and blend to form a purée.

Mix the purée with the cooled syrup, pour into a shallow freezer container. Cover and freeze for about 3 hours until mushy.

Whisk the egg white until stiff. Fold into the loosened sorbet. Re-freeze for 4 hours until firm.

Remove from the freezer and place in the refrigerator for 20 minutes to allow the sorbet to thaw slightly before serving. Slit open the lychees. Decorate the sorbet with the lychees and reserved zest.

SERVES 8
PER SERVING:
80 KCAL/0.2G FAT

4oz (100g) caster sugar
2 large ripe mangoes
zest and juice of 2 limes
1 egg white
fresh lychees to decorate

Kiwi fruit sorbet

Place the kiwi fruit and the Cointreau in a blender and blend until smooth. Pour the mixture into a bowl and freeze for about 2 hours.

Tip the mixture into a fresh bowl and whisk to break up the crystals. Beat the egg white until stiff and fold into the fruit purée. Place in a decorative bowl and freeze.

Remove from the freezer 20 minutes before serving and place in the refrigerator. Decorate with fresh fruit of your choice.

SERVES 4
PER SERVING:
155 KCAL/0.4G FAT

5 kiwi fruit, peeled and thickly
   sliced
2 tablespoons Cointreau
4oz (100g) caster sugar
1 egg white
fresh fruit to decorate

Apricot plum softie

Blend the dates and apricots with the yogurt in food processor or liquidiser until smooth.

Whisk the egg whites until they form stiff peaks then fold in the Canderel.

Carefully fold the date mixture into the egg white and spoon into 4 individual dishes. Leave to set.

Just before serving, decorate with the plum or apricot slices and the mint.

SERVES 4
PER SERVING:
73 KCAL/0.6G FAT

2oz (50g) fresh stoned dates
6oz (175g) fresh or dried (reconstituted) apricots
10oz (275g) thick low-fat natural yogurt
2 egg whites
2 tablespoons Canderel
2 plums or apricots, sliced
few sprigs of mint

Apple jelly with fromage frais

Peel and thinly slice the apples. Place in a saucepan with a little water and Canderel if desired. Cover with a tight-fitting lid and cook gently until stewed. Spoon the apple into individual dishes.

Make up the jelly with 16 fl oz (475ml) water and pour it over the apple. Leave to set.

When ready to serve, top with the fromage frais.

SERVES 4
PER SERVING:
141 KCAL/0.2G FAT

1lb (450g) cooking apples
Canderel to taste (optional)
1 packet jelly
4oz (100g) low-fat fromage frais

Tarte tatin

SERVES 6
PER SERVING:
240 KCAL / 1.5G FAT

2lb (900g) cooking apples
6oz (175g) caster sugar
1 tablespoon lemon juice
1 egg
2 tablespoons skimmed milk
8 sheets filo pastry

This Parisian upside-down dessert is famous all over the world. It was invented by two sisters who ran a hotel in the small town of Lamotte Beavron. The original recipe uses lashings of butter to fry the apples and then a butter pastry to seal in the flavour. This version uses low-fat filo pastry and cuts out the butter, still retaining the crisp pastry base and that delicious caramelised apple topping.

Preheat the oven to 220°C, 425°F, Gas Mark 7. Preheat a non-stick frying pan for 1 minute.

Peel the apples, cut into thick wedges and place in a bowl. Add the sugar and toss well.

When the pan is hot, tip in the cooking apples and sugar. Cook over a high heat for 6 minutes, moving the apples around with a wooden spoon. The sugar will start to caramelise. When it starts to turn a golden brown colour add the lemon juice and remove from the heat, taking care, as the caramel will reach a very high temperature and can burn severely. Pour into a round 8in (20cm) ovenproof flan dish, and allow to cool.

Beat together the egg and milk.

When the apple mixture is cool, place a sheet of filo pastry on top of the apples, brush with the beaten egg and milk, then add another pastry sheet. Continue until all the pastry is used up. Brush the top and place in the oven for 20–25 minutes.

Allow to cool for 5 minutes then turn out onto a tray or large serving plate. Serve with low-fat fromage frais.

Sparkling wine jelly

In this recipe, when you add the gelatine to the jug containing the wine, the wine will fizz. So add the gelatine slowly and make sure the jug is large enough to avoid any overspill.

Sprinkle the gelatine over 3 tablespoons of water and allow to stand until spongy. Dissolve the gelatine over a pan of hot water or place in the microwave for 20–30 seconds and stir until dissolved. Place the fruit squash, wine and 3fl oz (100ml) water in a large jug and stir in the dissolved gelatine.

Reserve a few raspberries for decoration and divide the remainder between 4 glasses. Fill the glasses with a little of the jelly. Place the glasses in the refrigerator for about 20 minutes until the jelly has set.

When set, pour in the remaining jelly (this sets the raspberries at the bottom of the glass, but if time is short, top up the glasses immediately). Chill the jellies for about 2 hours until set. Top with a little yogurt and the reserved raspberries.

SERVES 4
PER SERVING:
95 KCAL/0.10 FAT

1 × ¼oz (11g) packet gelatine
3 tablespoons concentrated
    summer fruit squash
¾ pint (450 ml) sparkling rosé
    wine
3oz (75g) raspberries
2 tablespoons Total 0% Greek
    Yogurt

Orange and ginger pashka

Pashka is a Russian sweet traditionally served at Easter. The original recipe is very rich and is made with full-cream cheese, double cream and lots of glacé fruits. This low-fat version is much lighter and can be enjoyed at any time of year, not just at Easter. This recipe must be made the day before it is required.

First prepare the mould. You will need either a small new flowerpot or a plastic yogurt or similar pot capable of holding about 1¼lb (500g). Punch several holes in the case (using a heated skewer is the easiest way to do this) and line with a piece of clean muslin. Set to one side until required.

 Drain and discard any liquid from the cottage cheese. Using a wooden spoon, press or rub the cottage cheese and quark through a sieve into a bowl. Stir in the yogurt.

Chop the 2 pieces of stem ginger and reserve the syrup. Grate the rind from 1½ oranges. Cut the segments from 1 orange and reserve. Cut the other orange in half. Cut the segments from one half and chop coarsely. Squeeze the juice from the other half orange and reserve.

Stir the chopped ginger, grated orange rind, chopped flesh from the half orange and the reserved syrup from the stem ginger into the cheese mixture and mix well. Add a little artificial sweetener if you wish. Spoon the mixture into the prepared mould and smooth over the top. Wrap the edges of the muslin over the top. Place the mould on a pastry cutter in a bowl or shallow dish with a light weight on top (about 12–16oz / 350–450g). Refrigerate overnight.

SERVES 6
PER SERVING:
113 KCAL / 1G FAT

8oz (225g) low-fat cottage cheese
8oz (225g) quark
¼ pint (150ml) low-fat natural yogurt
2 pieces stem ginger in 2 tablespoons syrup
2 oranges
artificial sweetener to taste (optional)
small piece crystallised orange peel
extra piece stem ginger
small piece crystallised angelica leaf
2 ripe passion fruits

Prepare the decoration by cutting thin diamonds or other shapes from the crystallised angelica leaf. These can also be prepared in advance and covered with cling film until required.

The next day, turn the pashka out onto a serving dish. On the top of the pashka arrange a spiral of orange slices in the centre and a decorative edging of the crystallised fruit shapes. Just before serving, cut the passion fruits in half, scoop out the centres and mix with the reserved orange juice. Add a little sweetener to taste if you wish. Do this at the last moment so that the full perfume and flavour of the passion fruits is appreciated. Pour the juice around the edge of the pashka and serve.

Rhubarb and orange fool

For the best flavour in this light and refreshing dessert, use young tender sticks of rhubarb.

Thinly pare the rind from one of the oranges, in one long piece if possible, taking care not to remove any of the pith. Place the rind in a stainless steel or enamel saucepan, then remove all the pith from the orange.

Remove the rind and pith from the remaining oranges, then one at a time, remove the segments from all 4 oranges, holding the oranges over a bowl to catch the juice and cutting each segment free of the connecting white tissue with a sharp knife. Squeeze the remaining tissue to extract all the juice.

Add 4 tablespoons of the orange juice to the orange rind in the saucepan, then cover the bowl containing the orange segments and juice and chill until needed. Add the prepared rhubarb and the Canderel to the saucepan, cover the pan and cook over a moderate heat for 5–6 minutes or until the rhubarb is soft. Meanwhile, place a nylon or stainless steel sieve over a bowl.

When cooked, pour the rhubarb into the sieve to drain. Return the juice to the saucepan and boil gently until it is reduced to about 4 tablespoonfuls.

Place the drained rhubarb in a bowl and remove the orange rind, then add the reduced juice and stir well so that the rhubarb pieces break down into a thick purée. Cover and chill for 2–3 hours.

Thirty minutes before serving, drain the juice from the orange segments (this will not be needed, but can be drunk or used for another purpose).

Fold the fromage frais into the rhubarb. Spoon half of the orange segments into 4 serving glasses and top with half of the rhubarb fool, then repeat. Chill until ready to serve. Just before serving, decorate with orange segments and mint.

SERVES 4
PER SERVING:
101 KCAL/0.4G FAT

4 large oranges
14oz (400g) [trimmed weight] rhubarb, cut into 1in (2.5cm) chunks
¼oz (10g) Canderel
4oz (100g) light fromage frais
orange segments and sprigs of fresh mint to decorate (optional)

Crunchy topped fruit fool

SERVES 4
PER SERVING:
128 KCAL / 5.6G FAT

1oz (25g) jumbo oats
2 teaspoons granulated sugar
8oz (225g) strawberries
11oz (300g) low-fat fromage
   frais
artificial sweetener to taste
   (optional)

Place a sheet of foil on the grill pan and spread the oats out on the foil. Sprinkle with the sugar. Lightly toast under the grill and allow to cool.

Reserve one strawberry for decorating. Mash the remainder with a fork and stir into the fromage frais. Sweeten to taste with the sweetener if desired. Spoon into serving glasses and chill.

Cut the reserved strawberry into 4 small slices.

Just before serving, sprinkle the fruit fool with the toasted oat flakes and decorate each glass with a slice of strawberry.

Peach and strawberry delight with raspberry coulis

Make the strawberry water ice in advance and store in the freezer.

Cut the fresh peaches in half and remove the stones. There is no need to skin them at this stage. Dissolve the sugar in $^1/_2$ pint (300ml) of water in a frying pan. Cover and simmer for a few minutes. Place the peaches in the water, skin side up, and simmer gently for 15–20 minutes, turning them over halfway through the cooking time. When they are tender, remove them from the pan and you will find the skins lift off very easily. Drain and leave to cool. The poaching liquor will keep for up to a week if stored in a covered container and kept in the refrigerator. You can use it for poaching other fruit or as a base for a fruit salad.

Cut a very small slice off the bottom of each peach so that the peach can sit firmly on a plate. Reserve until required.

Simmer the raspberries in a pan with 2–3 tablespoons of water until tender, then pass through a nylon sieve (a metal sieve will discolour the raspberries). Return the raspberry purée to a clean pan and sweeten to taste with sugar or sweetener and add a little lemon juice. Bring to the boil. Slake the arrowroot with a little water, add to the pan and return to the boil, stirring all the time. Adjust the sauce if necessary by adding a little more arrowroot or a little more water and/or lemon juice.

Pour a circle of the sauce into the centre of each of 4 dessert plates and, using the point of a skewer or cocktail stick, swirl a little fromage frais around the outside to give a decorative pattern. Place to one side until required.

Take the strawberry water ice from the freezer about 30 minutes before it is required and place in the refrigerator.

Just before serving, place a peach half in the centre of each decorated plate, and place a scoop of strawberry water ice in the centre. Halve the strawberries if necessary and arrange them attractively around each peach half. Serve immediately.

SERVES 4
PER SERVING:
111 KCAL/0.4G FAT

1 portion of strawberry water ice
   (see recipe on next page)
2 large peaches or 4 canned
   peach halves
2oz (50g) granulated sugar
8–12oz (225–350g) fresh
   raspberries
caster sugar or sweetener to
   taste
juice of $^1/_2$ small lemon
1 scant teaspoon arrowroot
1–2 tablespoons low-fat
   fromage frais
4–6oz (100–175g) small fresh
   strawberries to decorate

Apricot and brandy fool

SERVES 4
PER SERVING:
159 KCAL/0.2G FAT

4oz (100g) 'no-soak' dried
    apricots
artificial sweetener to taste
1 wineglass brandy
8oz (225g) quark
2 egg whites
mint and 4 dried apricots to
    decorate

Dried apricots, once reconstituted, have a much stronger flavour than fresh apricots and are sometimes much sweeter.

Place the apricots in a small saucepan with $\frac{1}{4}$ pint (150ml) water. Add artificial sweetener to taste, bring to the boil and simmer for 2–3 minutes until soft. Pour into a liquidiser, add the brandy and blend to form a purée.

Mix the apricot purée with the quark.

Whisk the egg whites until they stand in stiff peaks. Gently fold into the apricot and quark mixture and sweeten to taste. Spoon into 4 individual dishes and chill.

Strawberry water ice

SERVES 4
PER SERVING:
94 KCAL/0.2G FAT

5oz (50g) caster sugar
4 tablespoons orange juice
2 tablespoons lemon juice
1lb (450g) ripe strawberries

Place the caster sugar, orange and lemon juice in a saucepan. Add 4 tablespoons of water. Bring to the boil slowly, stirring frequently so that the sugar dissolves. Boil for about 5 minutes until the mixture becomes syrupy.

Hull the strawberries and add to the pan. Cook for 1–2 minutes. Remove from the heat and allow to cool.

When the mixture is cool, pass it through a fine nylon sieve to remove the seeds. Pour the mixture into a plastic container. Cover and freeze until the mixture starts to set. When the mixture is almost set, turn it out into a bowl and whisk until smooth. Return it to the freezer for a minimum of 4–5 hours. Use as required.

Fresh strawberry and lime pavlova

Preheat the oven to 140°C, 275°F, Gas Mark 1. Line 2 baking sheets with baking parchment.

Make the meringue by whisking the egg whites in a very clean dry bowl with an electric whisk for 4–5 minutes until thick. Whisk in the caster sugar a tablespoon at a time, allowing 20 seconds in between each one, until all the sugar is combined.

Place the meringue in a large piping bag with a star nozzle. Pipe a disc, 12in (30cm) in diameter, onto the baking parchment of one baking sheet and pipe another disc, 8in (20cm) in diameter, onto the other.

Place in the oven for approximately 2 hours or until the meringue has dried out and starts to colour. Remove from oven and allow to cool.

Peel away the baking parchment and place the large meringue on a serving dish, spread with yogurt and cover with sliced strawberries. Place the smaller meringue on top and decorate with the remaining strawberries.

Grate the zest of the lime with a fine grater all over the top of the meringue and dust with icing sugar.

SERVES 8
PER SERVING:
211KCAL/0.1G FAT

6 egg whites
12oz (350g) caster sugar
8oz (225g) Total 0% Greek
    Yogurt
1lb (450g) fresh strawberries or
    soft fruit, hulled and sliced
1 lime
icing sugar to dust

Pears alma

Choose small to medium pears for this dish. They need to be on the point of ripening but not completely soft. Rocha, Williams or Comice de Doyenne are the best types to use, since they have nice round shapes.

SERVES 4
PER SERVING:
192 KCAL/0.3G FAT

4 pears
7½fl oz (225ml) port
1 tablespoon caster sugar
1 tablespoon redcurrant jelly
1 orange
2–4 tablespoons low-fat
    fromage frais or Total %
    Greek Yogurt

Peel the pears and cut each one in half. Using the point of a small knife, cut a small notch in the end of each piece to remove the remains of the flower head, then cut a small v-shaped wedge from the core to the stalk to take out the stalk and the fibres which run down the centre of the pear. With a small teaspoon or ball-cutter, scoop out the core to form a nice round hollow.

Pour the port into a frying pan. Add the caster sugar and 2½fl oz (75ml) water. Place the pears cut-side down in the liquid. Bring to the boil, cover with a lid. Lower the heat and simmer gently until the pears are tender.

Turn the pear halves over in the liquid and leave for a moment or two, then remove them from the pan with a draining spoon and arrange neatly, cut-side up, in a round, shallow dish about 1in (2.5cm) deep.

Add the redcurrant jelly to the liquid in the pan. Bring to the boil and allow the jelly to dissolve. You may find it easier to use a balloon whisk and to whisk it into the liquid. Boil until the liquid has reduced by about a half. Pour over the pears and leave until cold.

In the meantime, pare the orange rind very thinly from half the orange and cut into very thin julienne strips. Place in a pan with a little water, bring to the boil and cook for a moment or two to soften the peel. Drain and reserve.

Place a teaspoon of fromage frais or yogurt in the centre of each pear and sprinkle a few strips of orange peel on top. Serve cold.

Raspberry roulade

SERVES 8
PER SERVING:
128 KCAL/0.3G FAT

12oz (350g) fresh or frozen
  raspberries
4 egg whites
4oz (100g) caster sugar
1 teaspoon vanilla essence
1 teaspoon each icing sugar and
  caster sugar
2 teaspoons gelatine powder
10fl oz (300ml) low-fat fromage
  frais

This is a delicious dessert but it's quite tricky to prepare, as rolling up the meringue roulade requires confidence! This end result is excellent, though, so do try it. Baking parchment is essential for this recipe.

Thaw the frozen raspberries (if using).

Preheat the oven to 170°C, 325°F, Gas Mark 3. Line a large Swiss roll tin with baking parchment.

Whisk the egg whites in a clean dry bowl until stiff. Whisk in 75g (3oz) of the caster sugar and add the vanilla essence. Spread the meringue mixture evenly into the Swiss roll tin and bake in the oven for 12 minutes.

Reduce the oven temperature to 150°C, 300°F, Gas Mark 2 and bake for a further 15 minutes.

Sprinkle a separate sheet of baking parchment liberally with the icing sugar and the caster sugar and tip the meringue carefully onto it. Leave to cool.

Wash the raspberries, if using fresh ones, and drain well. Mash the raspberries with a fork to form a purée. Spoon two-thirds of the raspberry purée into a separate bowl and place in the freezer until the purée forms crystals.

Dissolve the gelatine powder in a little hot water, then beat together the fromage frais and dissolved gelatine. Leave to chill until the mixture starts to thicken and set. Add the semi-frozen raspberry purée and then spread the mixture over the roulade. Roll up like a Swiss roll, wrap in baking parchment and freeze until required.

When ready to serve, remove the baking parchment, slice the roulade and serve with the remaining raspberry purée.

Tiramisu

Tiramisu is usually a truly forbidden dessert for anyone who is watching their waistline. In this low-fat alternative, I've used a branded cream substitute in place of double cream. While the sugar-free Dream Topping is high in fat in its powder form, when reconstituted with skimmed milk it becomes low fat. The end result is surprisingly tasty.

Mix the coffee with the brandy and make up to ¼ pint (150ml) with water. Reserve half the sponge fingers and dip the remainder in the brandied coffee. Arrange the brandied fingers on the base of a serving dish to form a layer.

Make up the Dream Topping with the milk and mix in the fromage frais. Spoon half the mixture over the sponge fingers in the dish. Dip the reserved sponge fingers in the remaining brandied coffee and place over the mixture in the dish. Top with the remaining fromage frais mix.

Just before serving, sprinkle a little powdered drinking chocolate on top.

SERVES 8
PER SERVING:
76 KCAL / 2.7G FAT

2 heaped teaspoons coffee granules or powder
2 teaspoons brandy
1 packet sponge fingers (approximately 12 fingers)
1 sachet Bird's Sugar-free Dream Topping
¼ pint (150ml) skimmed or semi-skimmed milk
12oz (350g) low-fat fromage frais
powdered drinking chocolate to decorate

Sherry trifle

SERVES 4
PER SERVING:
254 KCAL/0.9G FAT

1 packet sugar-free jelly
2 sherry glasses sweet sherry
2 medium bananas, peeled and
    sliced
1 × 15oz (425g) carton low-fat
    custard
2 × 5oz (2 × 150g) virtually fat-
    free vanilla flavoured yogurts
strawberry slices and lime zest
    to decorate (optional)

Vanilla-flavoured yogurt is a great substitute for cream and makes all the difference to this traditional recipe.

Make up the jelly in a large dish according to the packet instructions, but substitute 2 glasses of sweet sherry for 4fl oz (120ml) water. Divide the jelly between 4 individual diashes, add the bananas and leave to set.

When set, cover each with the low-fat custard and smooth the yogurt over the top. Decorate with strawberry slices and a little lime zest (if using).

Toffee yogurt meringue

Swirl the toffee yogurt into the fromage frais. Do not worry if it is not fully mixed, as this gives an attractive swirly effect.

Just before serving, place 2 rounded tablespoonfuls of the yogurt and fromage frais mixture into each meringue nest and dust with a light sprinkling of cocoa powder or drinking chocolate. Decorate each with a sprig of mint.

If you are not serving all the meringue nests at once, you can keep the yogurt and fromage frais mixture in the refrigerator for up to 4 days and then fill the nests when required.

MAKES 6
PER MERINGUE:
82 KCAL/0.3G FAT

1 × 150g (5oz) pot low-fat
   toffee yogurt
225g (8oz) low-fat fromage frais
6 meringue nests
a little cocoa powder or drinking
   chocolate
6 sprigs fresh mint to decorate

Apple and cranberry meringue

SERVES 6
PER SERVING:
143 KCAL/0.2G FAT

8oz (225g) fresh cranberries

approx. 1 tablespoon artificial
   sweetener or to taste

1–1½lb (450–675g) cooking
   apples

2–3oz (50–75g) mixed dried
   fruit

2 egg whites

4oz (100g) caster sugar

a little icing sugar *or*
   2 tablespoons cranberry
   sauce to decorate (optional)

This sweet is ideal for serving at dinner parties around Christmas time. To add a festive touch, you could decorate with 2 sprigs of fresh holly which has been washed well and dried.

Preheat the oven to 150°C, 300°F, Gas Mark 2.

Wash the cranberries and place them in a saucepan. Add the artificial sweetener and about ¼ pint (150ml) of water. Bring to the boil and simmer until all the cranberries have 'popped' (you will hear them doing this as they cook).

Peel and slice the apples and place in a pie dish. Cover with the cranberries and pour any juice over. Sprinkle the mixed fruit over the top.

Whisk the egg whites until they stand in stiff peaks. Sieve the sugar and fold it in gently in 2–3 batches. Pipe or spread the meringue over the top of the fruit so that it is completely covered.

Bake in the oven for 35–45 minutes until the apples are cooked and the meringue is slightly brown.

Decorate, if you wish, by sifting a little icing sugar over the top or by drizzling the warmed, sieved cranberry sauce over the meringue. Alternatively, use sprigs of fresh holly and arrange them decoratively on top of the meringue. Serve warm. If you wish, you can serve with custard made with skimmed milk and artificial sweetner in place of sugar.

Lemon meringue pie

Here is a delicious alternative to this traditional dessert. The fat-free sponge base is an ideal substitute for short-crust pastry, and the filling tastes every bit as good as the full fat version. Your dinner guests will adore it!

Preheat the oven to 180°C, 350°F, Gas Mark 4.

To make the sponge base, whisk together the eggs and sugar for several minutes until thick and pale in consistency.

Grease an 8in (20cm) flan case with a little vegetable oil then dust with caster sugar. Using a metal spoon, carefully fold the sifted flour into the egg mixture and then fold in the vanilla essence. Pour quickly into the flan case and level off with a knife. Bake in the oven for 20 minutes until golden brown.

Allow the sponge to cool. When cool, use a sharp knife to cut away a ½in (1cm) layer of sponge from the centre of the flan case, then use a spoon to scrape away any crumbs to leave a smooth surface.

To make the filling, finely zest the lemons on a fine grater and place in a small bowl. Squeeze the juice from the lemons into the bowl. Add the sugar and custard powder and mix to a paste. Heat the milk in a saucepan until boiling, pour onto the custard powder and mix well. Transfer to the saucepan and bring back to the boil until the mixture thickens. Pour it into the flan case and allow to cool.

To make the meringue, whisk the egg whites until stiff, then gradually fold in the caster sugar a tablespoonful at a time. Place in a piping bag with a star nozzle. Pipe the meringue in rosettes on the top of the cooled lemon mixture.

Bake in a low oven at 170°C, 325°F, Gas Mark 3 for 20–25 minutes until the meringue starts to colour. Allow to cool before serving.

SERVES 6
PER SERVING:
233 KCAL/2.4G FAT

2 eggs
3oz (75g) caster sugar
3oz (75g) self-raising flour, sifted
1 teaspoon vanilla essence

for the filling
2 lemons
1 tablespoon caster sugar
1 tablespoon custard powder
8fl oz (250ml) skimmed milk

for the meringue
2 egg whites
4oz (100g) caster sugar

Summer pudding

This old traditional pudding has been enjoyed as early as the 18th century, and possibly earlier. It is essential to use good-quality bread with an open texture in order for the delicious juices to be soaked up and form the casing for this stunning dessert. A farmhouse or tin loaf (uncut) gives the best results. Sliced supermarket bread won't work as well. If you prefer your pudding to be slightly tart, you can reduce the amount of sugar.

SERVES 6
PER SERVING:
372 KCAL/2.11G FAT

1½lb (675g) mixed soft berry fruits (strawberries, raspberries, blackberries, blackcurrants)
5–6oz (150–175g) caster sugar
1 large white farmhouse or tin loaf (unsliced)

Prepare the fruit by removing any stalks or leaves. Rinse the fruit well in a colander. Place in a large-bottom saucepan and sprinkle with the sugar. Bring to the boil over a low heat and simmer gently for 2–3 minutes until the sugar starts to dissolve. Remove the pan from the heat and place to one side.

Prepare the bread by removing all the crust with a sharp knife. Cut the bread into slices, about ½in (1cm) thick. Cut out a disc of bread from one slice and use to line the base of a 1½ pint (900ml) pudding basin. Place strips of bread around the inside edges of the basin, cut to shape, so that they fit tightly.

Strain the juice from the fruit through a fine sieve into a bowl. Spoon half the juice onto the bread in the basin. Turn each piece of bread over to allow the juice to soak through on each side.

Place the fruit in the centre of the basin and cover with the remaining slices of bread. Spoon most of the remaining juice over and turn the bread as before. Cover the basin with cling film and place a small plate on top. Place a heavy weight (such as a full tin or jar) on top of the plate to compress the pudding. Place in the refrigerator and leave to chill for at least 8 hours.

To serve, remove the weight and the plate. Loosen the edges of the pudding with a palette knife. Place a serving dish, upturned, on top of the pudding. Quickly turn the pudding over and shake 2 or 3 times. Remove the basin, and coat the pudding with any reserved juice.

Serve with fromage frais.

Low-fat pancakes

SERVES 4
PER SERVING:
157 KCAL/4.9G FAT

4oz (100g) plain flour
pinch of salt
1 egg
½ pint skimmed or semi-
　skimmed milk
4 teaspoons vegetable oil

This recipe makes 8 pancakes, allowing 2 pancakes per person. The oil is needed for frying the pancakes to give them a little crispness, but most of it is removed with the kitchen paper before cooking.

Sift the flour with the salt in a bowl and make a well in the centre. Pour the egg into the well and stir into the flour very carefully, slowly adding half the milk and stirring continuously. Beat until smooth. Add the remaining milk and leave the mixture to stand for 20–30 minutes. The batter should be the consistency of thick cream.

Preheat a non-stick frying pan with 1 teaspoon of oil, then wipe out the pan with kitchen paper, taking care not to burn your fingers (wear an oven glove if necessary). Take 2 tablespoons of batter for each pancake. Tilt the pan as you pour the batter so that the batter spreads evenly across the bottom of the pan. Cook until the underneath of the pancake is a golden brown colour, then wedge a wooden spatula around the edge of the pancake to raise it slightly. Flip the pancake over and cook for about 15 seconds on the other side. Repeat until you have 8 pancakes, adding a teaspoon of oil to the pan and wiping out after every 2 pancakes.

Serve immediately with fresh orange or lemon juice and honey or brown sugar.

Baked bananas with raspberries

If using frozen raspberries, allow them to thaw.

Preheat the oven to 180°C, 350°F, Gas Mark 4.

Peel the bananas and cut in half lengthways. Place each banana on a sheet of foil that is large enough to enclose the bananas during cooking. Divide the raspberries between the 2 parcels and add 2 tablespoons of orange juice to each parcel. Fold up to enclose the fruit.

Place on a baking sheet and bake in the oven for 15 minutes. Remove from the oven and serve each one in its foil parcel.

SERVES 2
PER SERVING:
118 KCAL/0.5G FAT

4oz (100g) fresh or frozen
    raspberries
2 bananas
4 tablespoons orange juice

Grilled pineapple with honey and lime

Slice the pineapple into quarters lengthways. Remove the centre core if hard. Cut the pineapple flesh into segments, taking care not to cut through the skin. Place the pineapple quarters on a baking sheet.

Place the honey and the lime zest and juice in a bowl and mix well. Spoon the mixture over the pineapple quarters and sprinkle with demerara sugar.

Place under a hot grill until golden and caramelised.

SERVES 4
PER SERVING:
213 KCAL/0.2G FAT

1 large ripe pineapple
4 tablespoons clear honey
zest and juice of 2 limes
4 tablespoons demerara sugar

Pear and ginger
upside down pudding

SERVES 6
PER SERVING:
175 KCAL/1.4G FAT

1 × 8oz (225g) can pear
   quarters in juice
2 tablespoons ginger preserve
4oz (100g) quark
4oz (100g) caster sugar
1 egg
5oz (150g) plain flour
2 teaspoons baking powder
3 tablespoons lemon juice
2 teaspoons ground ginger

Here, the quark replaces the butter or margarine normally used in sponge puddings.

Preheat the oven to 180°C, 350°F, Gas Mark 4.

Drain the pears and place them in the bottom of an ovenproof dish. Dot the ginger preserve over the pears.

Beat together the quark and the caster sugar. Add the egg and beat well. Fold in the flour, baking powder and ground ginger. Add the lemon juice and mix well. Spread the mixture over the pears.

Place in the oven and bake for 20–25 minutes.

When cooked, turn out onto a serving dish and serve with low-fat yogurt or fromage frais.

Baked cranberry pumpkin

Thaw the frozen cranberries, if using.

Preheat the oven to 180°C, 350°F, Gas Mark 4.

Place the cranberries, pumpkin, apple and raisins in an ovenproof dish. Pour the orange juice and zest over the fruit. Stir in the honey and the salt. Cover and bake in the oven for 25–30 minutes.

Serve with low-fat fromage frais.

SERVES 6
PER SERVING:
58 KCAL/0.3G FAT

$\frac{1}{2}$ cup fresh or frozen
    cranberries
1$\frac{1}{2}$lb (675g) pumpkin, chopped
1 small apple, peeled and
    chopped
$\frac{1}{4}$ cup chopped raisins
zest and juice of 1 orange
1$\frac{1}{2}$ tablespoons honey
dash of salt

Blueberry cobbler

This American dessert also works well with peaches or pears. Try it with a splash of white wine instead of water on the fruit.

Preheat the oven to 180°C, 350°F, Gas Mark 5.

Place the blueberries in a shallow ovenproof dish. Sprinkle with 2 tablespoons of sugar. Add $\frac{1}{4}$ pint (150ml) water.

Sift the flour and baking powder into a large bowl. Add the remaining sugar and the fromage frais and skimmed milk. Beat together until smooth.

Blob spoonfuls of the mixture on top of the blueberries. Place in the oven and bake for 20 minutes or until golden.

Just before serving, dust with a little icing sugar. Serve hot with low-fat fromage frais or yogurt.

SERVES 8
PER SERVING:
152 KCAL/0.5G FAT

1lb (450g) blueberries
4 tablespoons caster sugar
8oz (225g) plain flour
2 teaspoons baking powder
2oz (50g) virtually fat-free
    fromage frais
7fl oz (200ml) skimmed milk
icing sugar to serve

Low-fat fruity bread pudding

SERVES 4
PER SERVING:
185 KCAL/0.8G FAT

3oz (75g) mixed dried fruit
$\frac{1}{4}$ pint (150ml) apple juice
4oz (100g) diced stale brown
    bread
1–1$\frac{1}{2}$ teaspoons cinnamon
    powder or mixed spice
1 large banana, sliced
$\frac{1}{4}$ pint (150ml) skimmed milk
1 tablespoon demerara sugar

If you adore bread pudding, try this low-fat alternative.

Preheat the oven to 200°C, 400°F or Gas Mark 6.

Place the dried fruit and apple juice in a small pan. Bring to the boil and remove from the heat.

Stir the bread, spice or cinnamon and the banana into the fruit. Spoon into a shallow ovenproof dish. Pour the milk over the mixture and sprinkle the sugar on top.

Bake in the oven for 25–30 minutes until golden brown.

Serve hot or cold with low-fat custard.

Low-fat chocolate and black cherry pudding

SERVES 8
PER SERVING:
199 KCAL/3G FAT

3 large eggs, separated
4oz (100g) caster sugar
3oz (75g) self-raising flour
1oz (25g) cocoa powder
1 × 14oz (390g) can black
    cherry pie filling

Preheat the oven to 180°C, 350°F, Gas Mark 4.

Whisk the egg whites until stiff. Add the yolks and whisk in. Add the caster sugar and whisk until all the sugar has dissolved.

Sift the self-raising flour with the cocoa powder. Using a figure-of-eight action, fold half the flour into the egg and sugar mixture. When the flour is almost folded in, add the remaining flour in the same way until the mixture is smooth. Place on one side.

Spoon the pie filling onto the base of a lightly greased casserole dish. Spoon the sponge mixture over the top. Bake in the oven for approximately 40 minutes or until golden brown.

When cooked, leave to cool for a few minutes, then loosen the pudding with a palette knife and turn out onto a flat dish.

Serve with low-fat fromage frais.

Baked egg custard

Preheat the oven to 160°C, 325°F, Gas Mark 2.

Place the milk in a pan and heat until it 'steams'.

Lightly beat the egg yolks in a bowl until smooth.

Pour the hot milk onto the eggs and mix well. Sweeten to taste with sugar or sweetener. Strain into a small pie dish and sprinkle a little nutmeg over (if using).

Half fill a small roasting tin with water. Place the pie dish in the roasting tin and place in the oven. Bake for about 1 hour until the custard is set and firm to touch.

SERVES 2
PER SERVING:
109 KCAL/5.6G FAT

½ pint (300ml) skimmed milk
2 egg yolks
sugar or sweetener to taste
a little nutmeg (optional)

Low-fat Christmas pudding

SERVES 10
PER SERVING:
280 KCAL/2.5G FAT

3oz (75g) currants

3oz (75g) sultanas

4oz (100g) raisins

4 tablespoons brandy, rum or beer

3oz (75g) glacé cherries, halved

3oz (75g) plain or self-raising flour

1 teaspoon mixed spice

$\frac{1}{2}$ teaspoon cinnamon

2oz (50g) fresh breadcrumbs

2oz (50g) Muscovado or caster sugar

2 teaspoons gravy browning

zest of $\frac{1}{2}$ lemon

zest of $\frac{1}{2}$ orange

4oz (100g)) grated apple

4oz (100g) finely grated carrot

1 tablespoon lemon juice

2 eggs

4 tablespoons skimmed milk

2 tablespoons molasses or cane sugar syrup

4 tablespoons rum or brandy for reheating

This is an old faithful recipe that tastes even better than the full-fat traditional pudding. No one will guess this is low fat – not even the greatest sceptics!

You can deep freeze the pudding, but do take care to thaw it thoroughly before reheating.

Soak the currants, sultanas and raisins in the rum, brandy or beer and leave overnight.

When ready to make the pudding, shake the cherries gently in the flour, then add the spices, breadcrumbs, sugar and gravy browning.

Mix in the lemon and orange zest, grated apple and carrot and the lemon juice. Add the soaked fruit. Beat the eggs with the milk and molasses and slowly add to the mixture, stirring well. Mix together gently and thoroughly.

Place in a 2 pint (1.2 litre) ovenproof basin. If you are going to microwave the pudding, place an upturned plate over the basin and microwave on High for 5 minutes. Leave to stand for 5 minutes, then microwave for a further 5 minutes. If steaming the pudding, cover with foil or a pudding cloth, and then steam gently for 3 hours (this makes a moister pudding).

After cooking, allow the pudding to cool, then wrap it in aluminium foil and leave in a cool, dry place until required.

To reheat, pierce the pudding several times with a fork and pour some more rum or brandy over the top. Steam for 1–2 hours.

◀ *Low-fat Christmas pudding.*

Cakes, buns and loaves

It is surprising how many delicious cakes can be made with low-fat ingredients. The only danger is that they can be so moreish! Most of us find the aroma of freshly baked cakes and breads hard to resist. After cooking, cover them with a tea towel while they are cooling and store in airtight containers or, better still, wrap well and freeze until required. Remember, out of sight out of mind.

All these recipes can be incorporated into a low-fat eating plan. If you are trying to lose weight, you can eat a portion for dessert with lunch or dinner, providing the calories are counted into your allowance. And if you are just seeking to maintain your existing weight, you can even eat a portion between meals, again as long as you don't exceed your daily quota of calories.

Ginger marmalade cake

SERVES 10
PER SERVING:
204 KCAL/1G FAT

8oz (225g) mixed dried fruit

½ pint (300ml) cold tea

8oz (225g) self-raising flour

4oz (100g) caster sugar

1 egg, beaten

3 tablespoons ginger
    marmalade

1 tablespoon molasses

1 teaspoon ground ginger

This dark, moist cake has a real ginger flavour coming through. The cake tends to eat better 2–3 days after making. Store in an airtight container or wrap well in greaseproof paper.

Soak the mixed fruit in the tea overnight until the fruit swells.

Preheat the oven to 180°C, 350°F, Gas Mark 4. Line a 1½lb (675g) loaf tin with greaseproof paper, or use a non-stick tin.

In a bowl, combine the flour, sugar, egg and marmalade, then add the molasses and ground ginger. Mix well and place in the loaf tin. Bake in the oven for 1 hour.

Leave to cool before slicing.

Prune and almond cake

SERVES 10
PER SERVING:
165 KCAL/2.1G FAT

8oz (225g) ready-to-eat prunes

6oz (175g) plain flour

2 teaspoons baking powder

6oz (175g) caster sugar

3 eggs

2 teaspoons mixed spice

1 teaspoon almond essence

icing sugar to serve

You may find this cake has a slightly chewy texture, but the texture will improve with age.

Soak the prunes in a mug of hot black tea overnight.

Preheat the oven to 180°C, 350°F, Gas Mark 4. Line a 2lb (900g) loaf tin with greaseproof paper.

Drain the soaked prunes and purée half of them in a food processor or liquidiser. Mix the prune purée with the flour, baking powder, sugar, eggs and spice in a large bowl.

Chop the remaining prunes and fold the chopped prunes and almond essence into the mixture in the bowl.

Pour the mixture into the loaf tin and bake in the oven for 35–40 minutes.

Dust with icing sugar before serving.

Carrot and mango cake

Preheat the oven to 180°C, 350°F, Gas Mark 4. Line a 1lb (450g) round cake tin with greaseproof paper or baking parchment, or use a non-stick tin.

In a bowl, mix together the flour, baking powder, sugar, ground ginger, coriander, spice, sultanas and diced mangoes. Add the grated carrots and stir well.

Mix the beaten egg with the milk. Stir into the mixture and mix well. Pour the mixture into the prepared tin and bake in the oven for 50–55 minutes. To test if the cake is cook, insert a skewer into the cake. The skewer should come out clean.

Leave to cool.

Before serving, make the topping (if using) by mixing together the quark, orange zest and icing sugar until smooth. Spread over the top of the cake. Sprinkle with poppy seeds.

SERVES 10
PER SERVING:
207 KCAL/1.1G FAT

8oz (225g) plain flour
3 heaped teaspoons baking powder
6oz (175g) dark brown soft sugar
1 teaspoon ground ginger
1 teaspoon ground coriander
1 teaspoon mixed spice
4oz (100g) sultanas
4oz (100g) fresh mangoes, diced
1lb (450g) carrots, grated
1 egg, beaten
8fl oz (250ml) skimmed or semi-skimmed milk

for the topping (optional)
4oz (100g) quark
zest of 1 orange
4oz (100g) icing sugar
a few poppy seeds

Apple gâteau

SERVES 8
PER SERVING:
144 KCAL/2.5G FAT

3oz (75g) plain flour
3 eggs
4$\frac{1}{2}$oz (125g) caster sugar
pinch of salt
1 teaspoon icing sugar

for the filling
1lb (450g) eating apples
zest and juice of 1 lemon
1 tablespoon apricot jam
artificial sweetener to taste
   (optional)

Preheat the oven to 190°C, 375°F, Gas Mark 5. Very lightly grease an 8in (20cm) cake tin. Dust with a little caster sugar then with a little flour. Shake out the excess.

Sift the flour. Place the eggs and caster sugar in a mixing bowl and whisk with an electric whisk or mixer for 5 minutes at top speed until thick and mousse-like. Fold in the sifted flour and salt. Pour the mixture into the prepared tin.

Bake in the centre of the oven for 25 minutes or until the cake is golden brown and has shrunk from the edges of the tin a little. Run a blunt knife around the inside of the tin and turn out the cake onto a wire rack to cool.

To make the filling, peel and slice the apples and place the apple slices in a saucepan. Add the lemon zest and juice and the jam. Heat slowly. Add artificial sweetener to taste if required. Cover and cook until the apples are just tender. Allow to cool.

When the cake is cool, slice it across with a large knife to make 2 layers. Spread the bottom half with the cooled apple filling and cover with the top half of the cake. Sprinkle the cake with icing sugar.

Spicy fruit and apple cake

This spicy apple cake doubles up as a quick and tasty pudding – just cut into slices, steam for 1–2 minutes and serve with low-fat custard.

Soak the dried fruit in the hot tea overnight.

Preheat the oven to 170°C, 325°F, Gas Mark 3. Line a 2lb (900g) loaf tin or round cake tin with greaseproof paper.

Place the soaked fruit in a bowl and add the remaining ingredients. Combine well. Transfer the mixture to the prepared loaf or cake tin and bake in the oven for 2 hours.

When cooked, leave the cake to cool in the tin.

SERVES 10
PER SERVING:
205 KCAL/1G FAT

12oz (350g) dried mixed fruit
$\frac{1}{4}$ pint (150ml) hot black tea
6oz (175g) soft brown sugar
4oz (100g) cooking apple, diced
12oz (350g) self-raising flour
1 egg, beaten
2 teaspoons mixed spice
1 teaspoon ground cinnamon

Apricot loaf

Preheat the oven to 180°C, 350°F, Gas Mark 4. Line a 2lb (1kg) loaf tin with greaseproof paper.

Sift the flour, sugar, salt, baking powder and bicarbonate of soda into a large bowl. Add the raisins and apricots and mix well.

Place the orange juice in a cup and top up with more juice or orange squash.

Make a well in the centre of the flour and apricot mixture. Stir the milk, egg, orange zest and juice into the mixture.

Place in the prepared loaf tin and bake in the oven for 50–60 minutes.

Remove from the oven and leave to cool. When cool, place in an airtight container and store for 24 hours before using.

SERVES 10
PER SERVING:
225 KCAL/1.1G FAT

14oz (400g) plain flour
6oz (175g) sugar
$\frac{1}{2}$ teaspoon salt
$1\frac{1}{2}$ teaspoons baking powder
$\frac{1}{2}$ teaspoon bicarbonate of
    soda
3oz (75g) raisins
6oz (175g) ready-to eat or dried
    apricots, cut small and soaked
    in a little water
zest and juice of 1 orange
2 tablespoons skimmed milk
1 egg, beaten

Bran loaf

SERVES 8
PER SERVING:
145 KCAL/0.4G FAT

1 cup branflakes or All-Bran
1 cup sultanas
1 cup skimmed milk
$\frac{1}{2}$ cup brown sugar
pinch of mixed spice (optional)
1 cup wholemeal self-raising
   flour

Place all the ingredients except the flour in a bowl and leave for 1 hour.

Preheat the oven to 170°C, 325°F, Gas Mark 3. Lightly grease a 1lb (450g) loaf tin and line the base with greaseproof paper.

Add the flour to the bran mixture in the bowl and stir well. Place in the prepared loaf tin and bake in the oven for 1 hour 10 minutes.

Remove from the oven, turn out onto a wire rack and leave to cool.

Quick soda bread

SERVES 10
PER SERVING:
159 KCAL/0.8G FAT

12oz (350g) strong white flour
4oz (100g) wholemeal flour
1 teaspoon salt
4 teaspoons baking powder
3 tablespoons low-fat yogurt
$\frac{1}{2}$ pint (300ml) tepid water

Traditionally, soda bread is made using buttermilk, the by-product of butter production. This recipe substitutes low-fat yogurt for the buttermilk, and the end result is still a moist light soda loaf.

Preheat the oven to 220°C, 425°F, Gas Mark 7.

Sieve the flours together into a large bowl. Using a fork, mix in the salt and baking powder. Rub in the yogurt. Bind the mixture with the water, adding the water gradually. If the dough is too stiff, add a little more water.

Transfer the dough onto a floured board. Knead the dough and form into a smooth ball. Place on a non-stick baking sheet. Cut a cross in the top of the dough with a sharp knife.

Bake in the oven for 30–35 minutes.

To test if the bread is cooked, turn it over and tap the underneath. It should sound hollow when fully cooked.

Vanilla swiss roll with lemon curd

This is a sumptuous swiss roll. The home-made lemon curd filling just melts in your mouth. It makes a luxury cake, good enough to grace any tea party, and also works well as a dinner party dessert.

Preheat the oven to 180°C, 350°F, Gas Mark 4. Line a non-stick swiss roll tin with parchment paper.

Whisk together the eggs and sugar in a bowl for several minutes until thick and creamy and pale in consistency. Sift the flour and, using a metal spoon, carefully fold the flour and sugar into eggs and sugar, then fold in the lemon zest and the vanilla. Pour quickly into the prepared swiss roll tin.

Bake in the oven for 25–30 minutes until golden brown and firm to the touch.

Turn the sponge out onto sugared greaseproof paper and roll up with the paper. Leave to cool with paper still wrapped around the roll.

To make the lemon curd, place the lemon zest and juice in a measuring jug and make up to 1 pint (600ml) with skimmed milk. Mix the custard powder and sugar with a little of the lemon mixture into a paste.

Place the remainder of the lemon mixture in a saucepan and bring to the boil. Pour onto the custard powder, mix well and return to the pan. Bring back to the boil, whisking continuously until the curd thickens. Allow to cool.

When the lemon curd is completely cool, unroll the sponge, remove the parchment paper, and spread the lemon curd mixture onto the sponge and roll up again.

SERVES 8
PER SERVING:
148 KCAL/1.7G FAT

2 eggs
3oz (75g) sugar
3oz (75g) self-raising flour
fine zest of 1 lemon
1 teaspoon vanilla essence

for the lemon curd
fine zest and juice of 4 lemons
3/4 pint (450ml) skimmed milk
2 tablespoons custard powder
1 1/2 tablespoons caster sugar

Rock cakes

These lemon-spiked rock cakes are deliciously fruity. The quark is used as a replacement for butter or margarine.

Preheat the oven to 180°C, 350°F, Gas Mark 4.

Sift the flour and baking powder into a large mixing bowl. Rub in the quark. Add the sugar, raisins and lemon zest and mix well. Combine with the milk.

Shape the mixture into 12 balls and place on a non-stick baking sheet. Decorate with the cherries.

Bake in the oven for 20–25 minutes.

When cooked, glaze each cake with a little apricot jam.

MAKES 12
PER CAKE:
158 KCAL/0.4G FAT

12oz (350g) plain flour
3 teaspoons baking powder
3oz (75g) quark
3oz (75g) caster sugar
3oz (75g) raisins
zest of $\frac{1}{2}$ lemon
3fl oz (75ml) skimmed milk
4oz (100g) glacé cherries, cut in half
apricot jam to glaze

Honey and lemon scones

Again, low-fat yogurt is used as a replacement for butter or margarine.

Preheat the oven to 220°C, 425°F, Gas Mark 7.

Sift the flour with the baking powder in a bowl. Mix in the sugar and lemon zest. Rub in the yogurt and bind the mixture with $\frac{1}{4}$ pint (300ml) water to form a soft dough.

Roll out onto a floured board to a thickness of 2in (5cm).

Using a small cutter, stamp out 10 scones and place on a non-stick baking sheet.

Bake in the oven for 20–25 minutes.

While the scones are still hot, glaze the tops with honey, using a pastry brush, then place on a wire rack to cool.

MAKES 10 SCONES
PER SCONE:
219 KCAL/0.6G FAT

1lb (450g) plain flour
4 teaspoons baking powder
4oz (100g) caster sugar
fine zest of 1 lemon
3 tablespoons low-fat yogurt
2 tablespoons clear honey to glaze

Raisin and cinnamon muffins

MAKES 9 MUFFINS
PER MUFFIN:
170 KCAL/1G FAT

8oz (225g) plain flour
1 tablespoon baking powder
5 tablespoons caster sugar
1 egg
½ pint (300ml) skimmed milk
1oz (25g) Lighter Bake (virtually fat-free baking medium)
3oz (75g) raisins
1 teaspoon cinnamon

Preheat the oven to 180°C, 350°F, Gas Mark 4. Place 9 muffin cases in muffin tins.

Sift the flour, baking powder and caster sugar together in a bowl and make a well in the centre.

Beat together the egg, milk and Lighter Bake. Add to the well in the flour mixture and mix well with a fork. Fold in the raisins and cinnamon. Spoon the mixture into the muffin cases and bake in the oven for 20 minutes until well risen.

Meringue biscuits

MAKES 30 BISCUITS
PER BISCUIT:
28 KCAL/NIL FAT

4 egg whites
8oz (225g) caster sugar

These meringues can be stored in an airtight container for up to 2 weeks.

Preheat the oven to 110°C, 225°F, Gas Mark ¼. Whisk the egg whites until they stand in stiff peaks. Add 1oz (25g) of the caster sugar and continue whisking for 1 minute. Fold in the remaining caster sugar.

Place the meringue mixture in a large piping bag with a large nozzle (any pattern nozzle will do). Gently pipe the egg whites into small pyramids onto a non-stick baking sheet.

Place in the oven for approximately 2 hours or until crisp and beige in colour. The meringues should easily come away from the baking sheet. If they don't, gently prise them off with a sharp pliable knife.

Caramel meringue pyramids

These golden gems with a chewy centre taste like caramel toffees – and no fat in sight!

Preheat the oven to 150°C, 300°F, Gas Mark 2. Line a baking sheet with silicone paper.

Whisk the egg whites with a pinch of salt until they stand in stiff peaks. Gradually add the sugar, continuing to whisk for 1 minute. Place the mixture in a piping nozzle with a large star nozzle. Pipe 12 small pyramids onto the lined baking sheet.

Place in the oven for 2 hours or until crisp.

MAKES 30 PYRAMIDS
PER PYRAMID:
26 KCAL/NIL FAT

4 egg whites
pinch of salt
8oz (225g) soft brown sugar

Filo pastry mince pies

Filo pastry is the only pastry that is acceptable on a low-fat diet. These mince pies make a tasty alternative to the traditional ones.

Preheat the oven to 190°C, 375°F, Gas Mark 5.

Stack the filo pastry sheets on top of each other on the work surface. Using scissors, cut the stack into 6 square-shaped sections, so that you end up with 36 individual squares.

Take 6 non-stick patty tins. In each patty tin, place 4 individual pastry squares in layers, placing the squares at slight angles to each other and brushing with beaten egg white in between each layer. Place a half tablespoonful of mincemeat in the centre of each pastry case.

Brush the remaining 12 pastry squares with egg white and scrunch them up to make crinkly toppings for the pies. Place 2 scrunched-up squares on top of each portion of mincemeat.

Bake in the oven for 10 minutes until the pastry is crisp and golden.

Just before serving, dust with a little icing sugar (if using).

MAKES 6 MINCE PIES
PER MINCE PIE:
144 KCAL/1.5G FAT

6 sheets filo pastry (12 × 8in/ 30 × 20cm)
1 egg white, beaten
3 tablespoons spicy fat-free mincemeat (see recipe, page 394)
icing sugar to decorate (optional)

Spicy fat-free mincemeat

Peel, core and grate the cooking apples. Place the grated apples and the dried fruit in a saucepan. Add the mixed spice and cider. Simmer for about 20 minutes or until the mixture forms a pulp and most of the liquid has evaporated. Stir in your choice of spirit. Allow to cool.

When cool, pack the mincemeat in sterilised jars and store in the refrigerator until required. The mincemeat will keep in a refrigerator for 4 months. Once opened, use within one week.

MAKES 1LB (450G)
PER 1LB (450G):
775KCAL/1.1G FAT

1¼lb (500g) cooking apples
2lb (900g) mixed dried fruit
2 teaspoons mixed spice
1 pint (600ml) sweet cider
2 tablespoons brandy, whisky or
    rum

Mincemeat fruit crunch

Preheat the oven to 150°C, 300°F, Gas Mark 2. Line a 7–8in (18–20cm) square tin with greaseproof paper.

Mix all the ingredients together and place in the prepared tin.

Bake in the oven for approximately 1¼ hours until firm to the touch.

When cooked, leave in the tin to cool. When cool, cut into squares or chunks.

MAKES 20 SQUARES
PER SQUARE:
109 KCAL/0.72G FAT

8oz (225g) mincemeat (see
    above recipe for spicy fat-free
    mincemeat)
4oz (100g) cornflakes
9oz (250g) dried fruit
2 eggs
1 level teaspoon mixed spice
1 × 14oz (400g) can condensed
    milk (made with skimmed
    milk)
1–2oz (50g) glacé cherries,
    quartered

Sauces

come into their own in low-fat cooking, because we need the moisture to enhance the flavour of foods to make up for the lack of fat. In this section I have included a selection of both savoury and sweet sauces that I have used for many years, together with some new ones to widen the variety. As you'll see from these recipes, you really don't need to cook with fat to make a good sauce.

White sauce

SERVES 4
PER SERVING:
55 KCAL/0.2G FAT

½ pint (300ml) skimmed milk
1 onion, sliced
6 peppercorns
1 bay leaf
4 teaspoons cornflour
salt and freshly ground black pepper

You can also use this sauce to make a low-fat parsley sauce. Simply add chopped parsley to taste after thickening the sauce and continue to cook for the last 3-4 minutes.

Heat all but 2fl oz (50ml) of the milk in a non-stick saucepan, and add the onion, peppercorns, bay leaf and seasoning. Heat gently and cover the pan. Simmer for 5 minutes. Turn off the heat and leave milk mixture to stand with the lid on for a further 30 minutes or until you are ready to thicken and serve the sauce.

Mix the remaining milk with the cornflour and when almost ready to serve, strain the flavoured milk through a fine sieve, add the cornflour mixture and reheat slowly, stirring continuously, until it comes to the boil. If it begins to thicken too quickly, remove from heat and stir very fast to mix well.

Cook for 3–4 minutes and serve immediately.

Mushroom sauce

Heat all but 2fl oz (50ml) of the milk in a non-stick saucepan, and add the onion, peppercorns, bay leaf and salt and pepper. Heat gently, cover the pan, and simmer for 5 minutes. Turn off the heat and leave the milk mixture to stand with the lid on for a further 30 minutes. Strain the milk through a fine sieve into a jug.

Rinse out the saucepan. Return the milk to the pan and add the thyme, marjoram and chicken stock cube. Reheat until the mixture is almost boiling.

Mix the cornflour and the remaining milk into a paste and slowly add this to the hot milk mixture. Add the sliced mushrooms and gently heat until boiling, stirring continuously. Continue stirring and cooking for a further 2 minutes. Taste to ensure there is sufficient seasoning and adjust as necessary.

SERVES 4
PER SERVING:
63 KCAL/0.6G FAT

½ pint (300ml) skimmed milk
1 onion, diced
6 peppercorns
1 bay leaf
½ teaspoon dried thyme
½ teaspoon dried marjoram
1 chicken stock cube
2 teaspoons cornflour
4oz (100g) button mushrooms, thinly sliced
salt and freshly ground black pepper

Bread sauce

Pour the milk into a pan and slowly bring to the boil. Add the chopped onion, cloves and bay leaf. Remove from the heat, cover the pan and leave for 15–20 minutes to allow the flavours to infuse.

Remove the cloves and bay leaf, add the breadcrumbs and black pepper and return to the heat, stir gently until boiling. Season with salt and black pepper.

Remove from the heat and place in a small covered serving dish (a small bowl covered with foil would work just as well). Keep warm until ready to serve.

SERVES 8
PER SERVING:
41 KCAL/0.2G FAT

½ pint (300ml) skimmed milk
1 small onion, chopped
3 cloves
1 bay leaf
6–8 tablespoons fresh breadcrumbs
salt and freshly ground black pepper

Cranberry and port sauce

SERVES 4
PER SERVING:
55 KCAL/0.13G FAT

8oz (225g) cranberries
$\frac{1}{2}$ pint (300ml) cranberry juice
    drink
2 tablespoons port
artificial sweetener to taste
    (optional)

Place the cranberries in a saucepan. Add the cranberry juice drink. Bring to the boil, then simmer gently for about 5 minutes until soft. Push the mixture through a sieve to purée it and return to the pan.

Stir in the port and heat through. Add a little artificial sweetener if desired.

Mustard sauce

SERVES 4
PER SERVING:
59 KCAL/1.2G FAT

$\frac{1}{2}$ pint (300ml) skimmed milk
1 vegetable stock cube
4 teaspoons cornflour
$1\frac{1}{2}$ tablespoons Dijon mustard
1 tablespoon chopped fresh
    parsley (optional)
salt and freshly ground black
    pepper

This is a good base sauce for lasagne or a pasta bake. It is also delicious served with gammon.

Heat the milk and stock cube in a non-stick saucepan until the stock cube has dissolved.

Mix the cornflour with a little water to form a paste, then add slowly to the milk, stirring well, until it comes to the boil. Cook for 2–3 minutes, then stir in the mustard and parsley (if using) and adjust the consistency with a little water if required.

Season to taste.

Chilli barbecue sauce

Place the onion and garlic in a small pan. Add the remaining ingredients and mix well. Bring slowly to the boil and simmer for 15 minutes or until the onion is soft. Add a little water if necessary to prevent the sauce from becoming too thick.

Check the seasoning and adjust the consistency with more water at the end of the cooking time. Serve hot.

SERVES 6
PER SERVING:
48 KCAL / 0.2G FAT

1 onion, sliced
1 garlic clove, crushed
$\frac{1}{4}$ pint (150ml) tomato juice
2 tablespoons Worcestershire
    sauce
1 teaspoon medium hot chilli
    powder or to taste
4 tablespoons white wine vinegar
2 tablespoons clear honey
2 tablespoons soy sauce
1 teaspoon French mustard
salt and freshly ground black
    pepper

Red pepper sauce

This thick pepper sauce is ideal served with fish or meat and braised vegetables. It can be thinned down with a little vegetable stock if necessary.

Preheat the oven to 200°C, 400°F, Gas Mark 6.

Slice the peppers in half lengthways, remove the seeds and discard. Place the peppers, onion and garlic in a non-stick roasting tin and season well with salt and pepper. Place in the oven for 30 minutes until the vegetables soften.

Remove from the oven and spoon into a food processor or liquidiser. Add the passata and purée until smooth. Pass through a fine sieve to remove any stray seeds or skin. Add Tabasco to taste. Reheat as required.

SERVES 4
PER SERVING:
76 KCAL / 2G FAT

3 red peppers
1 large onion, chopped
3 garlic cloves, finely chopped
salt and freshly ground black
    pepper
$\frac{1}{2}$ pint (300ml) tomato passata
dash of Tabasco sauce

Hot chilli sauce

SERVES 6
PER SERVING:
38 KCAL/1.6G FAT

1–2 red chillies
2–3 spring onions or 1 small
    onion
1–2 tablespoons lemon juice
1 × 200g (7oz) can chopped
    tomatoes
2 tablespoons tomato purée
salt
1–2 teaspoons caster sugar or
    artificial sweetener to taste

Red chillies are the very hot ones, so do take care when using them. Start with just one chilli and add an extra one if necessary. When preparing chillies, make sure you do not touch your eyes, mouth or any tender skin with your hands. The seeds are also hot, so remove them if you want a much milder sauce. This is meant to be a thick sauce, but you can dilute it with vegetable stock if you wish, although this will dilute the taste of the chillies. The sauce can be deep frozen.

Trim the chillies and remove the seeds if you wish. Chop the chillies finely. Trim the spring onions and slice finely, or peel the onion (if using) and chop finely.

Heat a non-stick pan, add the onions and some or all of the chopped chillies, according to your preference. Cook gently until the onions are just soft but without colour. Add 1 tablespoon of the lemon juice and the chopped tomatoes and tomato purée. Season to taste with salt, sugar or artificial sweetener and extra lemon juice if required. At this stage you may also wish to add more chopped chilli. Bring to the boil and simmer for 6–7 minutes. Taste again and adjust the seasoning if required.

Spicy tomato and basil sauce

This sauce may be frozen and stored for up to 2 months.

Dry-fry the chopped onions in a non-stick pan, using a little water if necessary to prevent them from burning.

When the onions are cooked, stir in the remaining ingredients and bring slowly to the boil, stirring continuously. Simmer, uncovered, for 10–15 minutes so that the mixture reduces and becomes thicker. Taste and adjust the seasoning if necessary.

SERVES 2
PER SERVING:
32 KCAL/0.1G FAT

2oz (50g) onions, chopped
$\frac{1}{2}$ teaspoon chilli powder
4oz (100g) canned plum
   tomatoes
2 teaspoons tomato purée
1 teaspoon caster sugar
$\frac{1}{4}$ teaspoon oregano
1 tablespoon chopped fresh
   basil
a little salt and freshly ground
   black pepper

SAVOURY SAUCES: *top row (left to right) red pepper, bread, mustard, parsley; bottom row (left to right) mushroom, spicy tomato and basil.*

SWEET SAUCES: *top row (left to right) custard, strawberry yogurt, apricot; bottom row (left to right) orange, minted fromage frais, lemon.*

Brandy sauce

This sauce is superb as an alternative to brandy butter as an accompaniment to Christmas pudding.

Reserve 4 tablespoons of the milk. Pour the remainder into a saucepan and add the almond essence. Heat until almost boiling, then remove from the heat.

Mix the cornflour with the reserved cold milk and slowly pour it into the hot milk, stirring continuously, until the mixture begins to thicken. Return to the heat and bring to the boil. Continue to cook, stirring continuously. If the sauce is too thin, slowly add some more cornflour mixed with cold milk until you achieve the consistency of custard. Sweeten to taste.

Add the brandy a few drops at a time and stir well. Pour into a jug, cover, and keep warm until ready to serve.

SERVES 8
PER SERVING:
69 KCAL/0.1G FAT

1 pint (600ml) skimmed milk
3 drops almond essence
2 tablespoons cornflour
liquid artificial sweetener
3 tablespoons brandy

Apricot sauce

Wash the dried apricots (if using), place in a bowl, cover with cold water and soak overnight.

Place the apricots in a pan with 7fl oz (200ml) of the water in which they were soaked. Cook over a gentle heat until tender.

Purée the stewed or canned apricots with their juice in a food processor or liquidiser until smooth. Add sugar or artificial sweetener to taste. Stir in the rum (if using).

Serve hot or cold.

SERVES 6
PER SERVING:
71 KCAL/0.2G FAT

8oz (225g) dried apricots or
    1 × 14oz (400g) can apricots
    in juice
caster sugar or artificial
    sweetener to taste
2–3 tablespoons rum (optional)

Minted fromage frais

SERVES 4
PER SERVING:
19 KCAL/0.1G FAT

1 lemon
¼ pint (150ml) virtually fat-free
    fromage frais
1 tablespoon chopped fresh
    mint
artificial sweetener to taste

This is delicious served with stewed apple or baked fruit.

Using the fine section of a grater, gently grate the outside zest from the lemon, taking care not to remove any of the white pith which may make the sauce bitter. Squeeze out the juice from the lemon.

Mix the lemon zest and juice with the fromage frais, chopped mint and artificial sweetener to taste. Pour into a sauce boat.

Orange or lemon sauce

SERVES 4
PER SERVING:
72 KCAL/0.1G FAT

½ pint (300ml) skimmed milk
zest and juice from 2 oranges or
    2 lemons
3 teaspoons arrowroot
artificial sweetener to taste
2 teaspoons orange liqueur
    (optional)

This sauce is good with pancakes or a baked apple.

In a non-stick saucepan, heat the milk with the orange or lemon zest and juice until almost boiling.

Mix the arrowroot with a little water to form a paste. Slowly stir into the hot milk and continue stirring to form a smooth sauce. Sweeten to taste and add the liqueur (if using).

Serve hot.

Strawberry yogurt sauce

This simple sauce is ideal for serving with poached fruit if you find the taste of natural yogurt too sharp on its own.

Combine the yogurt and strawberry jam and whisk until smooth. Serve with any poached fruits of your choice.

SERVES 4
PER SERVING:
50 KCAL/0.27G FAT

1/4 pint (150ml) low-fat natural
　　yogurt
2–3 tablespoons sieved
　　strawberry jam

Low-fat custard

Heat most of the milk in a non-stick saucepan. Mix the remainder of the milk with the custard powder and add slowly to the heated milk, stirring continuously.

　　Add the artificial sweetener and continue to stir until boiling.

　　Simmer for approximately 5 minutes. Add more sweetener if required.

SERVES 2
PER SERVING:
101 KCAL/0.3G FAT

1/2 pint (300ml) skimmed milk
8 artificial sweetening tablets
　　or 2 tablespoons granulated
　　sugar substitute (e.g.
　　Canderel)
1 tablespoon custard powder

Dressings

The secret of a good salad is in the dressing. We are so used to being served oily dressings that they become something of a habit. The key is to learn how to make a good dressing without using oil, and it really isn't that difficult. Try it, and you'll be amazed how quickly your taste buds adapt. Once you've followed a low-fat diet for any length of time, you'll find the taste of oil becomes extremely unpalatable.

Herb vinegar

Vinegar can be flavoured with your favourite herb or a selection of several. The vinegar will infuse with the herbs, adding a special individual flavour to all your salads.

Simply choose fresh, good quality herbs, wash and pat dry with kitchen paper. Place into an attractive bottle or jar and cover with your choice of vinegar. Leave to infuse for 3–4 days and use within 6 months.

Spiced vinegar

Red wine vinegar can be spiced-up using cinnamon, cloves, cardamom and star anise.

Mix the cinnamon, cloves, cardamom, star anise and peppercorns together and place in a bottle or jar. Cover with the vinegar. Seal the bottle or jar and leave the vinegar to infuse for 3–4 days. Use within 6 months.

MAKES ½ PINT (300ML)
PER TABLESPOON:
3 KCAL/NIL G FAT

1 cinnamon stick
3 whole cloves
3–4 cardamom pods, crushed
2 star anise
6 whole black peppercorns
½ pint (300ml) red wine
    vinegar

Balsamic dressing

Balsamic vinegar is a dark, sweet vinegar from Modena in Italy. Its rich syrupy consistency makes a delicious fruity dressing.

Combine all ingredients in a small bowl and whisk until smooth. Place in a sealed jar or bottle and use as required. Use within 5 days.

MAKES 6½ FL OZ (180ML)
PER TABLESPOON:
12 KCAL/0.2G FAT

¼ pint (150ml) apple juice
2 tablespoons balsamic vinegar
1 tablespoon Dijon mustard
pinch of sugar
salt and freshly ground black
    pepper

Fat-free mayonnaise

MAKES 7 1/2 FL OZ (220ML)
PER TABLESPOON:
9 KCAL/0.02G FAT

6oz (175g) virtually fat-free
fromage-frais
2 tablespoons cider vinegar
1 tablespoon lemon juice
1/4 teaspoon ground turmeric
2 teaspoons sugar
salt and freshly ground black
pepper

Real mayonnaise contains egg yolks and oil, two very high-fat ingredients. This low-fat dressing can be substituted for mayonnaise in any recipe. The turmeric adds a rich golden colour to the finished dressing.

Combine all the ingredients together in a small bowl and whisk until smooth. Store in the refrigerator and use within 3 days.

Honey and orange dressing

MAKES 1/4 PINT (150ML)
PER TABLESPOON:
11 KCAL/0.02G FAT

6 tablespoons orange juice
4 teaspoons thin honey
1 tablespoon white wine
vinegar
1/2 teaspoon Dijon wholegrain
mustard
1 teaspoon grated orange rind
2 teaspoons chopped fresh
chives and parsley, mixed
salt and freshly ground black
pepper to taste.

Place the orange juice, honey and vinegar in a pan. Add the Dijon mustard and orange rind. Bring to the boil, then allow to cool.

When cool, add the chopped chives and parsley and season to taste with salt and black pepper. Place in a bottle or jar, seal the top and place in the refrigerator. Use within 7 days.

Fresh basil yogurt dressing

Basil has a strong and perfumed flavour. Its affinity with tomatoes is longstanding. Spoon this dressing over a simple tomato and red onion salad and leave to marinade for 20 minutes. Perfect!

Combine all the ingredients in a small bowl and whisk until smooth. Season well with salt and pepper. Store in the refrigerator and use within 4 days.

DRESSINGS AND VINEGARS: *(left to right) herb vinegar, fresh basil yogurt dressing, oil-free vinaigrette, spiced vinegar, lemon dressing, balsamic dressing.*

SERVES 4
PER SERVING:
22 KCAL/0.3G FAT

5oz (150g) low-fat natural
  yogurt
1 tablespoon lemon juice
2 tablespoons chopped fresh
  basil
1 garlic clove, crushed
salt and freshly ground black
  pepper

Oil-free vinaigrette

MAKES 7FL OZ (200ML)
PER TABLESPOON:
9 KCAL/0.1G FAT

$1/4$ pint (150ml) white wine
    vinegar or cider vinegar
2fl oz (50ml) lemon juice
3–4 teaspoons caster sugar
$1 1/2$ teaspoons French mustard
chopped fresh herbs, e.g.
    marjoram, basil or parsley
    (optional)
1 garlic clove, crushed (optional)
$1/2$ teaspoon salt
$1/2$ teaspoon freshly ground
    black pepper

Mix all the ingredients together and pour into a screw top jar or other container with a tight-fitting lid. Shake well. Taste and add more salt, pepper or sugar if you wish. Store in the refrigerator and shake well before using.

Garlic and yogurt dressing

SERVES 4
PER SERVING:
20 KCAL/0.3G FAT

1 garlic clove, crushed
5oz (150g) low-fat natural
    yogurt
1 tablespoon wine vinegar
1 teaspoon reduced-oil salad
    dressing
salt and freshly ground black
    pepper to taste

Mix all the ingredients together in a container, seal, and shake well. Taste and add more salt or sugar as desired.

Marie Rose dressing

Mix all the ingredients together and store in a sealed jar in the refrigerator. Use within 2 days.

SERVES 2
PER SERVING:
73 KCAL/1G FAT

2 tablespoons tomato ketchup
1 tablespoon reduced-oil salad
  dressing
4 tablespoons low-fat natural
  yogurt
dash of Tabasco sauce
salt and freshly ground black
  pepper to taste

Lemon dressing

Place all the ingredients in a screw-top jar or container. Seal, and shake well. Keep in the refrigerator and use within 3 days.

MAKES 7 1/2 FL OZ (220ML)
PER TABLESPOON:
2 KCAL/0.04G FAT

4fl oz (120ml) fresh orange juice
2fl oz (50ml) lemon juice
2fl oz (50ml) white wine
  vinegar
1 teaspoon Dijon mustard
salt and freshly ground black
  pepper

Index of recipes